SUPREME MYTHS

SUPREME MYTHS

*Why the Supreme Court
Is Not a Court and Its Justices
Are Not Judges*

ERIC J. SEGALL

 PRAEGER

AN IMPRINT OF ABC-CLIO, LLC
Santa Barbara, California • Denver, Colorado • Oxford, England

Library of Congress Cataloging-in-Publication Data

Segall, Eric J.
   Supreme myths : why the Supreme Court is not a court and its justices are not judges / Eric J. Segall.
      p. cm.
   Includes bibliographical references and index.
   ISBN 978-0-313-39687-8 (hardcopy : alk. paper) —
ISBN 978-0-313-39688-5 (ebook)
1. United States. Supreme Court.   2. Constitutional law—United States.   I. Title.
   KF8742.S434   2012
   347.73'26—dc23   2011042906

ISBN: 978-0-313-39687-8
EISBN: 978-0-313-39688-5

16   15   14   13   12   2   3   4   5

This book is also available on the World Wide Web as an eBook.
Visit www.abc-clio.com for details.

Praeger
An Imprint of ABC-CLIO, LLC

ABC-CLIO, LLC
130 Cremona Drive, P.O. Box 1911
Santa Barbara, California 93116-1911

This book is printed on acid-free paper ∞

Manufactured in the United States of America

To, For, and Because of Lynne

Contents

Preface

It is no great secret that the Supreme Court's constitutional law decisions reflect the personal values of the Justices. Law professors and other Court watchers have long described the Justices as politicians in robes. But these critics, by and large, suggest only that the Court should take law more seriously, and do not advocate fundamental change. I wrote this book, not to repeat this well-worn critique, but to argue that the problem with how the Supreme Court operates extends far beyond the great subjectivity that infects the Court's decision making. The unfortunate truth is that, for an array of different reasons, the Supreme Court does not function as a true court and its Justices do not decide cases like true judges. In other words, that politics and personality affect the Court's decisions is only the beginning of the story.

This book is written for academics and nonacademics as well as lawyers and nonlawyers. I hope it will interest not just those who follow the Supreme Court but anyone who wants to learn more about important and controversial issues such as abortion, affirmative action, freedom of religion, and gun control. I will show how the Court prevents the American people and our elected leaders from resolving these issues democratically through our representative system of state and federal elections. That political system is by no means perfect, and it too needs to be reevaluated. But when people in a democracy reasonably disagree over difficult policy questions not obviously resolved by their Constitution, those differences should be resolved by public debate and elections, not by the personal opinions of unelected, life-tenured Justices, and the supreme myths, disguised as law, the Justices create.

Acknowledgments

I would like to thank the many colleagues, friends, and family members who provided so much help with this project. The Georgia State law faculty has indulged my passion for this topic for years, and many of their insights are incorporated in this book.

Eric Berger, Clark Cunningham, Joel Goldstein, Mark Kendre, Neil Kinkopf, Dahlia Lithwick, Caren Morrison, Pete Dominick Miguel Schor, Robert Nagel, Anne Tucker, and Mark Tushnet read drafts of the book and provided helpful comments. Judge Richard Posner gave me more feedback and inspiration than I could ever have imagined.

I received advice from my friends Amy Chamberlain, Janet Collins, Patrick Connors, Rob Kaufman, Art and Marli Pasternak, and Laura Sciortino. Their perspectives dramatically improved the quality of the book.

Carolyn Wood read every word from around the corner, and Bill Hausdorff read every word from thousands of miles away. These two dear and brilliant friends have been challenging and improving my intellectual abilities for decades, and this book is much better because of their efforts to make me think more deeply and responsibly.

Ron Goldfarb, Dick Goldman, and Valentina Tursini believed in this project from the very beginning, and this book would not have been published without their efforts. I also want to acknowledge the fine work of Denver Compton and the entire Praeger team.

I received valuable help from my research assistants Russell Britt, Sarah Chambers, Rebecca Shepard, and Robert Steele, as well as my amazing administrative assistant Christine Nwakamma.

A special thank you goes to Russ Weaver who has invited me to a number of constitutional law workshops and conferences over the years where the ideas expressed herein have been debated and sharpened.

My wonderful family has been behind me from the start. Mom, Dad, Liz, and Pete, thank you for all your love, faith, encouragement, and support.

Anyone who has ever taught in a law school knows how much our success depends on the dean. In my case, I have been lucky that, for the last five years, Steve Kaminshine has been not only the best dean anyone could ever hope for, but also one of my closest friends. He has provided me with his generosity, counsel, and advice. This book specifically, and my professional and personal development generally, have benefitted from our relationship beyond what words could possibly express.

To my daughters, Jessy, Sara, and Katie, your warmth, love, and sunshine radiate over me every day of my life. To Lynne, because you are my soul mate, and also provided so much help with the book, you get double billing.

Prologue

If changing judges changes law, it is not even clear what law is.

—Judge Richard Posner

On June 20, 1860, Susan P. Hepburn of Louisville, Kentucky, borrowed $11,250 from Henry Griswold. At the time she issued her promissory note, the only legal currency in the United States was gold or silver coin. Mrs. Hepburn did not pay back her note so Mr. Griswold sued her for the balance owed. In today's economy, the debt was well over $200,000. Neither party likely foresaw that this lawsuit would change the course of American history.

On February 25, 1862, Congress passed the Legal Tender Act, which, for the first time in American history, made paper money (called greenbacks) legal tender to pay private debts.[1] The Lincoln administration made this dramatic decision because of the desperate financial situation of the federal government. The North had to fund the ongoing Civil War, and the government was out of money.[2] Soldiers needed to be paid and the army required supplies and weapons.

Mrs. Hepburn eventually came to court and offered to pay $12,720, the full amount of the principal plus interest, in United States paper money. Mr. Griswold refused this offer arguing that he had the right to be paid in gold or silver not greenbacks, which had less value. The court, however, accepted the payment and discharged Mrs. Hepburn's debt. Mr. Griswold appealed the case, which went all the way to the United States Supreme Court. He argued that the

United States Congress had no legal authority to make paper money legal tender.

Although it may seem obvious today that Congress has this power, the issue sharply divided the country in the post–Civil War era. The leading economists, academics, and judges of the time disagreed on the question, both as a matter of fiscal policy and constitutional law.

In terms of economics, the issue was divisive because the federal government had printed more and more money resulting in great inflation. Because preexisting debts now could be paid with cash instead of coin, debtors were helped and creditors hurt as the paper money depreciated. Most influential Democrats at the time were against the Legal Tender Act while many Republicans supported it.

As a matter of constitutional law, Congress has the authority to "coin Money [and] regulate the Value thereof."[3] There is nothing in the Constitution, however, that gives the government the authority to issue "paper money," and opponents of the Legal Tender Act argued that the term *coin* referred only to metals not paper currency. They also believed that, if Congress had the authority to make paper money legal tender where that authority did not expressly exist in the Constitution, the federal government's power would expand uncontrollably, and the framers' desire for a limited national government would forever be lost.

Congress does have the power to "regulate commerce," and to "borrow Money on the credit of the United States."[4] Advocates argued that these provisions, along with Congress's implied authority to exercise its enumerated powers, justified the decision to issue paper money. These supporters also contended that the Constitution should be interpreted to allow Congress to respond to new and unforeseen events like the Civil War. Both sides of the debate felt passionately, and this issue, arising after the worst crisis in this nation's history, raised fundamental questions about the nature of our national government, how our economy should be structured, and the appropriate balance of power between the Congress, the states, and the American people.

On February 7, 1870, the Supreme Court of the United States announced its decision in *Hepburn v. Griswold*, holding that Congress did not have the power under the Constitution to make paper money legal tender.[5] The majority (four Democrats plus one Republican) held that no provision in the Constitution gave Congress that authority, and doing so would give the federal government far too much power.[6] Additionally, the Court found that the Legal Tender Act unconstitutionally interfered with preexisting contracts because creditors expected to be paid in gold or silver, not paper money.[7] The dissenters (all Republicans) took issue with each of these points with one Justice boldly arguing that Congress needed to have the power to issue paper money and, without it, the government would have perished "and, with it, the Constitution."[8] Less important, perhaps, Mrs. Hepburn had to pay Mr. Griswold in silver or gold coin not greenbacks.

At the time of the decision, the Court had only eight Justices, and one of them had announced his resignation a week before.[9] Thus, on the same day that the *Hepburn* decision was made public, President Grant nominated two new Republican Justices, William Strong and Joseph Bradley, to the Court. Both were eventually confirmed, giving the Republicans a clear majority. There is little debate that Grant would only have nominated people for the Court who believed in the validity of the Legal Tender Act.[10] Although the president made his nominations the day *Hepburn* was announced, it appears that his administration was told of the decision two weeks prior.[11]

The *Hepburn* case not only had a major effect on the post–Civil War economy but also set forth a new and significant interpretation of the limited powers of Congress and the kind of national government the Constitution anticipated. Because of its importance, *Hepburn* had been "argued and reargued by numerous and distinguished counsel. It is probable that never in the history of the Court has any question been more thoroughly considered before decision."[12]

Despite the enormity of the *Hepburn* decision, however, both its result and rationale were short lived. Just over a year later, in May 1871, the two new Republican Justices joined with the three Republican dissenters in *Hepburn* and explicitly reversed the case in *Knox v. Lee (The Legal Tender Cases).*[13] This new majority argued that the legal tender provisions were urgently needed to fight the Civil War, and Congress should have broad powers to deal with that kind of emergency.[14] Both contentions had been specifically raised and then rejected only 15 months earlier by a majority of the Court in *Hepburn* (four of whom now dissented). The new majority pointed to no new facts or arguments supporting its reversal of the prior decision.[15]

The decision upholding Congress's power to make paper money legal tender was met with mixed reviews in the leading periodicals of the day. The *New York Times,* the *New York Herald,* and *Harper's*

Weekly "expressed the pleasure and gratification of the common people," while those periodicals with conservative tendencies criticized the decision and accused President Grant of packing the Court.[16] The *New York World* reported that, "The decision provokes the indignant contempt of thinking men. It is generally regarded not as the solemn adjudication of an upright and impartial tribunal, but as a base compliance with Executive instructions by creatures of the President placed upon the Bench to carry out his instructions."[17]

The decisions in the *Legal Tender Cases* illustrate three major problems with how the Supreme Court operates that continue to this day. First, although the opinions and dissents in these cases purported to be based on constitutional language and history, neither source could definitively support the result advocated by any of the Justices. As one scholar has written, "the language of the Constitution leaves the question open, and the debates in the Convention do not reveal any consensus of opinion."[18]

This description of the indeterminate nature of the issues raised by the validity of the Legal Tender Act is equally true for virtually every constitutional question litigated in the United States Supreme Court. For example, neither the text of the Constitution nor its history sheds any more light on the validity of laws concerning affirmative action, abortion, or gun control than it sheds on Congress's power (or lack thereof) to make paper money legal tender. Law (defined as constitutional text, the text's history, and prior case law) and legal reasoning simply cannot answer these questions, especially when the Supreme Court is free to, and often does, reverse its own decisions.

Second, even though prior law did not give rise to a concrete answer in the *Legal Tender Cases,* the Justices in both the majority and the dissent wrote their opinions as if their preferred results flowed naturally from that law. This pretense—that law drove the results—is problematic because judges have an important obligation to be candid about the actual reasons for their decisions. Supreme Court Justices, however, rarely admit that they are doing anything other than applying prior "law" to new facts, which is simply not how they resolve constitutional law cases. Instead, the Court's decisions are based on the Justices' personal and controversial value judgments.

Third, the Court in the *Legal Tender Cases* changed its mind on one of the most important policy questions ever to face this country *only* because President Grant had the opportunity to appoint two new Justices whom he knew supported Congress's power to make paper money legal tender.[19] The Supreme Court frequently reverses itself on important constitutional law issues for no other reason than the composition of the Court changes. The problem with this back and forth, in addition to the instability it causes, is that the Supreme Court's legitimacy stems in part from its intended role as a traditional court whose judges apply the "law." But, as was the case with the *Legal Tender Cases,* and as will be true for most of the issues discussed in this book, "if changing judges changes law," then it is uncertain whether the law controls judges or the other way around. In other words, the nature and history of the Supreme Court calls into serious question the axiom that we are a government of laws not people, at least when it comes to Supreme Court decision making.

The purpose of this book is to present an accurate picture of the Supreme Court of the United States, and present a few proposals to help cure the problems caused by the overreaching of the Justices. Because the Court functions much more like a political veto council than a court of law, and because the Justices decide cases more like a traditional council of elders than typical judges, the Supreme Court's power to overturn the important decisions of other governmental officials should be seriously reevaluated. Perhaps having an ultimate veto council is a good idea for a representative democracy whose people believe in limited government. But if so, we should be honest about how the council is structured and actually operates. It is well past time to pull back the curtain on, and then reassess, the Supreme Court of the United States.

CHAPTER 1

Supreme Mythology

The Supreme Court's rules and structures, along with those of
the American political system in general, give life-tenured justices
enormous latitude to reach decisions based on their personal
policy preferences. Members of the Supreme Court can further
their policy goals because they lack electoral or political accountability, have no ambition for higher office, and comprise a court
of last resort that controls its own caseload.
—Jeffrey A. Segal and Harold J. Spaeth

THE MYTHS

This book's argument that the Supreme Court does not act like a court
and its Justices do not decide cases like judges will strike many read-
ers as implausible. After all, Supreme Court Justices work in a courtroom, wear black robes, and decide cases brought before them. But
all that proves is that the Justices *look* like judges. It does not demonstrate that they *decide cases* like judges. How the Justices resolve
legal issues, how truthfully they explain their decisions, and what limits (if any) are placed on their authority are the important factors to
consider when determining whether the Court functions more like a
court of law or more like an ultimate political veto council.

Why should the American people care whether the Supreme Court
functions more like a court of law or a political veto council? The
answer is that the Court frequently prevents elected governmental
officials from implementing important policy decisions favored by

the voters and/or their representatives. For example, if a majority of voters in Chicago want to prohibit handguns in order to reduce homicides and fatal accidents, or if a majority of people in South Dakota wish to criminalize abortion because of concerns for the sanctity of human life, or if Congress wants to enact meaningful campaign finance reform to lessen the corrosive effects of corporate money on federal elections, the people and their representatives are not allowed to implement those decisions because the Supreme Court has made those policy choices illegal. Sometimes the Court favors liberal policies, sometimes conservative ones, and often the Court splits the difference. But on virtually every occasion that the Supreme Court of the United States removes an important policy question from the hands of voters and politically accountable governmental officials, the American people lose some of their power to govern themselves and our representative democracy becomes a little less representative and a little less democratic. This loss might be tolerable if the Justices were acting like traditional judges applying preexisting law to difficult legal problems. But the Court's decisions are based much more on personal and contestable value judgments than legal reasoning.

WHAT ARE JUDGES SUPPOSED TO DO?

How do we expect judges to resolve hard legal issues and how is that different from how the Supreme Court actually operates? From ancient times to the present, whether in America, Europe, or other democracies, judges are supposed to resolve cases by faithfully interpreting legal texts and prior cases and then applying that law to the facts before them. Of course, there are many cases where the governing legal text is vague, the facts truly in dispute, and the applicable law unhelpful, incomplete, or contradictory. No one suggests that judges can act like computers and simply apply clear law to agreed-upon facts and derive right or wrong legal answers. But even when the law does not point to solutions or provides significant discretion, judges remain obligated to examine and interpret legal materials such as constitutional language, relevant history, and prior cases to arrive at the best decision they can.

Not only are judges supposed to carefully examine prior law, but because judges are governmental officials who exercise coercive power, it is important that they explain their legal decisions with honesty and transparency. This requirement does not mean that judges have to justify in writing every decision they make, but there is general agreement that they ought to make public the reasons why they rule one way or the other on difficult legal issues, especially in contested constitutional law cases. One eminent law professor has expressed this idea as follows:

> Because of the inescapability of judgment in the interpretation and application of the Constitution, candor is essential if the justices . . . are to ask the rest of us to take them seriously. . . . Only if you and I understand the true grounds of the decision can we assent to its correctness . . . even though we think it wrong in substance. Because the Constitution is not a crossword puzzle with only one right answer . . . , playing the constitutional game fairly demands that the players be clear about why they give the answers they do. *Candor is indispensable if the system is to retain its moral dignity.*[1]

The Justices of the United States Supreme Court, however, do not treat prior law in a way that generates their constitutional decisions nor do they consistently offer the true justifications for the results they reach. Instead, the Justices employ the fancy but misleading jargon of constitutional law (text, history, and prior cases) to hide the personal value judgments that actually support their decisions. Thus, both in terms of their adherence to prior law, and their obligation to transparently explain legal decisions, the Justices fail to act like true judges.

One reason that prior law does not generate the Justices' decisions in constitutional cases is that most of the cases they choose to hear involve vague terms such as *due process of law, equal protection of the law, establishment of religion,* and *liberty.* These concepts simply cannot be defined without controversial and subjective interpretations. Imagine a legal directive requiring that Supreme Court Justices decide whether the government is acting *right,* or *fair* or requiring the Court to determine whether people are treated *equally* by the government or whether their *liberty* has been denied by the government. Would it make sense to say the Court is following or interpreting prior legal directives when determining what words like *fair, equal,* or *liberty* mean? Yet, these are the words that have generated the Court's decisions on abortion, affirmative action, privacy, and gay rights, among many others. When the Justices give meaning to phrases like *equal protection of the law* and *due process of law,* they are employing their own ideas of right and wrong formed by personal life experiences, not interpreting prior law.

Another reason Supreme Court Justices do not act like other judges is that, whereas most judges have to abide by the decisions of higher courts (as well as legislatures), which serves as a legal constraint on their judging, there is no court review of Supreme Court constitutional cases, and the Supreme Court does not now and never has taken its own precedent seriously. Essentially, that means the Court is free to change its prior decisions, and thus the law, as it sees fit, and it does so frequently.

The Justices of the Supreme Court do act like judges in the sense that they hear cases brought by opposing parties and decide who wins and loses. In this way, they are *judges,* just as people who decide beauty contests are judges in the common usage of that term. But, beauty contest judges are not *judges of law* because, among other reasons, the criteria these "judges" use to determine the winners are much more about subjectivity and taste than logic and reason, and the same is true for the Justices of the United States Supreme Court. As Judge Richard Posner has explained, the Justices decide constitutional cases:

> Only on the basis of a political judgment and a political judgment cannot be called right or wrong by reference to *legal* norms. . . . One may be able to give reasons for liking or disliking the decision . . . and people who agree with the reasons will be inclined to say that the decision is correct or incorrect. But that is just a form of words. One can, for that matter . . . give reasons for preferring a Margarita to a Cosmopolitan. The problem, in both cases, is that there are certain to be equally articulate, 'reasonable' people who disagree and can offer plausible reasons for their disagreement, [but] there will be no common metric that will enable a disinterested observer (if there is such a person) to decide who is right. . . . *From a practical standpoint, constitutional adjudication by the Supreme Court is also the exercise of discretion—and that is about all it is* [emphasis added].[2]

There is simply no way to privilege an answer to the question whether a Margarita is better than a Cosmopolitan, and there is similarly no way to privilege an answer to the question whether the United States Constitution protects the right of women to have abortions, whether cities may prohibit all handguns, or whether admissions committees at public schools may use racial quotas for affirmative action purposes, as well as most other constitutional questions decided by the Supreme Court. These are all questions of policy, judgment, and taste, and the Court has unfettered discretion to resolve them as the Justices see fit.

The vagueness of the sources of constitutional law, the Court's privilege to reverse prior cases without constraint, and the inherently value-laden nature of the entire enterprise explain why brilliant and skilled Justices like Justices Antonin Scalia and Ruth Bader Ginsburg disagree on virtually every contested issue of constitutional law. These Justices view the Constitution differently not because they have better or worse legal abilities or one is more skilled than the other at constitutional interpretation, but because they embrace vastly different fundamental values and have had different life experiences. When nine such people are not constrained by prior cases or any higher court, and need at least five votes to produce an outcome, it is not surprising that their decisions resemble the work of a political veto council much more than a court of law.

WHY IT MATTERS THAT THE COURT ACTS LIKE A VETO COUNCIL NOT A COURT OF LAW

If it is true that the Supreme Court does not apply prior law in a judgelike manner, then the original and most plausible justification for allowing the political preferences of these *unelected* governmental officials to trump the value judgments of *elected* officials simply disappears.

The justification for judicial review embraced by the Founding Fathers and supported by most people today is that "We the People" agreed to fundamental principles in our Constitution (and its Amendments) limiting future governments, and then we assigned the enforcement of those principles to judges. Under this system of limited government (as opposed to a country where the legislature is supreme or kingly tyranny), judges act as agents for the people who drafted the constitutional rules for future governments. In other words, the Constitution is the supreme law of the land and trumps ordinary legislation and other political decisions. To make this constitutional democracy work, judges do not need to and should not substitute their own policy choices for those of other political officials, but they are under an obligation to make sure that the Constitution's preexisting rules (to the extent they are ascertainable) are enforced.

The problem is that this "agency" theory of judicial review does not even remotely describe nor justify how the Supreme Court actually makes constitutional decisions. The Court frequently invalidates the policy choices of other governmental officials even where the relevant constitutional text is vague and its history indeterminate. Supreme Court cases overturning laws dealing with abortion, campaign finance reform, gun control, affirmative action, and many other important social issues cannot be justified on the basis that those laws violate either clear constitutional text or uncontested accounts of the will of the people who wrote and/or ratified that text. Unless the Court's decisions can be supported in that way, however, it is difficult to justify the Supreme Court's substitution of its own value judgments for those of the Congress, the president, and the states on difficult and controversial policy questions.

WHY THE MYTHS CONTINUE

The Court has not acted like a true court when overruling the laws of the elected branches for a long time, raising the question why the myths continue. The answer is partly that law professors, Supreme Court Justices, and United States senators have few incentives to describe the Court's decision-making process accurately. If Supreme Court decision making is much more about values than law, constitutional law professors (and I am one) might not be the most qualified "experts" to suggest what results the Court should reach. After all, my views on the validity of affirmative action programs, abortion laws, or gun control regulations, or the opinions of any other legal academic, are no "better" than anyone else's views because the resolution of these, and most other constitutional issues, implicates values, life experiences, and politics much more than law and logic. To many constitutional law professors, the myth that the Justices decide constitutional cases like traditional judges helps the professors protect their intellectual turf.

The Justices themselves have little incentive to be transparent about the job they do because, if the American people truly understood that the Court's decisions are more about values than law, the Justices would have a much harder time justifying both their power and life tenure. As Justice Scalia once famously quipped in a right-to-die case, the Justices of the Supreme Court are no better equipped to decide hard questions about the end of life than nine people picked at random from the Kansas City telephone directory. Unfortunately, neither Justice Scalia nor any other Justice acts consistently with this idea because both liberal and conservative Justices frequently overturn policy decisions of the elected branches and the states without a solid grounding in constitutional text, prior cases, or history. Public officials tend to lose their humility when they are given awesome and largely unreviewable governmental power for life, and Supreme Court Justices are no exception.

Most senators won't acknowledge that the Court's constitutional cases are more about values than law because if they did their constituencies might demand that judicial nominees provide real answers to hard questions during Supreme Court confirmation hearings—a result few senators favor. Under the current myths, nominees will not discuss prior cases or specific legal doctrine usually arguing that prospective judges should not disclose how they would decide legal issues that may come before them. But this practice only makes sense with traditional judges who are constrained to a significant degree by law and/or other courts. The Senate's confirmation process, as it now operates, serves to reinforce the false idea that Supreme Court Justices simply apply the preexisting law of the Constitution when overturning the acts of other political officials when, in fact, the Court is actually imposing its own controversial value judgments.

The myth that the Supreme Court acts like a court of law is especially problematic because our Justices are the only judges in the world who occupy seats on a country's highest court for life. When other democracies studied the American legal and political system in the middle and late 20th century and adopted the idea of judicial review, none of those countries chose to create a Supreme Court staffed by judges with life tenure. The reason is obvious—in a democracy no person should be given a governmental position for life where he or she wields significant power over some of the most important and controversial issues a nation has to resolve.

The false notion that the Supreme Court operates like other courts needs to be dispelled because the American people have a right to know how the third branch of the national government truly operates. Both the executive and legislative branches have changed dramatically since the founding of the country. The Court, however, functions substantially the same way it did in the 19th century, and it is well past time for a change. Liberals and conservatives; Republicans and Democrats; the rich, the poor, and the middle class; the religious and the agnostic; in short, all Americans, have a vested interest in fundamentally reevaluating the third branch of the national government and seeing it for what it really is, an ultimate political veto council.

It is important to briefly highlight what this book does not argue. Nothing here should be interpreted as making the claim that Supreme Court decision making simply comes down to partisan politics. Sometimes conservative Justices issue decisions that would be favored by the Democratic Party and more liberal Justices reach results Republicans would like. But the fact that the individual Justices don't always vote the preferences of their political party does not mean that the Justices are deciding cases *under the law*. Political preferences drive the Justices' constitutional decisions to some degree but so do their life experiences, religious and moral values, and other subjective beliefs. The myth this book is devoted to debunking is that legal considerations play a significant role in generating Supreme Court decisions. Text, history, and precedent simply don't count for much when the Court decides constitutional cases, and certainly count less than politics, values, and personal beliefs separate from prior positive law.

This book also does not claim, as some academics have suggested, that there are no relevant differences between Supreme Court Justices and legislators like senators and members of the House of Representatives. Because the Court is limited by the Constitution to deciding "cases and controversies," the Justices can only rule on issues that are brought to them by injured parties. Therefore, there are some limitations on the policy questions the Court can decide whereas legislators are free to pursue their own personal agendas.

Another difference between Supreme Court Justices and legislators is that the Justices are supposed to decide cases pursuant to preexisting law, whereas politicians are free to vote their consciences in an "all things considered manner." This is the difference that many academics point to as distinguishing the work of judges from the work of legislators. The central thesis of this book, however, is that Supreme Court Justices, because they (1) often deal with vague text and contestable historical accounts, (2) are allowed to overturn their own cases whenever they wish, and (3) cannot be overturned by any other court, are not bound by preexisting law in any meaningful sense of the word *bound*. The Justices are not legislators in the ordinary sense, but neither are they legal judges in the ordinary sense.

This book does not tackle issues raised by the criminal law provisions of the Constitution. When the Court decides whether searches are "unreasonable," or punishments "cruel and unusual," or jeopardy is "double," the Court is deciding issues directly relevant to their courtrooms, what evidence can be admitted, and other traditional tasks judges must perform (such as sentencing). Although the Court's treatment of these questions supports the view that its decisions are much more about values than law, there is a substantial difference between asking the Court to govern the courtroom and asking the Court to decide social issues such as abortion, gun control, and affirmative action. Those differences require different treatment and must await another book.

My last caveat is that the descriptive account herein is limited to the Court's duties under the Constitution. When the Court decides cases by interpreting federal statutes or state law, the Court can be overturned by a majoritarian process (i.e., Congress can change the law or state legislatures can modify state law). The Supreme Court only has the final say over the meaning and interpretation of the United States Constitution, and how it performs that task is the subject of this book.

CHAPTER 2

Marbury v. Madison and the Birth of Judicial Review

It is emphatically the province and duty of the Judicial Department to say what the law is.

—John Marshall

The Constitution on this hypothesis is a mere thing of wax in the hands of the judiciary, which they may twist and shape into any form they please.

—Thomas Jefferson

THE BACKGROUND

On January 31, 1801, a little more than a decade after the United States Constitution was ratified, John Marshall was confirmed as the fourth Chief Justice of the Supreme Court. Just a few weeks later, Marshall swore in Thomas Jefferson as America's third president. Although both men hailed from Virginia, were distant cousins, and two of this nation's greatest patriots, they profoundly disliked each other. Jefferson, a staunch antifederalist, believed strongly in state autonomy and local decision making. Marshall, on the other hand, was a dedicated federalist who believed in a more robust national government. Both men spent much of their careers applying their respective visions of government to the problems facing the brand new country.

The two men also had significant personal differences perhaps caused in part by John Marshall marrying a woman whose mother had rejected Thomas Jefferson's hand in marriage. As the years went by, and both men advanced in government, they frequently criticized each other publicly. For example, when opposing Marshall's election to the House of Representatives, Jefferson said that Marshall had "lax, lounging manners," which at the time was a grave insult, and later Jefferson said that Marshall was adept at "twistifications."[1] On the other hand, Marshall opposed Jefferson's presidency on the grounds, that "[h]is foreign prejudices seem to me totally to unfit him for the chief magistracy of a nation which cannot indulge those prejudices without sustaining deep and permanent injury," and because "[b]y weakening the office of President [Jefferson] will increase his personal power . . . diminish his responsibility, [and] sap the fundamental principles of the government."[2] The personal antagonism between these two important Founding Fathers, as well as their sharply differing views on the appropriate role of the brand new national government, provides the context for the first, and probably most important, constitutional law decision in this country's history.

The story begins on February 27, 1801, less than one week before Jefferson was sworn into office as the new president (replacing the incumbent John Adams), when the outgoing federalist Congress authorized the appointment of 42 judges for the District of Columbia, as well as a host of new federal judges. The District of Columbia positions were important because the judges were responsible, not only for deciding cases, but also for maintaining the public order.[3]

A few days later, on the second-to-last day of his presidency, John Adams appointed these judges many of whom were members of his own Federalist Party. The lame-duck Senate confirmed them the next day in the hopes of stacking the judiciary with men of their own political persuasion before the government was turned over to their bitter rivals (known at the time as the Democratic-Republican Party), the very next day.

In a bizarre twist of history, the person responsible for sealing and delivering the commissions to the new judges was none other than Chief Justice John Marshall, who also happened to be serving temporarily as John Adams's secretary of state. With the help of his brother, Justice Marshall delivered many of the commissions, but the two men didn't have time to deliver them all. One of the commissions that didn't get delivered was for William Marbury. Marshall later explained that, given the shifting administrations, the State Department was short-handed that night and, in any event, he didn't view the delivery of the commissions as legally necessary believing they were valid when signed and sealed.[4]

Thomas Jefferson was sworn into office as president the next day and discovered the commissions that hadn't been delivered. He directed his acting Secretary of State Levi Lincoln not to deliver them to the new federalist judges, including Marbury. Eventually, Marbury, and a few other federalists who weren't made judges, filed a lawsuit in the Supreme Court arguing that, once Congress authorized their judgeships and the president appointed them, they were entitled to become judges. Marbury asked for a legal remedy called a writ of mandamus, which is a court order requiring an executive official to perform an act required by law.

Marbury's lawsuit made Thomas Jefferson so angry that he ordered his attorneys not to show up at the oral argument. Jefferson also made it clear that he believed the Supreme Court, led by his rival John Marshall, had no legal authority to direct the president of the United States to take any action, much less make someone a judge. This might have made Marshall think that if he ruled against Jefferson and ordered him to make Marbury a judge, the president might refuse to obey the Court order, which could lead to a constitutional crisis a few short years after the country was founded.

The friction over the appropriate role of the federal courts in the new country transcended the *Marbury* case. For example, in what was viewed as a partisan move given that Marshall was Chief Justice, Jefferson convinced the new Congress to abolish the terms of the Supreme Court that were to take place in June and December of 1802. At the same time, Congress, with Jefferson's support, began impeachment proceedings against a few federalist judges and repealed the law passed by the prior Congress authorizing the creation of new federal judges. The nation's two political parties were fighting each other on many fronts, but the nature, scope, and legitimacy of the federal judiciary was the most important battleground. It was against this backdrop of nasty, partisan politics, as acrimonious as anything we have today, that the case of *Marbury v. Madison* finally came before the Court in 1803.[5]

THE DECISION

The Court hearing in *Marbury v. Madison* may have been "one of the oddest" in "the history of American litigation."[6] It began in a small committee room in the Capitol (no Supreme Court building existed at the time), and was later moved to a hotel for the benefit of one of the infirm Justices. Marbury's lawyer, former Attorney General Charles Lee, had to first establish the underlying facts (i.e., that Marbury had been granted a commission that had not been delivered). The problem was that the Senate and Jefferson's State Department refused to produce any relevant documents. Lee did subpoena Levi Lincoln (the current attorney general of the United States and former acting secretary of state) to testify, but Lincoln refused to answer questions on the grounds that a high-ranking executive branch officer could not be forced by the Court to testify about official business. There seemed to be an impasse until Lincoln agreed to answer written questions from Charles Lee. He answered them the next day saying that he had seen a number of the commissions on March 4, 1801, but he did not recollect whether Marbury's was among them. Lincoln did admit that he had not given the commissions to the incoming Secretary of State James Madison but never revealed what actually happened to them.[7]

The great irony of the proceedings was that "the person who would have been the best witness, the person responsible for the fiasco—was sitting in the presiding chair as Chief Justice. . . . Everyone in court knew exactly what had happened, but no one could, or would, provide the formal evidence."[8] Eventually, relying on the testimony of a state department clerk, as well as affidavits from John Marshall's brother, Charles Lee simply announced he had proven the facts and moved on to his legal argument that Marbury had a right to his commission.[9] Because Jefferson did not see fit to send his lawyers to the hearing, there was no objection.

After Lee set forth his view of the law, the Court adjourned. On February 4, 1803, almost two years after Marbury was supposed to receive his commission, the Court rendered its unanimous decision holding that the Court did not have jurisdiction over the case (meaning Marbury would not get his commission), but also setting forth the first judicial defense of judicial review over both congressional and executive actions thereby strengthening the Court's power at the very moment that its authority was being threatened the most. Marshall made the astute political judgment that he would announce the great principle of judicial review in a case where, ultimately, the president would prevail, and Congress would be largely indifferent. In deciding the case the way he did, however, Marshall committed three clear legal errors demonstrating that he cared much more about making important policy decisions than acting like a true judge.

First, John Marshall should never have decided the case . Marshall began his opinion by asking whether physical delivery of the judicial commission to Marbury was necessary to make it legally binding. Not surprisingly, Marshall's answer was that delivery was unnecessary because, of course, it was John Marshall himself who had been responsible for that delivery and failed to complete the task! Had the commission been delivered in time, Marbury would have become a judge, and there would have been no case. Thus, Marshall was involved in the underlying facts of the case and, by any standards, should have recused himself. Moreover, there can be no argument that recusal was a concept foreign to the Chief Justice because during the same time period he recused himself in the important case of *Martin v. Hunter's Lessee*,[10] which established that the Supreme Court could overturn acts of the states as well as those of the federal government. No judge should ever decide a case where the plaintiff's injury stems, in part, from the judge's own actions, and *Marbury v. Madison* should not have been an exception.

The second legal mistake made by Marshall has to do with the order in which he decided the issues in the case. The two substantive legal issues in *Marbury v. Madison* were (1) whether the delivery of the judicial commission was necessary to make it effective, and, (2) if the commission was effective without delivery, did the Supreme Court have the power to order the president of the United States to give Marbury his judgeship? There was, however, a jurisdictional defect with the case because Marbury filed his suit originally in the Supreme Court and not some lower court.

It was and remains a fundamental rule of our judicial system that a court must first decide whether it has jurisdiction over a case and then, only if it finds it has jurisdiction, can it move on to discuss the substance or merits of that case.[11] In *Marbury*, however, Justice Marshall improperly reversed this normal order so that he could achieve his political goals.

Discussing the merits first, Marshall decided both that the commission was legally binding even without delivery, and that the Court, *if* it had proper jurisdiction, could order the president to comply with the law. In this part of the opinion, Marshall persuasively argued that, to be a country of laws not men, the president had to be answerable to the Court when he violated vested legal rights (assuming proper jurisdiction of course). The problem, as discussed below, was that Marshall also decided that such jurisdiction was lacking in this case making his discussion of the Court's power to order the president to comply with the law completely unnecessary to the decision in the case. This move would turn out to be brilliant strategy because Marshall announced that the Court had power over the president in a case the president actually won on other grounds. Marshall was able to avoid a constitutional confrontation at the same time that he added significantly to the Supreme Court's authority. He achieved this political goal, however, only by failing to act like a true judge who should decide jurisdictional issues before looking at the merits of the case.

Marshall's third legal error was that, even when finally turning to the jurisdictional issue in the case, he did not act like a judge who is supposed to interpret the law in good faith. The issue was whether Marbury had filed his suit in the right court because he sued initially in the Supreme Court not in a lower court. There are several ways to bring a case to the United States Supreme Court. The plaintiff can file a lawsuit in federal or state court asserting a federal issue and then, if he loses, appeal it all the way to the Supreme Court. A plaintiff can also try to file a case *originally* in the Supreme Court, which is what Marbury did. The problem was that, under the unambiguous language of Article III of the Constitution, the Supreme Court only has original jurisdiction in cases involving foreign "ambassadors, ministers and consuls," and where a state is a party to the case.[12] Marbury's case, however, did not fall under any of these categories of *original* jurisdiction. Thus, Marshall should simply have dismissed the case on the grounds that Marbury's suit could not be heard by the Court as an *original* matter. There should have been no discussion of the president's power, the legality of the commission without delivery, or any other issue.

The problem with that approach for Marshall was that he wanted to establish, not only that the president had to abide by Court orders, but also that the Court could exercise judicial review over acts of Congress inconsistent with the Constitution. He could not reach that goal by simply dismissing the case because it fell outside of Article III, so he created a false conflict between a federal law and the Constitution.

There was a federal statute, the Judiciary Act of 1789, which provided that the Supreme Court had the power to issue "writs of mandamus, in cases warranted by the principles and usages of law, to any . . . persons holding office, under the authority of the United States."[13] This statute was intended to allow the Court to issue a writ of mandamus (a traditional legal remedy) when it was legally "warranted" in a case with proper jurisdiction. Marshall, however, interpreted the law to *grant original* jurisdiction to the Supreme Court in *any* and *every* case where a plaintiff asked for a writ of mandamus, and Marbury was seeking such a writ.

The problem was that the Judiciary Act did not come close to saying what Marshall said it did and, had it done so, it would have been completely inconsistent with the clear text of Article III, which sets forth the three narrow situations where Supreme Court original jurisdiction is allowed (and asking for a writ of mandamus is not one of them). In fact, the primary drafter of the section of the Judiciary Act Marshall was talking about was Oliver Ellsworth, the Chief Justice before Marshall, as well as a member of the First Congress and a delegate to the Constitutional Convention.[14] Marshall had the temerity to argue that Ellsworth drafted a federal statute that violated a part of the Constitution (Article III) that Ellsworth also helped write. Of course, the Judiciary Act was never intended to provide for original jurisdiction in the Supreme Court simply because the plaintiff sought a writ of mandamus, and thus Ellsworth did not, in fact, write a statute that was inconsistent with Article III.

Nevertheless, because Marshall suggested (implausibly) that Congress had intended in the Judiciary Act to allow for original jurisdiction every time a plaintiff sought a writ of mandamus (an impossible reading of the law), he was able to address the issue of judicial review—what should the Court do when presented with a law that is inconsistent with the Constitution?

Despite literally making up a question that didn't exist, and making a mockery of a judge's job to interpret the law accurately, Marshall did eloquently lay out the reasons why the Court needed to have the power of judicial review over the acts of the elected branches. Echoing many of the ideas expressed during the preratification debates on the issue, and noting that the United States was intended to be a government of limited powers, Marshall explained that:

> Certainly all those who have framed written Constitutions contemplate them as forming the fundamental and paramount law of the nation, and consequently the theory of every such government

must be that an act of the Legislature repugnant to the Constitution is void.

It is emphatically the province and duty of the Judicial Department to say what the law is. Those who apply the rule to particular cases must, of necessity, expound and interpret that rule. If two laws conflict with each other, the Courts must decide on the operation of each. . . . This is the very essence of judicial duty.

If, then, the Courts are to regard the Constitution, and the Constitution is superior to any ordinary act of the Legislature, the Constitution, and not such ordinary act, must govern the case to which they both apply. [15]

Marshall's rationale for the necessity of judicial review makes sense, but it is unfortunate that he articulated his justification in a case that (1) he shouldn't have decided in the first place (because he should have recused himself), and (2) the issue should never have arisen because there was no true conflict between a law of Congress and the Constitution. In any event, because Jefferson won the case on jurisdictional grounds, and Marshall invalidated part of a law that didn't really exist in the first place, there was little opposition to the case other than Jefferson's public criticism that was largely ignored by the public and the press.

One more point about Marshall's reasoning in *Marbury* must be emphasized. Although *Marbury* formally announced that the Supreme Court had the power to overturn acts of the elected branches, there is reason to believe that the kind of judicial review contemplated by Marshall was quite different from the kind the Court would eventually exercise. In *Marbury*, Marshall gave examples as to why he believed judicial review was necessary. He noted that the clear text of the Constitution requires that treason has to be proven either by two witnesses or by confession in open court.[16] What would happen, he asked rhetorically, if Congress passed a law allowing treason to be proven with only one witness? The answer, obviously, would be that the law would be invalid; otherwise "constitutional principle" would have to yield to a "legislative act," and that would be inconsistent with the entire notion of a written Constitution.[17] Other examples provided by Marshall also involve violations of unambiguous constitutional text.[18] One must wonder what Marshall would have thought of the Supreme Court prescribing abortion codes, affirmative action regulations, and campaign finance reform guidelines, among many other current policies, pursuant to the vague language of the First and Fourteenth Amendments.[19] Although Marshall definitely favored a strong role for the Court in the American system of checks and balances, it is highly unlikely that he would have approved of the Court acting as a super legislature and influencing so many of our economic, social, and political questions.

Marbury v. Madison is as important for its lawlessness as it is for being the first case granting the federal courts the power of judicial review over both the Congress and the president. After all, if the first and arguably most important case in constitutional law could be decided by a Justice flagrantly violating core conceptions of judicial recusal, judicial power, and statutory interpretation, why should the Court act like a responsible court in cases involving freedom of speech, abortion, the right to own guns, and so forth? With *Marbury,* the Supreme Court's exercise of judicial review was divorced from the practice of deciding cases like true judges from the very start.

CHAPTER 3

Racial Discrimination: *Dred Scott, Plessy,* and the Reconstruction Amendments

How much would it be worth to a young man upon the practice of law to be regarded as a white man rather than a colored one? Six-sevenths of the population are white. Nineteen-twentieths of the property of the country is owned by white people. Ninety-nine hundredths of the business opportunities are in the control of white people. . . . Probably most white persons if given a choice would prefer death to life in the United States as colored persons. Under these conditions, it is not possible to conclude that the reputation of being white is not property. Indeed, is it not the most valuable sort of property, being the master-key that unlocks the golden door of opportunity.

—Albion Tourgee, lawyer for Homer Plessy

SLAVERY AND DRED SCOTT

After *Marbury v. Madison* was decided, the Supreme Court did not invalidate a single federal law for 54 years, although it did overturn numerous state laws.[1] This may have been due to the fact that our economy had not yet moved westward or industrialized, and Congress did not enact many laws important enough to be challenged in court. This trend, however, ended in 1857 when the Court decided the infamous *Dred Scott* case holding that African Americans were not citizens of the United States, and Congress had no power to abolish slavery in the territories.[2] Any discussion of the role the Supreme Court has played in American history must take into account this important and tragic case.

The practice of slavery was a major issue during the debates leading to American independence, and the Founding Fathers wrote into the Constitution a number of provisions dealing with the issue. Congress was prohibited from ending slavery until 1808; slaves were counted as three-fifths of a person for purposes of apportionment; and the Constitution required states to "deliver up" escaped slaves and prohibited the states from discharging them.[3] There can be little doubt that the Constitution would not have been ratified without these proslavery provisions.[4]

When the Supreme Court eventually became involved in the slavery issue, the Justices tended to overturn modestly progressive laws designed to limit the institution. For example, in *Prigg v. Pennsylvania*,[5] the Supreme Court held unconstitutional a state law prohibiting the removal of a black person from Pennsylvania by force or violence in order to detain him as a slave. The Court believed that the federal Constitution gave slave owners unqualified rights in their property, and therefore state laws could not interfere with those rights.[6] Furthermore, the Court held that Congress had the power to help owners recover escaped slaves, and all state laws to the contrary were unconstitutional.[7] The Court, as a policy matter, was lagging behind at least some of the states in the desire to limit the effects and practice of slavery.

The Court's landmark decision in *Dred Scott* involved a slave in Missouri who was taken by his owner to Illinois, a free state.[8] After his master died, Scott offered to pay the master's widow $300 for his freedom, but the widow refused. Scott then sued the administrator of the estate claiming that he was a free man because he now lived in Illinois.[9] His grounds for jurisdiction were diversity of citizenship, which allows citizens of one state to sue citizens of another state in federal court.[10] He lost in the lower federal court and appealed to the Supreme Court of the United States.

Seven of the Justices at the time had been appointed by proslavery presidents from the South, and of these, five Justices were from slave-holding families. Thus, it was not surprising that Scott faced an uphill battle. Chief Justice Taney, writing the opinion for the Court, held that Scott could not sue in federal court because a "negro" ancestor of a former slave was not and could not be a citizen of the United States, regardless of his current status. In other words, almost 70 years after the country was founded, blacks were invisible to the laws of the United States.

In addition to finding that Scott could not sue as a "citizen," the Court went on to hold that the Missouri Compromise, which had forbid slavery in certain territories, was unconstitutional.[11] The Court said that Congress had no power to pass such a law, and that, because slaves were property, their owners' rights could not be extinguished without violating the due process clause of the Fifth Amendment.[12]

There are numerous problems with the *Dred Scott* decision beyond the obvious harm caused by the Court's decision that Congress could not end slavery in the territories and the holding that descendants of slaves could not be citizens. First, while the case was pending, president-elect James Buchanan wrote a letter to Supreme Court Justice John Catron asking him when the case would be decided. Buchanan hoped that a decision against Scott would settle the slavery issue once and for all.[13] After Buchanan received an answer, he successfully pressured Justice Robert Grier, a Northerner, to join the Southern majority to prevent the appearance that the decision was made along regional lines.[14] These were improper *ex parte* contacts even by the judicial standards of the time. Yet, the Court ignored the improprieties and issued its infamous decision without a word about the presidential interference, something a true court should never have done.

Second, the Court's decision that the Missouri Compromise exceeded Congress's powers and prevented it from forbidding slavery in the territories ignored clearly settled law and violated unambiguous constitutional text. Article IV of the Constitution provides that "Congress shall have power to dispose of and make all needful Rules and Regulations respecting the Territory or other Property belonging to the United States."[15] Pursuant to this language, the newly formed Congress, in 1789, passed the Northwest Ordinance, which prohibited slavery in the territory northwest of the Ohio River.[16] It is virtually impossible to believe that the Founding Fathers who passed this law in 1789, the year after the Constitution was ratified, would have believed that Congress lacked the power to limit slavery in the territories outside the states. If the *Dred Scott* Court had been truly interested in acting like a court and making a decision based on preexisting positive law sources, as well as the original will of the people, the Missouri Compromise would have been upheld. As one of the dissents in the case pointed out, the Court's decision "had abandoned the law for politics and assumed an authority that rightfully belonged to the political branches."[17] But, as many scholars have observed, the

Court erroneously thought that it could end the slavery controversy with its opinion preventing Congress from taking any future efforts to lessen the impact of slavery.[18] The Court's policy objective was much more important to the Justices than giving a faithful reading to preexisting positive law. The *Dred Scott* ruling was a tragic mistake by an unaccountable political institution, and it helped lead to the Civil War.

THE RECONSTRUCTION AMENDMENTS

After the Civil War, the United States enacted the Thirteenth, Fourteenth, and Fifteenth Amendments to the United States Constitution. These amendments finally ended slavery, gave blacks the right to vote, guaranteed to citizens the "privileges and immunities" of citizenship, and prohibited the states from denying any person the "equal protection of the laws," or taking any person's "life, liberty, or property without due process of law."[19] In addition, Congress was explicitly given the power to enforce these amendments through "appropriate legislation."[20] Although the purposes of these amendments were to reverse the Court's decision in *Dred Scott* and give the newly freed slaves the status of full citizens and the right to vote, there were questions left open by these fundamental changes to the Constitution. These issues included the following:

1. Did the amendments prohibit racial segregation in public facilities and public schools?
2. Did the amendments give Congress the power to prohibit *private* discrimination in places of public accommodations like restaurants and hotels?
3. Did the amendments create significant new national "privileges and immunities" enjoyed by citizens and enforceable in the federal courts?

Over the next 30 years, the Court would provide answers to all of these questions. Unfortunately, the Court failed to deliver on the promise of equality that the drafters of these amendments intended to ensure to the newly freed slaves.[21]

The Court's first major interpretation of the new amendments came in a case that did not directly involve race relations but certainly had major implications for racial issues. In *The Slaughter-House*

Cases,[22] the Court had to decide the constitutionality of a Louisiana law that gave a monopoly to a company in the slaughter-house business in New Orleans and the surrounding territory. The plaintiffs were butchers who asserted that their "right to exercise their trade" was deprived by the statute.[23] They claimed, among other things, that the Louisiana monopoly law abridged their "privileges and immunities" protected by the Fourteenth Amendment.[24] The Court noted that this was its first opportunity to interpret the newly enacted amendment, and held that the "privileges and immunities" of the "citizens of the United States" only covered a narrow category of rights owing their existence to the national government, such as the right to habeas corpus and the right to the protection of the government when on the "high seas," and did not affect fundamental rights traditionally protected by the states such as the right to pursue an occupation.[25] The Court argued that the protection of these rights had to lie "where they have heretofore rested," with the governments of the states.[26]

In reaching this conclusion, the majority relied much more on its own judgment of the appropriate relationships among the states, the federal government, and the people than on constitutional text, the history of that text, prior case law, or the fact that the Reconstruction Amendments were specifically designed to alter the balance of power between the states and the federal government after the Civil War. The dissenting opinions did not ignore the enormity and significance of the majority's holding. Justice Field said the following:

> The question presented is . . . of the gravest importance, not merely to the parties here, but to the whole country. It is nothing less than the question whether the recent amendments to the Federal Constitution protect the citizens of the United States against the deprivation of their common rights by State legislation. In my judgment the fourteenth amendment does afford such protection, and was so intended by the Congress which framed it and the States which adopted it.[27]

As one commentator has observed, the majority's decision was based on the political reality that the Court "was more concerned about preserving the states' regulatory functions than in establishing national authority to [enforce the new Civil Rights Amendments]."[28]

After effectively reading the Privileges and Immunities Clause out of the Constitution by interpreting it so narrowly, the Court then had to answer the question whether Congress had the power to prohibit racial discrimination in hotels, restaurants, and other places of public accommodations. The Civil Rights Act of 1875 was Congress's attempt to end private racial discrimination by making it illegal for individuals to discriminate on the basis of race in "inns, public conveyances, and theatres."[29] The law was to some extent a reaction to the efforts of white supremacist groups and other private individuals and businesses to maintain separate living conditions and separate societies for whites and blacks, not only in the South, but throughout the entire country.

In *The Civil Rights Cases*,[30] the Court consolidated five lower court cases where blacks had been excluded from whites-only places of public accommodations. The plaintiffs had been excluded from a dining room in Topeka, Kansas, an opera in New York City, good seats in a San Francisco theater, and a railway car set aside for ladies on a train in an undisclosed location. The issue before the Court was whether Congress had the power pursuant to the Thirteenth and Fourteenth Amendments to abolish private racial discrimination. The Thirteenth Amendment ended slavery, and Section 5 of the Fourteenth Amendment gave Congress the power to "enforce by appropriate legislation" the rest of the Fourteenth Amendment, including its promise to all citizens of the "equal protection" of the laws.

In a relatively short 8–1 opinion, the Court held that Congress lacked authority to end racial discrimination by private individuals and only gave Congress the power to redress "state action."[31] The Court said that an "individual cannot deprive a man of his [rights]; he may, by force or fraud, interfere with the enjoyment of the right in a particular case; [but] unless protected in these wrongful acts by some shield of state law or state authority, he cannot destroy or injure the right."[32] Therefore, the Fourteenth Amendment is concerned only with official state practices, and the "[i]ndividual invasion of individual rights is not the subject-matter of the amendment."[33] Under this reasoning, Congress had no power to enforce the "equal protection of the laws," by regulating private discriminatory behavior.

The Court also had to wrestle with the plaintiffs' argument that the Thirteenth Amendment, which ended "involuntary servitude," authorized Congress to end private racial discrimination. The Court, although agreeing that Congress could reach private action to stop both slavery and its "badges and incidents," nevertheless held that the refusal to serve a black person in a place of public accommodation was not such a "badge or incident."[34] The Court held that refusal of service had nothing to do with slavery and the acceptance of such a theory "would be running the slavery argument into the ground."[35] Thus, Congress was not allowed to prevent private individuals and companies from discriminating on the basis of race.[36]

The dissent saw the matter differently. Justice Harlan believed that both the Thirteenth and Fourteenth Amendments gave Congress the authority to regulate private action that discriminated against African Americans.[37] He said that the majority's narrowing of the new amendments reduced them to "baubles, thrown out to delude those who deserved fair and generous treatment at the hands of the nation. Citizenship in this country necessarily imports at least equality of civil rights among citizens of every race in the same state."[38] He also argued that, even if the Fourteenth Amendment required state action to be enforced, "[i]n every material sense . . . railroad corporations, keepers of inns, and managers of places of public amusement are agents or instrumentalities of the State, because they are charged with duties to the public, and are amenable, in respect of their duties and functions, to governmental regulation."[39] Justice Harlan would have allowed Congress to prohibit racial discrimination in stores, hotels, and restaurants to make good the promise of equal protection under the law for the newly freed slaves, but he was the lone voice on a Supreme Court determined to keep the unjust and unequal social order firmly in place. That the Justices other than Harlan held those views is reflected in an entry made in his private journal by the author of the *Civil Rights Cases,* Joseph Bradley. He wrote that "depriving white people of the right of choosing their own company would be to introduce another kind of slavery."[40] It is most unfortunate that Justice Bradley had the legal authority to impose this social/political view on a Congress wishing to end racial discrimination.

The third important public policy question the Court had to answer concerning the new Civil Rights Amendments was whether official state action that segregated whites and blacks in buses, trains, hotels, and restaurants was constitutional. This was a different question from the one presented by the *Civil Rights Cases.* The issue there was whether *Congress* could prohibit racial discrimination as a matter of federal law not whether the Reconstruction Amendments prevented the *states* from requiring segregation as a matter of state law. Unfortunately, on this issue, once again, the Court failed to deliver on the promises made by the Reconstruction Amendments.

The landmark case testing the validity of state segregation laws was actually a planned challenge by an organization called the Citizens' Committee to Test the Constitutionality of the Separate Car Law, a group of black professionals in New Orleans.[41] It wanted to file a lawsuit seeking to overturn a Louisiana law titled rather ironically "An Act to Promote the Comfort of Passengers," which required railroads to provide separate but equal accommodations for whites and blacks. The group's strategy was to have a person with mixed blood violate the law, get arrested, and then challenge the conviction in court.[42]

Homer Plessy, a native of Louisiana who was seven-eights white, agreed to challenge the law and be the test case. On June 7, 1892, Plessy boarded the whites-only part of a train and was arrested by a private detective who had arrest powers. The whole incident had been arranged beforehand with the railroad's knowledge because it was also opposed to the law that required it to add more cars to its trains. Plessy and the Committee (and the railroad) lost in lower court and the case of *Plessy v. Ferguson*,[43] went all the way to the Supreme Court of the United States where the Justices dealt a devastating blow to the movement to give African Americans equal status under the law.

Writing for the majority, Justice Henry Billings Brown held that Louisiana's statute was not discriminatory because whites were separated from blacks just as much as blacks were separated from whites.[44] The Court said that the policy did not violate the equal protection clause because it was not a classification that was "capricious, arbitrary, or unreasonable."[45] In words that would echo through history, the Court found that the forced separation of the races by the state did not, by itself, "stamp the colored race with a badge of inferiority," but rather that such a badge was there "solely because the colored race chooses to put that construction upon it."[46] The Court concluded that "if one race be inferior to another socially, the Constitution cannot put them on the same plane."[47]

Once again, Justice Harlan dissented. He objected to the "arbitrary separation of citizens on the basis of race" and argued that this separation was a "badge of servitude" that could not be justified on "any legal ground." And, in a famous passage, he wrote:

[I]n view of the Constitution, in the eye of the law, there is in this country no superior, dominant ruling class of citizens. There is no caste here. Our Constitution is color-blind, and neither knows nor tolerates classes among its citizens. In respect of civil rights, all citizens are equal before the law. The humblest is the peer of the most powerful. The law regards man as man, and takes no account of his surroundings or of his color when his civil rights as guaranteed by the supreme law of the land are involved.[48]

With *Plessy*, the Supreme Court's narrowing of the Civil Rights Amendments was complete. The Court emasculated the Privileges and Immunities Clause; held that Congress did not have the power to prohibit private racial discrimination in commercial establishments; and officially sanctioned *state-required* segregation of whites and blacks in trains, hotels, schools, and restaurants. As the dissents in each of these cases amply demonstrated, the decisions could easily have gone the other way had there been different Justices on the Court who held different values and who were inclined to interpret the Reconstruction Amendments in a more textually honest and egalitarian manner. These cases were decided by judges with a specific vision of the social, legal, and political relationships between whites and blacks. It is difficult to fathom how much different (and better) our country could have been (and would be now) had the Court held that Congress could in fact forbid private racial discrimination and the states were not allowed to require it. Our entire dark history of racial discrimination, Jim Crow, and segregated schools may well have taken a healthier course toward equality. Tragically, the Court's rubber stamping of the forced separation of the races and its rejection of Congress's efforts to outlaw private discrimination increased racial tensions in this country for generations to come.

CHAPTER 4

The Economy

The Constitution is not intended to embody a particular economic theory. . . . It is made for people of fundamentally differing views.

—Oliver Wendell Holmes

OVERVIEW AND EARLY CASES

Historians agree that the founding fathers' major motivation for ratifying the United States Constitution was to give Congress the authority to regulate the national economy and the power to prevent the states from engaging in protectionist and discriminatory economic legislation.[1] Under the Articles of Confederation, the legal document governing the new country before the Constitution was ratified, Congress did not have any power over commerce or even the ability to raise its own money. Soon after the government was formed under the Articles, however, states began taxing each other and hoarding their own resources. As one historian has observed, "[t]he states passed tariff laws against one another as well as against foreign nations; and, indeed, as far as commerce was concerned, each State treated others as foreign nations. There were retaliations, discriminations, and every manner of trade restrictions and impediments. . . . Merchants and commercial bodies were at their wits' ends to carry on business and petitioned for a general power over Commerce."[2] The new Constitution was meant to give Congress the means to solve these economic problems.

The framers put into the new Constitution a number of provisions dealing with economic freedom. The Fifth Amendment prohibits the taking of property without "due process of law," and says that private property shall "not be taken for public use, without just compensation," while Article I, Section 10 prohibits the states from "impairing the obligation of contracts." In addition to these limitations, Article I, Section 8 gives Congress the affirmative power to regulate "commerce among the states," and the authority to enact laws that are "necessary and proper" to the execution of all other national powers.

The ability of the new national government to regulate the economy under the Constitution was first questioned in the landmark case *Gibbons v. Ogden*.[3] This dispute began when, in 1808, New York gave a monopoly to Robert Fulton and Robert Livingston to operate their steamboats on the state's waters, which included the Hudson River. This monopoly hurt New Jersey's economy so the states' leaders passed a number of laws authorizing its citizens to operate boats on the river. These efforts were thwarted by New York courts enforcing the monopoly given to Livingston and Fulton. In 1820, however, New Jersey passed a new law giving its citizens a right to collect damages from any person who obtained a court order continuing the monopoly. This New Jersey law was enacted, to some extent, at the behest of Cornelius Vanderbilt, who wanted to operate boats on the Hudson River. In essence, the states of New York and New Jersey were fighting over who could and could not operate commercial ships on waters between the two states.[4]

After the death of Robert Fulton, Aaron Ogden was licensed by the estate to continue the steamboat monopoly. A rival of his, Thomas Gibbons, operated a steamboat pursuant to a license issued by an act of Congress. Ogden filed a lawsuit in New York trying to stop Gibbons from operating his boats arguing that his New York monopoly was valid even on interstate waters. Despite being represented by the great lawyer Daniel Webster, Gibbons lost in the New York courts and he appealed to the Supreme Court of the United States. The issue was whether Congress's power to regulate "commerce among the states" authorized it to license Gibbons's boats despite the New York monopoly. Although the parties to this case were technically Gibbons and Ogden, the controversy was also between the sovereign states of New York and New Jersey as well as Cornelius Vanderbilt.

Ogden argued that the word *commerce* as used in the Constitution meant only the buying and selling of commodities, not navigation, and thus Congress lacked the power to regulate New York's waters. Chief Justice Marshall, writing for the Court, disagreed and interpreted the Commerce Clause broadly to include not only navigation but "every species of commercial intercourse" that "concerns more states than one."[5] In a common sense interpretation of the phase "commerce among the states," Justice Marshall said that the Commerce Clause allows Congress to regulate all of those "concerns" that affect the states generally, although the "internal commerce of a state . . . [is] reserved for the state itself."[6] Assuming the matter being regulated affects more states than one, Marshall said the only limitations on Congress's powers to regulate came from other constitutional provisions. Thus, Congress could regulate the steamboat business, and New York's monopoly had to give way to superior federal law. Gibbons was allowed to operate his steamboat, and he and Vanderbilt made their money.

Marshall's opinion in *Gibbons* had several major effects on this country's economy and on the Supreme Court's power to interpret the Constitution. First, there is a wide consensus among historians that Marshall's decision to overturn New York's monopoly had significant beneficial economic effects for the young nation. The opening of the Hudson River and Long Island Sound helped New York become a major center of commerce and trade.[7] A year after *Gibbons* was decided, the number of steamboats operating in New York's waters grew from 6 to 43.[8] Moreover, removal of the threats of similar monopolies of the railroad and coal industries amounted to the "emancipation proclamation of American commerce."[9]

The breadth of Marshall's decision in *Gibbons,* however, would eventually lead to a crisis in constitutional law because, in addition to giving Congress the power to regulate the national economy, the framers also wanted to ensure that the federal government would not be so powerful as to swallow up the states. To that end, the Ninth and Tenth Amendments had been added to the original Constitution to make clear that Congress would only have those powers delegated to it in Article I, and that the listing of specific rights in the Constitution did not preclude the people from having additional ones.[10] As our country and its economy grew larger in the late 19th and early 20th centuries, however, the debate over whether to allow Congress to regulate all economic matters affecting more states than one, or to leave to the states significant regulatory powers of their own, divided academics, economists, and federal judges. The problem was, and still is, as can be seen by the contemporary debate over health care, that although it may be true that in a national economy there are few local activities that do not affect the entire economy, if Congress can regulate all commerce for that reason, little will be left to the states, and the framers' desire for a limited national government will be lost. The tension is between the need for efficient national economic regulation and the desire for significant state autonomy, and it is a conflict that has divided the Justices of the Supreme Court for well over 100 years.

THE ECONOMIC CONSTITUTION: 1900–1990

In the late 19th century, private economic power was on the rise and the industrialization of America had begun. With these developments, state legislatures and Congress began regulating business in new and more progressive ways. The Court was at first quite hostile to this economic legislation.

The decision that best exemplifies this judicial antagonism was *Lochner v. New York*,[11] where the Court reviewed a New York law limiting baker's hours to 60 in a week and 10 in a day.[12] The law had been enacted partly at the behest of New York progressives in order to protect bakery workers from long days in hot and dusty conditions, and partly at the behest of larger bakeries looking to drive smaller, mostly immigrant-run bakeries out of business.[13] The law had been approved unanimously in both houses of the New York legislature.[14]

The plaintiff bakery owner claimed that the law violated the Fourteenth Amendment because it deprived him of his "liberty" to enter into contracts with his employees, and the Court agreed.[15] The Court conceded that states have the police power to safeguard the health, morals, and safety of its citizens, but found that the New York maximum hours law did none of those things because bakery employees did not need special protections, and because "clean and wholesome" bread did "not depend upon whether the baker works [only] ten hours per day or only sixty hours a week."[16] The Court was also concerned that, if the hours of bakery employees could be limited by the government, so could the hours of "doctors, lawyers, scientists, all professional men, as well as athletes and artisans."[17] The Court concluded that New York's attempt to protect bakery employees was "not . . . a health law, but . . . an illegal interference with the rights of individuals, both employers and employees, to make contracts regarding labor upon such terms as they may think best."[18]

Justices John Harlan and Oliver Wendell Holmes filed important dissenting opinions, which would eventually be adopted by later Supreme Courts. They argued that judges should not second guess reasonable economic regulations. Harlan cited several experts who asserted that bakers worked long, arduous, and potentially unsafe hours, and therefore New York could have reasonably believed this law necessary to protect their safety.[19] He also argued more broadly that there was a logical connection in all trades between hours worked and the health and safety of workers, and therefore New York's law was reasonable and should have been upheld. Holmes agreed and argued that different economists might have conflicting views on the value of New York's law, but a Constitution "is not intended to embody a particular economic theory, whether of paternalism . . . or of laissez faire. It is made for people of fundamentally differing views."[20] For Harlan and Holmes, the question was whether the New York law was reasonable, but for the Justices in the majority the issue was whether the law was important enough to override what they viewed as the fundamental right of liberty to contract.

The Court's divisions over economic regulations would continue over the next 25 years. In 1916, Congress passed progressive economic legislation regulating child labor throughout the United States. Because many states did not have child labor laws, and some of those that did would not enforce them, large numbers of children were working long hours under dangerous conditions for extremely low wages. The situation was so dire that the House Labor Committee reported that "the entire problem has become an interstate problem rather than a problem of isolated States and is a problem which must be faced and solved only by a power stronger than any State."[21]

Congress passed its child labor law under the authority granted it by the Commerce Clause of Article, I, Section 8, which gives Congress the power to regulate "commerce . . . among the states."[22] The law forbade the delivery or shipment in interstate commerce of any article produced or manufactured by children who worked more than a specified number of hours in a day or more than six days in a week or who worked at night.[23] Congress had every reason to believe this law would pass constitutional muster because over the years preceding its passage, the Supreme Court had upheld similar laws prohibiting the interstate shipment of lottery tickets, meat that had not been federally inspected, mislabeled eggs, and women transported for purposes of prostitution.[24] The key to all of those cases was that Congress was regulating the shipment of goods or people across state lines, and therefore the laws were within Congress's express power to regulate commerce among the states. For reasons having nothing to do with legal analysis, application of prior cases, law, or logic, however, the child labor law met a different fate.

Were the Supreme Court truly concerned with wrestling with its past decisions in a good faith manner, it would have had only two choices: (1) overrule the prior cases upholding Congress's power to regulate the shipment of goods in interstate commerce in order to overturn the child labor law; or (2) uphold the child labor law. After all, there is no constitutional difference between Congress prohibiting the movement across state lines of goods made by children, and Congress prohibiting the movement across state lines of lottery tickets, or meat that was not federally inspected. Nevertheless, in *Hammer v. Dagenhart,*[25] the Court struck down the child labor law while ostensibly affirming its prior decisions.

The Court said its previous cases dealt with goods and products that were themselves dangerous to interstate commerce, whereas the products made by child labor were "of themselves harmless."[26] What the Court meant by this distinction is unclear, especially when considering the laws it had previously upheld prohibited the transportation of women across state lines for immoral purposes and the buying and selling across state lines of lottery tickets, neither of which were harmful "of themselves," but were prohibited nonetheless. Moreover, as Justice Holmes said in dissent in the child labor case, the Commerce Clause gives Congress the power to regulate the interstate shipment of products that are bought and sold without any limitation except for other constitutional limitations, such as those contained in the First Amendment.[27] In fact, nearly 100 years earlier, in the first Supreme Court case to interpret the Commerce Clause, Chief Justice John Marshall unambiguously held that Congress's power over interstate commerce is plenary and is limited only by other express constitutional provisions.[28] Nevertheless, despite the numerous cases upholding Congress's power in this area and the clear text of the Commerce Clause, the *Hammer* Court overturned Congress's efforts to end the evils of child labor.

The Justices in *Hammer* said they were concerned that, if Congress could prohibit goods made by children from crossing state lines, then its power would be unlimited and destroy the balance of power between the state and national governments. The Court believed that Congress was not truly concerned with interstate commerce, but instead wanted to regulate the working conditions of children, and such regulation should be left to the states.[29] In response to the argument that Congress was concerned that states with child labor would compete unfairly with states that prohibited such labor, the Court said that Congress had no business interfering in the open markets for goods and services.[30] Finally, in an overly dramatic concluding paragraph, the Court warned the country what would happen if Congress were allowed to outlaw child labor by limiting the interstate shipment of goods made by children:

> The far reaching result of upholding the act cannot be more plainly indicated than by pointing out that if Congress can thus regulate matters entrusted to local authority by prohibition of the movement of commodities in interstate commerce, all freedom of commerce will be at an end, and the power of the States over local matters may be eliminated, *and thus our system of government be practically destroyed* [emphasis added].[31]

The negative effects of the child labor decision cannot be overstated. It would take more than 20 years for the Court to reverse itself and allow Congress to help solve the problem of young children working under terrible conditions.[32] During this time period, thousands of innocent children were abused. It is not too dramatic to observe that the Supreme Court prevented the peoples' representatives from addressing a serious social evil *in a case where the unambiguous text of the Constitution and previous cases supported the exercise of congressional power.* In any system of judicial review of legislative acts there is a potential for mischief, and mistakes will be made. However, in *Hammer* the legal issue should not have been in doubt. As Justice Holmes said in dissent, "The act does not meddle with anything belonging to the states. . . . The statute . . . is within the power expressly given to Congress . . . [and] confines itself to prohibiting the carriage of certain goods in interstate or foreign commerce. Congress is given power to regulate such commerce in unqualified terms."[33] The *Hammer* decision is pernicious not just because of the social harm it caused, and not just because the Court reached an incorrect decision under the applicable law, but because the Court felt free to disregard positive law sources including constitutional text and Supreme Court precedent to reach a policy result inconsistent with those sources. An institution truly concerned with applying and following prior law simply could not have reached such a result.

In the first 35 years of the 20th century, the Court invalidated more than 200 state and federal laws addressing the economy.[34] Government regulation of prices, wages, and hours, as well as labor laws protecting unions and children were overturned by the Court.[35] Even after the Great Depression shocked the country, the Court struck down efforts by President Franklin Roosevelt and Congress to aid the flailing economy. Regulations of the railroad, poultry, and coal industries were all overturned by the Court despite Roosevelt's plea that national legislation was necessary to lessen the economic crisis felt across the United States.

In 1937, after Roosevelt was elected for a second time and by a large margin, he took his case directly to the American people by proposing his now-famous Court-Packing Plan, which would have allowed him to nominate a new Justice for every Justice over 70 who decided not to retire, up to a total of six newly appointed Justices. His motivation was to stop the Court from striking down economic legislation designed to implement the New Deal. This is what he told the American people in a nationwide "Fireside Chat" radio address on March 9, 1937:

> When the Congress has sought to stabilize national agriculture, to improve the conditions of labor, to safeguard business against unfair competition, to protect our national resources, and in many other ways, to serve our clearly national needs, the majority of the Court has been assuming the power to pass on the wisdom of these acts of the Congress—and to approve or disapprove the public policy written into these laws. . . .
>
> We have, therefore, reached the point as a nation where we must take action to save the Constitution from the Court and the Court from itself. We must find a way to take an appeal from the Supreme Court to the Constitution itself. We want a Supreme Court which will do justice under the Constitution and not over it. In our courts we want a government of laws and not of men.[36]

The radical Court-packing solution proposed by Roosevelt met great hostility in Congress and never came close to being enacted.[37] It also became unnecessary because, around the same time, Justice Owen Roberts changed his mind on the relationship between federal and state power, and the Court (by a 5–4 margin) adopted a new and almost entirely hands-off approach to economic regulation that has continued in large part until today. As to state legislation, the Court decided that the right of freedom of contract between employees and employers was not fundamental and thus subject to reasonable state laws. As to federal power, the Court changed its interpretation of the Commerce Clause to provide Congress virtually unlimited authority to make laws concerning the national economy. Several cases from this regulation-friendly New Deal period exemplify this new trend and also demonstrate that the Court's change of heart resulted entirely from political, not legal, concerns.

In 1923, the Court had invalidated a District of Columbia law granting women a minimum wage because the law violated the "liberty of contract."[38] In 1937, a mere 14 years later, the Court explicitly reversed this case, saying that the Court's only job was to determine whether minimum wage laws and other economic regulations could be "regarded as arbitrary or capricious."[39] This was a complete change of perspective by the Court (though implemented by the vote of a single Justice). Whether it was brought on by the Great Depression, the president's Court-Packing Plan, or other factors has been and will be debated by scholars and historians but one thing is clear: neither the text of the Constitution nor the history of its adoption changed between 1924 and 1937. What changed was Justice Roberts's views on the appropriate scope of state power to regulate the economy and the importance of freedom of contract to employees and their employers.

The issue in *NLRB v. Jones & Laughlin Steel Corp.*[40] was whether the federal government had the authority under the Commerce Clause to regulate labor relationships between employers and workers. In this case, a national steel company fired a handful of employees and refused to reinstate them as ordered by a federal agency. The company claimed that its labor relationships were local issues beyond the reach of the federal government—an argument the Court had previously accepted on numerous occasions. But, in *Jones & Laughlin,* the Court sided with the government agency and against private industry.

Retreating from previous tests it had used to overturn economic legislation, such as whether the law had a "direct" or "indirect" effect on commerce, the Court stated its new approach to economic legislation in language that Roosevelt could have written himself:

> When industries organize themselves on a national scale, making their relation to interstate commerce the dominant factor in their activities, how can it be maintained that their industrial

labor relations constitute a forbidden field into which Congress may not enter when it is necessary to protect interstate commerce from the paralyzing consequences of industrial war? We have often said that interstate commerce itself is a practical conception. It is equally true that interferences with that commerce must be appraised by a judgment that does not ignore actual experience.[41]

No one on the Court really believed there was going to be an "industrial war" if the Court refused to interfere in this case, but the Court was signaling that it would no longer second guess Congress's efforts to regulate the economy—at least as applied to large companies that operated on a national scale. Then, in *Wickard v. Filburn,* decided in 1942, the Court even applied its deferential approach to economic laws with only an attenuated connection to "commerce among the states."[42]

As part of the New Deal plan to pull the nation out of the Great Depression, Congress passed the Second Agricultural Adjustment Act of 1938, giving the federal government the authority to set quotas and prices for the sale and purchase of agricultural products.[43] Roscoe Filburn was a farmer who sold milk, poultry, and eggs on the open market and also harvested a small amount of wheat to feed his animals and family. In 1941, he planted 12 acres more than the federal quota permitted, and he was fined by the government.[44] Refusing to pay the fine, he lost his marketing card, which he needed to sell his wheat.[45] Filburn sued to reverse the penalty, and argued that Congress did not have the power under the Commerce Clause to regulate the wheat he harvested for personal use.[46]

By the time Filburn's case reached the Supreme Court in 1942, President Roosevelt had replaced eight of the nine Justices who made up the Court that had been so hostile to economic legislation.[47] Whereas at least five Justices of the old Court believed strongly in free markets, personal freedom of contract, and equality of bargaining power between employers and unions, the new Court was made up of men who believed that economic experts who worked for the national government could provide solutions to the country's economic woes. This new attitude, which had little to do with constitutional text, history, or case law, was evident in Justice Jackson's opinion for a unanimous Court in *Wickard*. He held that any activity, including purely local activity that had a "substantial economic effect on interstate commerce," could be regulated by Congress.[48] Moreover, the question was not whether the plaintiff's harvest of wheat created that effect but whether "his contribution, taken together with that of many others similarly situated," substantially impacted commerce among the states.[49] That Filburn's wheat was home grown for personal use was irrelevant because the "variability . . . [of] home grown wheat [has] a substantial influence on price and market conditions. . . . [The] record leaves us no doubt that Congress may properly have considered that wheat consumed on the farm . . . would have a substantial effect in defeating and obstructing its purpose to stimulate trade therein."[50]

The Court in *Wickard* held: (1) that Congress could regulate all local activity that had a substantial effect on commerce among the states; (2) that when looking at this question, Congress could consider the aggregate effect of all similar activity; and (3) that even crops never intended to be sold at market were subject to federal regulation. The Court abandoned the old free market ideology and gave the national government a free hand to regulate the economy of the United States.

In light of the Court's new attitude, it did not invalidate an exercise of Congress's Commerce Clause authority again for nearly 60 years. During that time period, it approved of Congress's use of its commerce power to regulate virtually every aspect of the relationship between unions and employers; to prohibit numerous local crimes such as loan sharking even by a single defendant; to prohibit racial discrimination in restaurants and hotels (restrictions the 19th-century Court held were beyond Congress's powers); and to enact numerous laws regulating all aspects of the economy such as minimum wage laws, pension regulations, and overtime rules. Most of these laws would have been constitutionally incomprehensible to the Justices of the pre–New Deal Supreme Court. Yet, it was not the Constitution that changed, nor our understanding of its history, but the values and political views of the Justices. When those values changed again with the Rehnquist Court, the Court took a step back in evaluating Congress's powers under the Commerce Clause, but only a modest step.

THE MODERN CASES

In 1990, Congress passed a law making it a federal crime to possess a gun in or near a school zone. A few years later, Alphonso Lopez Jr., a 12th-grade student at Edison High School in San Antonio, Texas, carried a concealed .38 caliber handgun and five bullets into the school. Acting on an anonymous tip, school officials confronted the boy, who admitted he was carrying the weapon. He was arrested under Texas law for firearm possession on school premises, but the next day the state charges were dismissed when federal agents charged him with violating the federal law prohibiting guns on school property. He challenged his arrest as being beyond federal power under the Commerce Clause, and the Rehnquist Court agreed with him in *United States v. Lopez*.[51]

In response to Lopez's argument that Congress's law prohibiting gun possession in schools was not a regulation of "commerce among the states," the government argued that gun possession in particular, and violent crime in general, posed serious threats to our educational system and was directly related to the economy in numerous and substantial ways. Here is Chief Justice Rehnquist's summary of the government's argument supporting the law:

> [T]he presence of guns in schools poses a substantial threat to the educational process by threatening the learning environment. A handicapped educational process, in turn, will result in a less productive citizenry. That, in turn, would have an adverse effect on the Nation's economic well-being. As a result, the Government argues that Congress could rationally have concluded that [the law] substantially affects interstate commerce.[52]

The prior Supreme Courts that had affirmed Congress's powers to regulate homegrown wheat, every aspect of labor relations, racial discrimination by small hotels and restaurants, and small local crimes such as loan sharking and arson, would have easily upheld this law. They likely would have reasoned (as the government argued and the dissent in this case accepted) that billions of dollars are spent on our nation's schools, that gun possession in those schools poses a serious threat to those schools, and that our national economy depends on an educated populace.[53] If the Supreme Court truly perceived its mandate to be applying preexisting law (precedent) to new cases honestly and transparently, the Court would have continued its deferential approach to federal economic legislation. But the Rehnquist Court had a more important agenda than following prior law, and that priority trumped the consistent application of legal principles.

Never answering the question whether Congress could have rationally found that gun possession around schools substantially affected commerce among the states, the Court focused on a very different question: if the government's arguments were accepted, would there be any limitation left on congressional authority under the Commerce Clause? Suggesting that the answer was no, the majority invalidated this federal law and overturned the defendant's conviction on the following grounds:

> Under the theories that the Government presents . . . it is difficult to perceive any limitation on federal power, even in areas such as criminal law enforcement or education where States historically have been sovereign. Thus, if we were to accept the Government's arguments, we are hard pressed to posit any activity by an individual that Congress is without power to regulate.
>
> To uphold the Government's contentions here, we would have to pile inference upon inference in a manner that would bid fair to convert congressional authority under the Commerce Clause to a general police power of the sort retained by the States. Admittedly, some of our prior cases have taken long steps down that road, giving great deference to congressional action. . . . The broad language in these opinions has suggested the possibility of additional expansion, but we decline here to proceed any further. To do so would require us to conclude . . . that there never will be a distinction between what is truly national and what is truly local. . . . This we are unwilling to do.[54]

The Court made these dire predictions despite Justice Breyer's dissenting argument (1) that gun possession around schools posed a particularly "acute" threat to our national educational system, and (2) prior cases offered substantial justifications for the federal law.[55] The Court made no serious response to Breyer's first argument, and as to the second, the Court said that all its previous cases dealt with laws regulating "commercial activities," but the law at issue in this case did not. In other words, the Court said that its previous decisions allowed Congress to regulate local activities that "substantially affected" commerce among those states, only if those activities were commercial in nature.[56] Gun possession, according to the Court, was not a commercial activity.

The majority never explained, however, why it was adopting this new commercial/noncommercial test, and it is hard to see why such a distinction matters if the activity Congress is regulating actually affects "commerce among the states." Moreover, had the majority wanted to reach a different decision, it could have characterized the case as a regulation of schools not a regulation of guns and then found, as Justice Breyer asserted in dissent, that given how much money is spent on our educational system, Congress could have rationally concluded that regulating schools was regulating a "commercial activity." One wonders, for example, whether the majority would have upheld a law prohibiting guns within a few feet of banks or tall office buildings. In any event, these arguments based in law, logic, and prior cases did not resonate with a Court determined to rewrite (to a limited degree) its prior law governing Congress's powers under the Commerce Clause.

Five years later, in *United States v. Morrison*,[57] the same Court sent another message to Congress that its Commerce Clause authority was not as broad as Congress may have liked. The case involved a female student at Virginia Tech who was allegedly raped by two football players. After she filed complaints against the boys through the school's disciplinary system, the charges against one were dismissed and the other's punishment was suspended. The victim then dropped out of school and filed a federal lawsuit against her alleged attackers under the Violence Against Women Act (VAWA), a federal law granting victims of gender-related violence a civil cause of action against their attackers. This law was passed only after Congress compiled an extensive record documenting that the economic cost of gender-related violence in 2004 was between $5 and $10 billion.[58] Congress looked at reports from task forces in 21 states, issued eight different reports put together by various congressional committees, and listened to numerous expert witnesses over four years of hearings.[59] Based on all of this evidence, Congress passed the VAWA, which provided that "all persons within the United States," have the right to be "free from crimes of violence motivated by gender," and created a federal civil cause of action on behalf of those injured by such violence and against the person who committed the violence.[60] The question before the Supreme Court was whether Congress had the authority to pass the VAWA under either the Commerce Clause or the Fourteenth Amendment.[61] The Court said neither provision provided constitutional authority for the law.

The Court said that gender-related violence is "not, in any sense of the phrase, economic activity."[62] The Court was concerned that if Congress could regulate all violent crime under the Commerce Clause because the aggregate effect of that crime substantially affected commerce, then there would be no limit to Congress's powers, and it could pass laws dealing with all activities that lead to crime as well as "marriage, divorce, and child-rearing," as all of those activities also affect our nation's economy. Although the Court conceded that Congress compiled extensive findings linking domestic and other gender-related violence to commerce among the states, such findings are "not sufficient . . . to sustain Commerce Clause legislation."[63] In short, by a 5–4 majority, with the Justices lining up exactly the same way they did in *Lopez,* the Court found that Congress did not have the power to give crime victims a federal cause of action to sue people who attacked them for gender-related reasons.

There are many reasons to believe the Court erred in striking down the VAWA. Congress spent years studying the problem, the costs to the economy in terms of women missing work, getting divorced, and incurring medical expenses are relatively obvious, and, perhaps most important, Congress found that the states were not enforcing their own laws against domestic violence. As the dissent observed, the National Association of Attorneys General supported the act *unanimously,* and attorneys general from 38 states urged Congress to create the civil remedy because the states' procedures for dealing with violence against women were inadequate.[64] Thirty–six states supported the VAWA when it was challenged in court, while only one took the position the law was unconstitutional.[65] For the Court to invalidate this law on the grounds that it invaded the rights of the states is perplexing and ironic given that the states overwhelmingly supported the law. As Justice Souter quipped, the Court required the states to accept this new view of the Commerce Clause and states' rights whether "they wanted it or not."[66]

The point here, however, is not whether *Morrison* was right or wrong as a matter of constitutional law. The point is that, as Justice Souter argued, the case would have come out differently had it been decided "at any time between . . . 1942 and . . . 1995."[67] A Court that allows the federal government to regulate every aspect of the employer/employee relationship, the amount of wheat one can grow on his own property for personal use, local crimes such as arson and loan sharking, and decisions by small restaurants and hotels about whom they must serve as customers, all because such practices in the aggregate substantially affect commerce, should also defer to a congressional judgment that gender-related violence is a serious, national economic problem when considered in the aggregate (as is gun possession around schools). Between 1942 and 1995, the Constitution did not change and the Commerce Clause was not amended, but the people on the Court and their values did. To these nine judges (or more accurately to five of them), problems of gun violence and attacks on women were state, not federal, problems. These are political decisions made by political actors about the proper relationship between the state and federal governments, not legal decisions informed by text, history, or precedent.

A few years after *Morrison,* the Court encountered a Commerce Clause problem involving, not guns or domestic violence, but illegal drugs. Although California allowed the use of marijuana for medical purposes, the Bush administration made it clear that it would enforce the federal prohibitions on marijuana despite the California law. Whereas in *Morrison,* most states wanted the federal government to intervene and help with problems of gender-based violence, in *Gonzales v. Raich,*[68] the State of California wanted the national government to leave it alone and show respect for its decision to decriminalize marijuana for medical purposes. Nevertheless, when the issue was state-sanctioned drug use, the Court's deference to congressional judgments returned in full force, and the Justices' states' rights sympathies vanished.

Angel Raich and Diane Monson lived in California and suffered from a variety of painful medical conditions. Under California's Compassionate Use Act of 1996, they legally used marijuana to alleviate some of their pain. Both women had been using marijuana for a number of years, and Raich's physician testified that, without the marijuana, Raich would suffer excruciating pain. None of the marijuana used by the women was bought or sold, and all of it was grown inside California.

After federal Drug Enforcement Agency agents seized and destroyed some of their plants pursuant to the Controlled Substances Act (CSA), the women filed a lawsuit claiming the law was unconstitutional to the extent it prevented them from possessing, obtaining, or growing marijuana for their personal medical use. They argued that no constitutional provision authorized Congress to pass such a law.

The Ninth Circuit Court of Appeals, not surprisingly, agreed with the plaintiffs relying on the Court's two prior Commerce Clause decisions *United States v. Lopez* and *United States v. Morrison.* The lower court believed that, after those two decisions, purely local noneconomic activities could not be regulated by Congress under its commerce power.

In *Gonzales v. Raich,* however, Justices Kennedy and Scalia took a different approach to the government's commerce authority than they had in *Lopez* and *Morrison*. They agreed with the moderates on the Court that the federal Controlled Substances Act could be validly applied to marijuana used for medical purposes, and therefore the federal law trumped California's desire to authorize such use. The rationale used by the majority to reach this result seemed at odds, to say the least, with the holdings in *Lopez* and *Morrison*.

Writing for the majority, Justice Stevens employed the following "logic" to affirm the federal drug statute as applied to homegrown marijuana. He said that Congress has the power to regulate purely local activities that are part of or related to an economic "class of activities that have a substantial effect on interstate commerce."[69] In effect, any activity (even noncommercial, local activities) may be "reached by Congress if it exerts a substantial economic effect on interstate commerce."[70] Even though there was nothing economic or commercial about the marijuana use in this case, and even though there was nothing bought or sold or moving from state to state, the majority held Congress could regulate such activity because it might substantially affect the national marijuana market. In other words, the use of homegrown marijuana could replace the need to buy it on the open market and interfere with the federal government's ability to extinguish that market. Through this reasoning, the use of homegrown marijuana in the privacy of one's home pursuant to a valid state law became an activity substantially affecting "commerce among the states."

Justices Thomas and O'Connor easily pierced the majority's logic. Thomas began his dissent by pointing out that "Diane Monson and Angel Raich use marijuana that has never been bought or sold, that has never crossed state lines, and that has had no demonstrable effect on the national market for marijuana. If Congress can regulate this under the Commerce Clause, then it can regulate virtually anything— and the Federal Government is no longer one of limited and enumerated powers."[71] Justice O'Connor more directly addressed the Court's reasoning by saying the following:

It will not do to say that Congress may regulate noncommercial activity simply because it may have an effect on the demand for commercial goods, or because the noncommercial endeavor can, in some sense, substitute for commercial activity. Most commercial goods or services have some sort of privately producible analogue. Home care substitutes for daycare. Charades games substitute for movie tickets. Backyard or window sill gardening substitutes for going to the supermarket. To draw the line wherever private activity affects the demand for market goods is to draw no line at all, and to declare everything economic. We have already rejected the result that would follow—a federal police power.[72]

The majority and dissenting opinions also sparred over whether *Raich* was consistent or inconsistent with the Court's most recent Commerce Clause decisions overruling Congress's efforts to prohibit guns around schools and providing people with a civil remedy for gender-motivated violence.[73] This sparring over doctrine, however, in all likelihood did not generate the results in these cases. The four moderates on the Court at the time (Breyer, Stevens, Souter, and Ginsburg) would have voted in favor of Congress in all three cases because they did not really believe the Court should limit how Congress acts under the Commerce Clause.[74] The three Justices most devoted to states' rights at the time (O'Connor, Rehnquist, and Thomas) all would have overruled the federal laws in all three cases. The important question is why two of the conservatives (Scalia and Kennedy) voted one way in *Lopez* and *Morrison* but the other way in *Raich*.

Justice Kennedy did not write separately, so we do not know his reasons, but Justice Scalia's concurring opinion relied heavily on Congress's efforts to outlaw illegal drugs, and he concluded that Congress could take all reasonable steps to advance that goal, even the criminalization of homegrown marijuana for medical use. It is not too hard to conclude that Justice Scalia is far more sympathetic to the war on drugs than he is to regulating guns or combating domestic abuse. Of course, those are not legal reasons, and one wonders how Justice Scalia will vote in the next difficult Commerce Clause case.

The public policy issues raised by *Raich* are arguably difficult. Congress has the power under the Commerce Clause to regulate and criminalize the buying and selling of drugs pursuant to its power to regulate "commerce among the states." But does that power give Congress the authority to regulate marijuana that is homegrown and neither bought nor sold? And if so, are Justices O'Connor and Thomas right that such a power would give Congress unlimited authority to regulate every aspect of people's lives? And, even if that is true, is that a price we have to pay for living in a country where virtually everything, in the aggregate, affects national markets? There do not seem to be persuasive legal answers to these hard questions raising fundamental issues concerning the proper relationship between the state and federal governments. Given the complexity and difficulty of these problems, however, it is fair to ask why we would delegate the resolution of these issues to Supreme Court Justices who have little knowledge of drugs, police practices, or the medical needs of people wanting to use marijuana to relieve pain, and no better insight into how to structure our federal/state system than any other political official. This case involved a dispute between the people of California and the federal government, and perhaps they should have been left alone to fight that battle without the interference of nine judges with no more expertise on this issue than anyone else involved in this difficult public debate.

CHAPTER 5

Abortion

The states are not free, under the guise of protecting maternal health or potential life, to intimidate women into continuing pregnancies.

—Harry Blackmun

The fact that a majority of the States . . . have had restrictions on abortions for at least a century is a strong indication, it seems to me, that the asserted right to an abortion is not so rooted in the traditions and conscience of our people as to be ranked as fundamental.

—William Rehnquist

Perhaps the most divisive constitutional question of the last 40 years has been whether women have a constitutional right to terminate their pregnancies. The Supreme Court's decisions on this issue have sharply divided the American people, the nation's political parties, and the Justices of the Supreme Court. The controversy over abortion has given rise to powerful organizations on both the left and the right and has played a major role in numerous elections and Supreme Court confirmation hearings. It is impossible to fully understand the Supreme Court's impact on American politics without paying careful attention to the issue of abortion.

People disagree about abortion because the issue raises fundamental questions about religion, women's rights, when life begins, and what interests the state rightfully has in the potential of human life. This book does not pretend to provide persuasive answers to these difficult questions but does suggest that the Supreme Court's interference in this difficult arena bears much more the marks of a political veto council whose members are applying their personal moral judgments than a court of judges interpreting prior law.

HISTORY

Few people realize that, prior to the middle of the 19th century, abortion was legal until "quickening," the moment when a woman could first detect fetal movement (usually around 16 weeks).[1] Even the Catholic Church accepted this idea until Pope Pius IX changed the Church's policy in 1869.[2] Thus, prior to the Civil War, women could legally secure abortions in the United States.[3]

In the mid-19th century, however, the law began to change with Connecticut being the first state to outlaw abortion and others quickly following suit. By the 1890s, every state had enacted anti-abortion laws.[4] This change occurred due to an alliance between "Anti-Vice" advocates who argued that abortion (and contraception) were undermining the traditional role of women as wives and mothers with doctors (including the newly formed American Medical Association (AMA)), who were trying to organize and enhance their reputations and their business prospects.[5] The doctors argued that only they (and not midwives) could safely deliver babies and that women should not be able to use contraception and abortion to avoid their natural destinies as wives and mothers.[6] One prominent doctor at the time said the following:

Were woman intended as a mere plaything, or for the gratification of her own or her husband's desires, there would have been need for her of neither her uterus nor ovaries, nor would the prevention of their being used for their clearly legitimate purpose have been attended by such tremendous penalties as is in reality the case. . . .

Is there then no alternative but for women, when married and prone to conception, to occasionally bear children? This, as we have seen is the end for which they are physiologically constituted and for which they are destined by nature. . . . [The prevention and termination of pregnancy] are alike disastrous to a woman's mental, moral, and physical wellbeing.[7]

From the turn of the century until the 1960s, these 19th-century laws stayed in effect although their enforcement varied dramatically from generation to generation and depending on geography and local politics.[8] From the 1880s to the 1920s, women, doctors, and especially midwives were often subject to prosecution and harassment especially if the woman suffered death or injury from an abortion.[9] The different attitudes toward sex that emerged during the 1920s, as well as the Great Depression, led to more lenient attitudes about abortion with some experts estimating that somewhere between 600,000 and 800,00 abortions occurred each year during that decade.[10] After World War II, however, attitudes shifted again as women were expected to leave their jobs and return to their roles as wives and mothers and abortion was linked by some to support Russian-style communism.[11] During the 1950s, prosecutorial efforts were directed mostly at doctors deterring many physicians from performing abortions and leading to the era of "back alley" abortions.[12] It became all too common for "motorcycle mechanics, bartenders, and real-estate agents" to perform abortions, and the dangers to women increased significantly.[13] Approximately a million abortions were performed each year but the number of women's deaths and serious injuries increased despite major improvements in medical techniques.[14] By the end of the 1950s, however, things began to change again as various reform movements, both among doctors and women's rights groups, began to emerge.

The possibility of legalizing abortion, or at least decreasing the penalties for it, erupted in the 1960s due to a wide array of factors including the sexual revolution, the women's liberation movement, and the increasing number of women going into the workplace and universities.[15] There was also widening concern about overpopulation leading former presidents Truman and Eisenhower to become co-chairs of Planned Parenthood.[16]

By the end of the 1960s, medical and legal organizations had dramatically changed their views on abortion. The AMA adopted the position that abortion was a medical matter "based on sound clinical judgment," and "informed patient consent."[17] The American Bar Association accepted a law that would have left the abortion decision to the woman and her doctor during the first 20 weeks of pregnancy, and the American Public Health Association issued similar standards.[18] At the same time, legislative reform movements were underway in numerous states to reduce the penalties for having or performing an abortion. A 1972 Gallup Poll showed that a majority of people, including a majority of Catholics, favored letting women and their doctors make the abortion decision outside the purview of the law.[19] Although the issue was still quite controversial, and only a few states had made abortions legal, by the time the Supreme Court decided *Roe v. Wade,* in 1973, our nation's attitudes toward abortion had shifted to a significant degree.

ROE V. WADE AND *DOE V. BOLTON*

In Texas in 1973, it was illegal for a woman to have an abortion unless the procedure was necessary to save her life. In the same year in Georgia, women could legally have abortions only if (1) continuation of the pregnancy would endanger the woman's life, or seriously and permanently injure her health, or (2) if the fetus would very likely be born with a grave and permanent mental or physical defect, or (3) if the pregnancy resulted from forcible or statutory rape. All abortions in Georgia had to be performed in an accredited hospital with at least three doctors concurring in writing that the woman satisfied one of the aforementioned conditions. These laws were representative of many state laws at the time the Court decided these cases.

Both *Roe v. Wade,* and its companion case, *Doe v. Bolton,* were lawsuits paid for and organized by various political groups interested in the legalization of abortion. The named plaintiff in *Roe,* whom we now know was a woman named Norma McCorvey, was a ninth grade drop-out who had been to reform school and had tried to end her pregnancy by consuming large amounts of drugs and alcohol.[20] Although there were other plaintiffs in *Roe,* including a sympathetic middle-class couple who were seeking an abortion because the health (though perhaps not the life) of the mother was at stake, history has focused on McCorvey's role in the case perhaps because she later claimed to have been used by her attorneys for political gain. She even eventually became a pro-life advocate.[21]

Justice Blackmun began his opinion in *Roe v. Wade* with a refreshingly honest account of the difficulty of the case:

> We forthwith acknowledge our awareness of the sensitive and emotional nature of the abortion controversy, of the vigorous opposing views, even among physicians, and of the deep and seemingly absolute convictions that the subject inspires. One's

philosophy, one's experiences, one's exposure to the raw edges of human existence, one's religious training, one's attitudes toward life and family and their values, and the moral standards one establishes and seeks to observe, are all likely to influence and to color one's thinking and conclusions about abortion. In addition, population growth, pollution, poverty, and racial overtones tend to complicate and not to simplify the problem.[22]

Unfortunately, in the very next paragraph, Justice Blackmun gave the Court's standard and misleading account of how it decides constitutional cases: "Our task, of course, is to resolve the issue by constitutional measurement, free of emotion and of predilection. We seek earnestly to do this. . . . We bear in mind, too, Mr. Justice Holmes' admonition . . . [that the Constitution] is made for people of fundamentally differing views, and the accident of our finding certain opinions natural and familiar or novel and even shocking ought not to conclude our judgment upon the question whether statutes embodying them conflict with the Constitution of the United States."[23] In other words, Justice Blackmun, and the six other Justices who joined his opinion, suggested that their own personal "predilections" would be set aside when deciding whether the anti-abortion statutes at issue were inconsistent with the Constitution. The Justices would have done better to recognize how much of a role their personal "predilections" actually played in the Court's analysis of the Texas and Georgia statutes.

The Court began its analysis with a lengthy summary of the abortion controversy and the history of abortion law. It then summarized the interest that Texas put forward to justify its regulations—the protection of the fetus as either human life or potential human life.[24] Then, the Court turned to the woman's interest. The Court conceded that nothing in the text of the Constitution specifically referred to abortion or a "right to privacy," but also observed that the Court had found the "roots" of such a right in a number of constitutional provisions such as the First Amendment (free speech), the Fourth and Fifth Amendments (criminal law protections), the Ninth Amendment (the enumeration of rights in the Constitution was not meant to "deny" other rights retained by the people), and the Fourteenth Amendment's protection of "due process of law."[25] Relying on past decisions involving the right to contraception, the right to marry, and the right to educate ones' children, the Court said that only personal rights that are "fundamental" or "implicit in the concept of ordered liberty . . . are included in this guarantee of personal privacy."[26] Locating the abortion right in the Fourteenth Amendment's Due Process Clause, the question then became whether a women's decision to terminate her pregnancy could be considered a *fundamental* right, and the Court answered that question as follows:

> This right of privacy . . . is broad enough to encompass a woman's decision whether or not to terminate her pregnancy. The detriment that the State would impose upon the pregnant woman by denying this choice altogether is apparent. Specific and direct harm medically diagnosable even in early pregnancy may be involved. Maternity, or additional offspring, may force upon the woman a distressful life and future. Psychological harm may be imminent. Mental and physical health may be taxed by child care. There is also the distress, for all concerned, associated with the unwanted child, and there is the problem of bringing a child into a family already unable, psychologically and otherwise, to care for it. In other cases, as in this one, the additional difficulties and continuing stigma of unwed motherhood may be involved.[27]

Rejecting the argument that because of these interests a woman has an absolute right to terminate her pregnancy "at whatever time, in whatever way, and for whatever reason she alone chooses," the Court nonetheless held that abortion was a fundamental right that could only be limited by the state to further a compelling governmental interest and through a law that is narrowly tailored to further that interest.[28] This test, known as "strict scrutiny," is the test the Court reserves for governmental action that interferes with our most fundamental rights such as freedom of speech, freedom of religion, and the right to be free of state-imposed racial discrimination. In other words, the Court held that the right to have an abortion was a fundamental freedom protected by the United States Constitution that states like Texas and Georgia could not restrict absent the most important governmental interest.

Texas argued that it had a compelling interest in prohibiting abortions because the fetus is a "person" within the meaning of the Constitution and entitled to equal protection under the law. The Court disposed of this argument in a few paragraphs saying that because abortion laws did not emerge until the mid-19th century there was no legal basis for suggesting that a fetus is a person protected by the Constitution.

Texas also argued that life begins at conception and Texas had a compelling interest in protecting that life even if the fetus is not yet a legal person. This is obviously a fundamental question in the abortion debate. The Court first responded that it "need not resolve the difficult question of when life begins. When those trained in the respective disciplines of medicine, philosophy, and theology are unable to arrive at any consensus, the judiciary, at this point in the development of man's knowledge, is not in a position to speculate as to the answer."[29] The Court then went on to say, however, the following:

> It should be sufficient to note briefly the wide divergence of thinking on this most sensitive and difficult question. There has always been strong support for the view that life does not begin until live birth. This was the belief of the Stoics. It appears to be the predominant, though not the unanimous, attitude of the Jewish faith. It may be taken to represent also the position of a large segment of the Protestant community, insofar as that can be ascertained. . . . [T]he common law found greater significance in quickening. Physicians and their scientific colleagues have regarded that event with less interest and have tended to focus either upon conception, upon live birth, or upon the interim point at which the fetus becomes "viable," that is, potentially able to live outside the mother's womb, albeit with artificial aid. . . .
>
> In areas other than criminal abortion, the law has been reluctant to endorse any theory that life, as we recognize it, begins before live birth or to accord legal rights to the unborn except in narrowly defined situations and except when the rights are contingent upon live birth. . . . In short, the unborn have never been recognized in the law as persons in the whole sense.
>
> In view of all this, we do not agree that, by adopting one theory of life, Texas may override the rights of the pregnant woman that are at stake.[30]

Although the Court said that it was not going to decide when life begins, the language cited above demonstrates that the Court, at the very least, rejected Texas's position that the fetus is a human life deserving of legal protection. The Court should have been honest and transparent that it was rejecting, as a legal matter, Texas's position that life begins at conception.

Although the Court did not accept Texas's beginning of life argument, it did hold that Texas had "important and legitimate" interests in protecting both the health of the mother and the *potential* human life she carried inside her.[31] These interests, according to the Court, grew stronger as the woman's pregnancy grew longer, eventually becoming compelling. Thus, the Court created (no one can plausibly argue this was a legal interpretation of constitutional text or history) the famous trimester framework that was the law of the land from 1973 until 1992. Pursuant to this scheme, states could not regulate abortions at all in the first trimester, could regulate them only for the health of the mother in the second trimester, and could prohibit all abortions after viability.[32] Given this framework, the Texas law was unconstitutional inasmuch as it prohibited all abortions unless the life of the mother was at stake, and most of the Georgia law at issue in the companion *Doe* case was also unconstitutional because it required all abortions to be performed in accredited hospitals and be certified by three doctors and approved by various committees. None of those requirements satisfied the *Roe* standards according to the Court.

In light of the controversy that *Roe* caused, many people forget that *Roe* was a 7–2 decision, not one of those 5–4 split outcomes with a key swing Justice making the difference. Justice Rehnquist filed one dissent in which he argued that Justice Blackmun's opinion echoed the now-discredited *Lochner* opinion by applying strict judicial review to a governmental action alleged to be a violation of the Due Process Clause of the Fourteenth Amendment. Justice Rehnquist argued that the Texas abortion statute should be constitutional as long as it was "rational," and he believed it satisfied that legal standard.[33] He also said that the Court's "decision . . . to break pregnancy into three distinct terms and to outline the permissible restrictions the State may impose in each one . . . partakes more of judicial legislation than it does of a determination of the intent of the drafters of the Fourteenth Amendment."[34]

Justice White dissented even more emphatically than Justice Rehnquist. He wrote that the Court valued "the convenience of the pregnant mother more than the continued existence and development of the life or potential life that she carries. Whether or not I might agree with that marshaling of values, I can in no event join the Court's judgment because I find no constitutional warrant for imposing such an order of priorities on the people and legislatures of the States."[35] He went on to say:

> I find nothing in the language or history of the Constitution to support the Court's judgment. The Court simply fashions and announces a new constitutional right for pregnant mothers and, with scarcely any reason or authority for its action, invests that right with sufficient substance to override most existing state abortion statutes. . . . As an exercise of raw judicial power, the Court perhaps has authority to do what it does today; but, in my view, its judgment is an improvident and extravagant exercise of the power of judicial review that the Constitution extends to this Court.[36]

There can be little debate that the decision in *Roe* dramatically changed our constitutional landscape in numerous important ways and also helped fuel a new political movement with serious consequences for our government and the American people. Before we turn to those developments, however, it is important to place the Court's decision in an accurate legal perspective.

Many legal scholars, politicians, and media personalities have argued that *Roe* is a particularly striking example of judicial activism and faulty legal reasoning. The argument normally goes something like this: There is not a word about abortion in the Constitution and the Court's trimester framework sounds much more like a legislative code than a legal decision. The Court has no business legislating from the bench on this highly contentious and difficult issue.[37] Even leading liberal law professors, who are strongly pro-choice as a legislative matter, have strongly criticized the Court's approach to abortion.[38]

The problem with this perspective is the suggestion that *Roe* is different in a material way from how the Court normally operates. Both liberal and conservative Supreme Courts before *Roe* and after *Roe* have created constitutional rights out of whole cloth without much concern over whether the right was justified by constitutional text or history, and these decisions often sound more like complex legal codes than constitutional law. For example, in *Griswold v. Connecticut,*[39] the Court invalidated a state law banning contraceptive use. Although this *result* is now uniformly considered correct even by conservative scholars and Justices (such as the current Chief Justice of the United States Supreme Court), there is not one word in the United States Constitution devoted to contraception. Moreover, like *Roe,* the *reasoning* of the opinion has been criticized and is still being criticized by those on both the left and the right of the legal academy. Nevertheless, as a matter of legal reasoning, if the result in *Griswold* is correct, and states are not at liberty to ban contraception, the result in *Roe* is also defensible.

To the objection that *Roe*'s trimester framework reflected more of a legislative than a judicial judgment, this criticism could be leveled at numerous other important areas of constitutional law. Professor David Kairys, in his excellent book *With Liberty and Justice for Some* argues that there are numerous arbitrary constitutional rules articulated by the Court that sound much more like legislative than judicial rules but that are not criticized on that basis. He provides the following examples: if a state wants to adopt a residency requirement for voting that requirement (as a constitutional matter) must be 50 days or less (not 60 nor 80); a criminal defendant has a right to a jury trial if the possible sentence exceeds 6 months (not 4 or 8 months); a suspect cannot be detained by the police for more than 48 hours (not 24 or 72) without a judicial hearing on probable cause; and, of course, there are the famous *Miranda* warnings where the Court set forth detailed instructions to police on how they may question suspects.[40] In the areas of freedom of speech and religion, the Court has concocted (there is simply no better word for it) complex and detailed rules for when the government must allow speech on its property, when religious symbols can be placed on public grounds, what kinds of assistance the government can offer to private religious schools, and what kinds of campaign finance restrictions are constitutionally permissible. In all of these areas, and many others, the Court created far-reaching codes of conduct for governmental officials that most people would associate more with legislative line-drawing than judicial reasoning. The decision in *Roe,* as Professor Kairys persuasively argues, is not different in kind than the typical Supreme Court decision based on ambiguous constitutional text (or even silence), indeterminate history, and malleable precedent.[41]

Far from being an outlier, the *real* problem with *Roe* is that it is far too familiar. Like virtually every constitutional issue the Court decides, neither the Constitution nor the cases decided under it can dictate the result. Yet, the Justices have a national veto power on this most difficult question. The consequences of that disconnect, as the next section demonstrates, have been significant for our political parties, our government, the development of constitutional law, and our people.

THE AFTERMATH

There were two major aftershocks of *Roe* that had far-reaching effects even apart from the specific consequences of the decision itself. Outside the legal academy, conservative politicians were able to use *Roe* as a rallying cry against the Democratic Party and the very idea of liberalism. Less than six years after *Roe*, the New Right became a powerful force in American politics. This broad coalition was made up of social conservatives who believed in "family values"; opposed busing, abortion, and affirmation action; and were led by televangelists like Jerry Falwell and Pat Robertson.[42] This movement (along with the poor economy and the Iran hostage crisis) had an influence on the 1980 presidential election in which Ronald Reagan captured most of the Southern states by a slim margin due in no small part to the large turnout of Christians who identified more with the once-divorced Hollywood actor than with Jimmy Carter, a born-again Christian.[43]

How much of a role the Court's decision in *Roe* played in all this is somewhat contested, but it is undeniable that the New Right was able to use the issue of abortion effectively as both a fund-raising tool and a call to action. One commentator has argued that "[n]ot only did *Roe* energize the pro-life movement and accelerate the infusion of sectarian religion into American politics, but it also radicalized many traditionalists."[44] Another national scholar has gone even further:

> [T]he decision may well have created the Moral Majority, helped defeat the equal rights amendment, and undermined the women's movement by spurring opposition and demobilizing potential adherents. At the same time, *Roe* may have taken national policy too abruptly to a point toward which it was groping more slowly, and in the process may have prevented state legislatures from working out long-lasting solutions based upon broad public consensus.[45]

This new right-wing movement repeated some of the "traditional roles for women" rhetoric that was so prevalent in the abortion debates of the late 19th century. People like Phyllis Schlafly, Jerry Falwell, Gary Bauer, and organizations such as the Heritage Foundation and Concerned Women for America have endorsed something called "The Natural Family: A Manifesto." The main idea behind this document is the following:

> We affirm that women and men are equal in dignity and innate human rights, but different in function. Even if sometimes thwarted by events beyond the individual's control (or sometimes given up for a religious vocation), the calling of each boy is to become husband and father; the calling of each girl is to become wife and mother. Everything that a man does is mediated by his aptness for fatherhood. Everything a woman does is mediated by her aptness for motherhood. Culture, law, and policy should take these differences into account. . . .
>
> Above all, we believe in rights that recognize women's unique gifts of pregnancy, birthing, and breastfeeding. The goal of androgyny, the effort to eliminate real difference between women and men, does every bit as much violence to human nature and human rights as the old efforts by the communists to create "Soviet Man" and by the Nazis to create "Aryan Man."[46]

At the same time that *Roe* was helping galvanize the Religious Right and Far Right movements outside the legal academy, inside America's law schools those in favor of the decision were desperately trying to find a way to justify the Court's reasoning. The most commonly used strategy was to argue that legitimate constitutional interpretation did not require that the Court's decisions be tied to the constitutional text.[47] The premise of this argument was that neither the constitutional text nor the usual sources of constitutional interpretation such as history, precedent, and tradition could justify many of the Court's most important cases.[48] One famous legal scholar rhetorically asked the following question in the title of a famous article: "Do We Have an Unwritten Constitution?"[49] His answer was an emphatic "Yes." Otherwise, he argued, cases involving desegregation, the rights of voters to have their votes count equally, and capital punishment (among many others) would have to be reversed.[50] Another scholar, arguing against the use of history in constitutional interpretation, made the claim that "strict originalism cannot accommodate most modern decisions under the Bill of Rights and the Fourteenth Amendment, or the . . . Commerce Clause."[51] As the 1980s rolled on, other legal scholars argued that the Court's job was to make the Constitution the best it could be by relying on moral philosophy, political values, and pragmatic reason.[52] The idea that the Supreme Court could only enforce those rights secured by clear constitutional text, history, or precedent was abandoned by these scholars. Any notion that the purpose of judicial review was tied to recreating the original will of the people was also left behind.

The link between these arguments and *Roe* made the work of these academics relatively easy targets for those on the right. Conservatives argued that liberals wanted to take the "Constitution" out of constitutional interpretation and the whole idea of "legislating from the bench" began to have traction in the public eye. Ronald Reagan's first Attorney General Ed Meese began attacking what he called the "living Constitution," in public speeches and law review articles.[53] Speaking at a conservative think tank, one commentator quipped that "[t]he question today is not so much how to read the Constitution as *whether* to read the Constitution."[54] These criticisms were accepted by those in the Reagan administration who were responsible for the selection of federal judges, and, by and large, only those individuals sympathetic to this critique were considered for appointment.

There can be little argument that *Roe* became one of the more contested Supreme Court decisions in our history. And just as in many other constitutional law areas where the Court strongly protects rights that are controversial and highly disfavored by vocal segments of our populations, the Court began to back off its decision in *Roe* relatively quickly as the elected branches tried to water down the effects of this controversial judicial effort to settle the abortion debate.

In the 10 years preceding *Roe,* a mere 10 bills were introduced in Congress relating to abortion. In the 10 years after *Roe,* more than 500 bills dealing with abortion were introduced.[55] Although Congress could not muster the necessary support to redefine life as beginning at conception or to pass a constitutional amendment overturning *Roe,* it did prohibit abortions at military hospitals and federal prisons. More important, just three years after *Roe,* Congress passed the Hyde Amendment, which prohibited the use of Medicaid funds for abortion unless the life (not just health) of the mother was at stake. When the prohibition came up for debate again the following year, Senator Henry Hyde, the bill's sponsor, said the following:

> Theology does not animate me; biology does. That is a human life: that is not a potential human life; it is a human life with potential. When a pregnant woman, who should be the natural protector of her unborn child, becomes its deadly adversary, then it is the duty of this legislature to intervene on behalf of defenseless human life.[56]

Prior to the Hyde Amendment, the federal government was spending approximately $45 million a year and paying for up to 300,000 abortions a year, roughly one-third of all abortions performed nationally.[57] After the Hyde Amendment, many poor women had a very difficult time securing safe abortions. The Hyde Amendment was, of course, attacked in the courts as being unconstitutional on the grounds that it was premised on the belief that abortion was murder; that it discriminated against indigent women; and that it was based on religious beliefs that violated the First Amendment.[58] In 1980, a federal district court judge in Washington, D.C., accepted some of these arguments and struck down the Hyde Amendment on the grounds that it violated women's rights to personal privacy and equal protection.[59]

This victory for pro-choice forces, however, was short-lived. In *Harris v. McRae*,[60] the Supreme Court held that Congress did not have a legal obligation to provide federal funding for abortions even if the life or health of the mother was at stake. The essence of the Court's decision was that "the financial constraints that restrict an indigent woman's ability to enjoy the full range of constitutionally protected freedom of choice are the product not of governmental restrictions on access to abortions, but rather of her indigency . . . [T]he Hyde Amendment leaves an indigent woman with at least the same range of choice in deciding whether to obtain a medically necessary abortion as she would have had if Congress had chosen to subsidize no health care costs at all. We are thus not persuaded that the Hyde Amendment impinges on the constitutionally protected freedom of choice recognized in *Wade*."[61]

Justice Brennan in dissent offered a different perspective by suggesting that by "funding all of the expenses associated with childbirth and none of the expenses incurred in terminating pregnancy," the government was coercing poor women not to have abortions, and it didn't matter that the government was using a "carrot rather than the stick."[62] Justice Brennan went on to argue that the government is not allowed to burden or condition the exercise of fundamental constitutional rights through its spending policies, and a woman's right to have an abortion was such a right.

The issue in *Harris* is not easy as a matter of constitutional law. The government has no constitutional obligation as an initial matter to pay any health care costs so when it voluntarily agrees to do so it makes sense that it can fund only those procedures it deems worthy. On the other hand, even though the government doesn't have to pay for health care in the first instance, when it agrees to do so it must do so constitutionally. For example, Congress could not pay for health care for whites but not blacks because that would violate the equal protection rights of blacks. So, does it violate the rights of women to pay for childbirth but not abortion? The Court has consistently said no and Congress has continued to refuse to allow federal money to be used for abortions (even the 2008 Democratic Congress). Regardless of how one views this constitutional question, however, the reality is that, because many states won't subsidize abortions, almost 40 years after *Roe* poor women still have a difficult time securing safe abortions. The effect of this is a "restoration of precisely the state of affairs that had troubled so many before *Roe*."[63] Rich women have safe abortions while the poor and disadvantaged face far more serious obstacles as well as significant health risks.

It was the Carter administration that argued and won the case in *Harris* but as soon as President Reagan was elected in 1980 the federal government became even more dedicated to pursuing an anti-choice agenda. President Reagan gave numerous speeches criticizing *Roe*, often comparing it to the infamous *Dred Scott* case where the Court declared that African Americans could not be citizens of the United States. In 1984, Reagan said the following:

Our nation-wide policy of abortion-on-demand through all nine months of pregnancy was neither voted for by our people nor enacted by our legislators—not a single state had such unrestricted abortion before the Supreme Court decreed it to be the national policy in 1973. But the consequences of this judicial decision are now obvious: more than 15 million unborn children have had their lives snuffed out by legalized abortions. That is over ten times the number of Americans lost in our nation's wars.[64]

Of course, the Supreme Court never held that any state must have "abortion-on-demand" for "nine months," and it always allowed state prohibitions on abortion after viability. One should pause to wonder how it is that the president of the United States can utter such a falsehood about an issue so important to so many and not be severely criticized for misstating the facts.

President Reagan did not only speak out against *Roe,* but his administration adopted policies and legal strategies to undermine the decision with the hope that it would eventually be overturned. He placed a moratorium on scientific research on fetal tissue (saying that women should not be encouraged to choose abortion on the grounds that it might help scientific advances), he prohibited family planning clinics receiving federal funds from discussing abortion (a regulation eventually approved by the Supreme Court), and, although publicly denying the charge, adopted a strategy for selecting federal judges at all levels of the federal judiciary who, at the very least, were skeptical of *Roe* and its progeny.[65]

Meanwhile, states also adopted numerous strategies to undermine *Roe* and make it more difficult for women to secure abortions. States limited where abortions could be performed, with what methods, what women had to be told about the fetus before an abortion could be performed, how long women would have to wait after their first visit to the doctor to get an abortion, and who, in addition to the woman, had to agree to the abortion.[66] Other than consent requirements for minors, all of these regulations were invalidated by the federal courts (and the Supreme Court) until 1992 and the landmark case of *Planned Parenthood of Southeastern Pennsylvania v. Casey.*[67]

The Supreme Court that decided *Casey* was very different politically and much more conservative from the Court that decided *Roe v. Wade.* Justices Scalia, O'Connor, Kennedy, Souter, and Thomas were not on the Court at the time of *Roe,* and all had been appointed by either Presidents Reagan or Bush. In addition, there had been conservative calls to overturn *Roe* for almost 20 years, numerous marches on Washington, and four Justices (Rehnquist, Scalia, White, and Kennedy) who had previously indicated that they would overrule *Roe,* while one Justice (O'Connor) had openly criticized the decision. No one knew how Justice Souter viewed the issue but he had been appointed by a pro-life president. Of the nine Justices on the bench at the time of *Casey,* only two, Justices Stevens and Blackmun, had openly stated that *Roe* should continue to be the law of the land, and only Justice Blackmun had been on the Court at the time *Roe* was decided.

Casey involved a challenge to numerous Pennsylvania regulations on abortion. These regulations required: (1) a woman seeking an abortion had to give her informed consent prior to the abortion procedure and then wait at least 24 hours before the abortion could be performed; (2) a minor had to obtain the consent of one parent before having an abortion (with a judicial bypass option) ; (3) a married woman seeking an abortion had to sign a statement saying she had notified her husband of her intended abortion (unless she signed a statement saying that notifying the spouse would put her or her family in danger); and (4) clinics that provided abortions had to comply with numerous, detailed, and expensive reporting requirements.[68] The law made exceptions for certain "medical emergencies." Although the U.S. government was not a defendant in the case, it made a special appearance to argue that *Roe v. Wade* should be explicitly overturned.

The drama leading up to *Casey* cannot be overstated. First, the lower court had upheld all of the regulations except the spousal consent requirement and had applied a different legal standard than the trimester framework set forth in *Roe*.[69] The lower court had counted the Justices' votes in pre-*Casey* cases and concluded that *Roe* did not need to be followed.[70] Two weeks prior to the argument, more than 500,000 people marched on Washington, to that point the most ever, demanding that *Roe* be overturned. Kenneth Starr, the solicitor general of the United States, argued in his brief that "no *credible* foundation exists for the claim that a woman enjoys a fundamental right to abortion."[71] And, with the new Justices seemingly receptive to these arguments, the words of Justice Blackmun's dissent in the last abortion case heard by the Court prior to *Casey* seemed to be falling on deaf ears: "I fear for the future. I fear for the liberty and equality of the millions of women who have lived and come of age in the 16 years since Roe was decided. I fear for the integrity of, and public esteem for, this Court."[72]

Between the time of the argument in *Casey* and the day the decision was issued, there was much media and academic speculation that *Roe* might be overturned. On the last day of the Court's 1992 term, and just a few minutes before the Court was to announce its decision, Justice Anthony Kennedy gave a rare interview to a reporter in his chambers. He was looking "out at the gathered crowd from his Chambers window," and said to the reporter, "Sometimes you don't know if you're Caesar about to cross the Rubicon," or rather "Captain Queeg cutting your own tow line." Then Kennedy asked to be left alone because he had to "brood."[73]

It turned out that the Court's decision in *Casey* did little to lessen the abortion debate. There were numerous opinions written by different Justices but the one that counted was written by Justices Kennedy, Souter, and O'Connor. Those three Justices said they were reaffirming the central holding of *Roe* that the Fourteenth Amendment protects a woman's decision whether or not to terminate her pregnancy. They claimed that principles of *stare decisis* (the need to follow prior cases) led them to this conclusion. Nevertheless, and notwithstanding their statement that they were reaffirming *Roe,* the three Justices gutted much of what *Roe* stood for. Their opinion discarded the trimester framework announced in *Roe* and replaced it with the following new test: the Court would uphold all regulations governing abortions before the fetus was viable if those regulations did not pose an "undue burden" on a woman's right to an abortion. This "undue burden" test, previously articulated by Justice O'Connor, and now the law of the land, placed far fewer restrictions on laws governing abortion than the *Roe* trimester and fundamental right tests. After viability, states could continue to outlaw abortion as long as the life of the mother was not at stake.

Whereas under the old regime, 24-hour waiting requirements and informed consent rules were held unconstitutional by the Court, in *Casey* these laws were upheld because the plurality found that they did not pose an undue burden on a woman's right to choose. In fact, the only regulation in *Casey* invalidated by the Court was the one requiring spousal notification. Although the press reported that *Roe* had been reaffirmed, the law of abortion changed dramatically with the *Casey* decision.

This new undue burden test made it much more difficult to predict which abortion laws would be upheld and which would not. For women who have to travel away from home to secure abortions, or for women having to endure angry pro-life protestors at the clinic performing the abortion, the 24-hour rule causes great hardship. But, is it an undue burden? The joint opinion in *Casey* said it wasn't, although it did not disagree with the lower court judge who had found that the 24-hour rule placed a "particular burden" in the way of women seeking abortions.[74] Now, lower court judges have to distinguish between "particular burdens," which are constitutional, and "undue burdens," which are not, no simple task.

As far as requiring spousal notification, the joint opinion invalidated that provision, mostly out of concern for women who would be put in danger by notifying their husbands, *even though the law created an exception for exactly that circumstance.* The joint opinion never explained adequately why the 24-hour provision did not amount to an undue burden but the spousal notification law did. Justice Scalia discussed the problems with the undue burden test in his opinion in *Casey:*

> The shortcomings of Roe did not include lack of clarity: Virtually all regulation of abortion before the third trimester was invalid. . . . [T]he [undue burden] standard is . . . inherently manipulable. . . . The inherently standardless nature of this inquiry invites a district judge to give effect to his personal preferences about abortion. By finding and relying upon the right facts, he can invalidate [almost] any abortion restriction that strikes him as "undue"—subject, of course, to the possibility of being reviewed by a Circuit Court or Supreme Court that is as unconstrained in reviewing his decision as he was in making it.[75]

If the Supreme Court announced that it would only approve those abortion regulations that didn't get in the way of women "too much," and invalidate those that did get in the way "too much," and lower courts could do the same subject to appellate review, the law on abortion would be the rule of what each judge preferred in each individual case not the rule of law. The "undue burden" standard, in effect, has given us the same type of nonlegal regime with similar abortion laws being approved or overturned by federal judges all over the country based not on legal rules, text, or history, but the judges' subjective sensibilities on the abortion question.[76]

PARTIAL-BIRTH ABORTION

Casey was not the Court's last word on abortion. In 2000, in *Stenberg v. Carhart,*[77] the Court reviewed a Nebraska law prohibiting so-called partial-birth abortions. The term *partial-birth abortion* has come to be associated with a medical procedure called "dilation and extraction" (D&X), which is a relatively rare method of performing mostly second-term abortions. The intact D&X involves the termination of a pregnancy by partially extracting a fetus from the uterus and then collapsing its skull to remove its brain. The fetus is then removed in as intact a manner as possible. The more common method of performing abortions after 20 weeks called the standard "dilation and evacuation" (D&E) is to dismember the fetus and pull out the parts. Some doctors and medical experts consider the standard D&E method less than ideal because it can involve substantial blood loss and may increase the risk of puncturing the cervix, which could impair the woman's ability to have children in the future.[78] Additionally, one of the reasons that an Ohio doctor developed the D&X procedure was that he wanted to find a method of performing second-trimester abortions that didn't require an overnight hospital stay because Ohio hospitals would not perform abortions after 18 weeks.[79] In any event, there is substantial disagreement about the pros and cons of both procedures although the standard, nonintact D&E is the more common method of performing second-term abortions.[80]

The Nebraska statute at issue in *Stenberg* prohibited any partial-birth abortion unless that procedure was necessary to save the life of the mother. It defined "partial-birth abortion" as a procedure in which the doctor "partially delivers vaginally a living unborn child before killing the . . . child," and defined the latter phrase to mean "intentionally delivering into the vagina a living unborn child, or a substantial portion thereof, for the purpose of performing a procedure that the [doctor] knows will kill the . . . child and does kill the . . . child."[81] Violation of the law was a felony, and could lead to the automatic revocation of a convicted doctor's license. Leroy Carhart, a Nebraska physician, brought a lawsuit claiming that the Nebraska statute violated the Constitution because it was unconstitutionally vague and placed an undue burden on his medical decisions and his female patients seeking abortions.[82]

The Court struck down the law by a 5–4 vote. Justice Breyer, writing for Justices Ginsburg, Stevens, Souter, and O'Connor, summed up the important nature of the case in the first paragraph:

We again consider the right to an abortion. We understand the controversial nature of the problem. Millions of Americans believe that life begins at conception and consequently that an abortion is akin to causing the death of an innocent child; they recoil at the thought of a law that would permit it. Other millions fear that a law that forbids abortion would condemn many American women to lives that lack dignity, depriving them of equal liberty and leading those with least resources to undergo illegal abortions with the attendant risks of death and suffering. Taking account of these virtually irreconcilable points of view, aware that constitutional law must govern a society whose different members sincerely hold directly opposing views, and considering the matter in light of the Constitution's guarantees of fundamental individual liberty, this Court, in the course of a generation, has determined and then redetermined that the Constitution offers basic protection to the woman's right to choose.[83]

Applying those principles, the majority found that the law was unconstitutional for two reasons. First, to the extent that that it barred not only the intact D&X procedure but also the much more commonly used D&E method where the fetus was dismembered before the abortion was complete, the law posed an undue burden on a woman's right to an abortion in violation of the *Casey* test.[84] Nebraska had conceded that if the law applied to the standard D&E it would be unconstitutional but argued that the law only applied to the D&X. The Court rejected that position as inconsistent with the text of the law and its legislative history.

The Court also held the law unconstitutional because it contained no exception for the health of the mother. Nebraska argued that the intact D&X was never necessary for a mother's health because the standard nonintact D&E could always be performed, but the Court said that medical evidence was conflicting on this point and Nebraska bore a heavy burden in showing that the D&X was *never* necessary for the health of the mother—a burden it could not meet.[85]

Not surprisingly, Justices Scalia, Rehnquist, and Thomas dissented as all three had been on record saying they would overturn *Roe* and *Casey,* and leave the issue of abortion to the states. Justice Scalia continued his attack on the *Casey* undue burden test by saying the following:

I never put much stock in *Casey's* explication of the inexplicable. In the last analysis, my judgment that *Casey* does not support today's tragic result can be traced to the fact that what I consider to be an "undue burden" is different from what the majority considers to be an "undue burden"—*a conclusion that cannot be demonstrated true or false by factual inquiry or legal reasoning*. It is a value judgment, dependent upon how much one respects (or believes society ought to respect) the life of a partially delivered fetus, and how much one respects (or believes society ought to respect) the freedom of the woman who gave it life to kill it. . . . [The result here] has been arrived at by precisely the process *Casey* promised—a democratic vote by nine lawyers, not on the question whether the text of the Constitution has anything to say about this subject (it obviously does not); nor even on the question (also appropriate for lawyers) whether the legal traditions of the American people would have sustained such a limitation upon abortion (they obviously would); but upon the pure policy question whether this limitation upon abortion is "undue"—*i.e.,* goes too far.[86]

Justice Scalia's critique of *Casey* is exactly right. Whether or not an abortion law unduly burdens a woman's right to have an abortion is not a legal question appropriate for judges because no constitutional text or history could possibly be relevant to the question. The problem with Scalia's dissent, however, is that his criticism would be just as applicable to many other areas of constitutional law and Scalia picks and chooses which of those he criticizes and which he joins in a manner also inappropriate for judicial actors. The real problem with *Casey* is not that it breaks with much of constitutional law in its open-endedness but that it is all too similar to so many other constitutional cases.

Scalia's rhetoric was no surprise but Justice Kennedy, who joined with Justices O'Connor and Souter in *Casey*, filed a vehement dissenting opinion that shocked many observers. He believed that Nebraska had a legitimate interest in prohibiting an abortion procedure where the fetus is removed more or less intact from the woman, and that the banning of just one type of procedure, where there was medical uncertainty relating to the necessity of that procedure, did not amount to an undue burden under *Casey*. And, he concluded the following:

The decision nullifies a law expressing the will of the people of Nebraska that medical procedures must be governed by moral principles having their foundation in the intrinsic value of human life, including life of the unborn. Through their law the people of Nebraska were forthright in confronting an issue of immense moral consequence. The State chose to forbid a procedure many decent and civilized people find so abhorrent as to be among the most serious of crimes against human life, while the State still protected the woman's autonomous right of choice as re-affirmed in *Casey*. The Court closes its eyes to these profound concerns.[87]

The debate over partial-birth abortion both inside and outside the Court was far from over. Congress had tried to enact two laws prohibiting the procedure in the 1990s but both were vetoed by President Clinton. In 2003, however, George Bush signed a new federal partial-birth abortion law prohibiting the procedure. Aware of the Court's earlier decision overturning Nebraska's law partly on the grounds that the law barred the standard D&E, Congress's statute very clearly defined the procedure that would be illegal. The law prohibited "deliberately and intentionally" delivering "a living fetus until, in the case of a head-first presentation, the entire fetal head is outside the body of the mother, or, in the case of breech presentation, any part of the fetal trunk past the navel is outside the body of the mother, for the purpose of performing an overt act that the person knows will kill the partially delivered living fetus."[88] Although Congress tried, with this language, to comply with the part of the Court's decision saying the Nebraska law was too vague, it did not address the Court's other concern in *Stenberg* that there was no exception for the health of the mother. Congress also failed to include such an exception. At the time, the Supreme Court had never approved an abortion regulation that did not include such an exception.

The federal partial-birth abortion law was immediately challenged in federal court and struck down by several judges on the grounds that it did not contain an exception for the health of the mother and was constitutionally indistinguishable from the law the Supreme Court had already struck down. Then, something happened unrelated to the abortion question that would alter the course of this issue. Justices Rehnquist and O'Connor both left the Court. Justice Rehnquist, who voted to uphold Nebraska's law, was replaced by Justice Roberts who was expected to vote the same way. Justice O'Connor, who was in the majority in *Stenberg*, and voted to strike down the statute, was replaced by Justice Alito, and that change in personnel, not any change in the law, turned out to make the entire difference. When the federal partial-birth abortion law came before the Supreme Court in 2007 in *Gonzalez v. Carhart*,[89] there were now five votes ready to strike it down (the three dissenters in *Stenberg* plus the new Justices Roberts and Alito). With the substitution of Justice Alito for Justice O'Connor, Justice Kennedy was able to turn his *Stenberg* dissent into the law of the land.

Justice Kennedy's opinion said that the main issue in the case was whether the federal partial-birth opinion law placed a substantial obstacle in the path of women seeking abortions.[90] After concluding that the law at issue only prohibited the intact D&X procedure and not the standard D&E procedure, Kennedy turned to identifying the reasons Congress enacted the law. He said that Congress was more offended by removing a fetus from the woman whole than cutting the fetus up first and then removing the parts from the woman. Kennedy noted that Congress found that the intact D&X procedure was a "brutal and inhumane procedure [which] . . . will further coarsen society to the humanity of not only newborns, but all vulnerable and innocent human life, making it increasingly difficult to protect such life."[91] According to Justice Kennedy, Congress was also concerned that the reputation and integrity of the medical profession would be damaged if allowed to perform partial-birth abortions because the procedure was very similar to infanticide. It must be pointed out, however, that aborting a viable fetus is illegal everywhere (unless the mother's health is at stake) so the intact D&X procedure is no closer to infanticide than the standard D&E procedure that Congress did not prohibit. Whatever differences there may be between the two procedures have nothing to do with any medical differences to the fetus. In one procedure the fetus is dismembered before removal (allowed), and in the other the fetus is destroyed after it is partially removed from the woman (not allowed). The fact that the Court found a legally significant difference between the two speaks more of personal sensibilities than legal argument.

In addition to suggesting that Congress had legitimate reasons to outlaw the D&X procedure, Justice Kennedy also said that Congress had a legally sufficient reason to protect women from having the procedure. This part of the opinion, joined by five Justices, is so alarming that the whole section needs to be quoted to make the point adequately:

Respect for human life finds an ultimate expression in the bond of love the *mother* has for her *child*. The Act recognizes this reality as well. Whether to have an abortion requires a difficult and painful moral decision. *While we find no reliable data to measure the phenomenon,* it seems unexceptionable to conclude some women come to regret their choice to abort the infant life they once created and sustained. Severe depression and loss of esteem can follow.

In a decision so fraught with emotional consequence some doctors may prefer not to disclose precise details of the means that will be used, confining themselves to the required statement of risks the procedure entails. From one standpoint this ought not to be surprising. Any number of patients facing imminent surgical procedures would prefer not to hear all details, lest the usual anxiety preceding invasive medical procedures become the more intense. This is likely the case with the abortion procedures here in issue.

It is, however, precisely this lack of information concerning the way in which the fetus will be killed that is of legitimate concern to the State. *The State has an interest in ensuring so grave a choice is well informed.* It is self-evident that a mother who comes to regret her choice to abort must struggle with grief more anguished and sorrow more profound when she learns, only after the event, what she once did not know: that she allowed a doctor to pierce the skull and vacuum the fast-developing brain of her *unborn child,* a *child* assuming the human form.[92]

There are a number of elements in this discussion that demonstrate how far removed Justice Kennedy's analysis is from standard legal argument. First is his assumption that a pregnant woman carrying a fetus she does not want already considers herself a mother to the "child" inside her. Such an analysis may not fit many women seeking abortions such as those who were raped, the victims of incest, or women who used birth control properly that simply failed. Moreover, who is Justice Kennedy to say that "respect for human life finds an ultimate expression in the bond of love the mother has for her child." What about the bond between father and son, husband and wife, and gay partners, among other important and fundamental "bonds" between people. This is not court made law but a value-laden discourse on "human relationships 101."

Second, Justice Kennedy conceded that there was no data to back up the claim that many women regret choosing to have an abortion and then live with despair. Obviously, some women may feel this way, but how many others regret not having an abortion and keeping the child or regret putting the child up for adoption? Moreover, why is it the Court's or the Congress's job to protect these women from their own choices? As Justice Ginsburg argued angrily in dissent, this paternalistic view of women treated them more like children than fully functioning members of our society.[93] Finally, Justice Kennedy laments in this section that women are not given the full details of the D&X procedure but concludes that the cure for that omission is, not to require the doctors to provide more accurate information, but instead to deprive women of a procedure they may need. Again, this is not law or logic but simply the enforcement of Justice Kennedy's view that the intact D&X procedure is somehow more disgusting than other methods of abortion.

Although these sections patronizing women are indefensible, the Court's legal analysis of the federal law is even worse. The law did not have an exception for the health of the mother, and the doctors who filed the suit argued that such an exception was necessary because sometimes it is better for women's health to use the intact D&X procedure than the standard D&E. This was exactly the same argument the Court accepted in *Stenberg* when it overturned Nebraska's partial-birth abortion law.

The *Gonzales* Court framed the issue as follows: "whether the Act has the effect of imposing an unconstitutional burden on the abortion right because it does not allow use of the barred procedure where 'necessary, in appropriate medical judgment, for [the] preservation of the . . . health of the mother.'"[94] The Court conceded that the law would be unconstitutional if it "subject[ed] [women] to significant health risks."[95] And, the Court did not refute the factual determination made by the *Stenberg* Court that "whether the Act creates significant health risks for women has been a contested factual question. The evidence presented in the trial courts and before Congress demonstrates both sides have medical support for their position."[96] The Court spent several paragraphs detailing the factual arguments for both sides and then concluding, *in direct contradiction to the Court's holding in Stenberg,* that the presence of medical uncertainty does not require a health exception for women. Under *Casey* and *Stenberg*, if there was uncertainty about the medical necessity of a medical abortion procedure, the tie would go to women's health, but now under *Gonzalez* a tie goes to those wishing to ban the procedure.[97] This new position did not occur because of a change in text, precedent, history, or even an open acknowledgment of a legal mistake. It came about simply because Justice Alito voted to uphold a statute legally identical to a statute that Justice O'Connor voted to overturn. This type of political behavior is inappropriate for our nation's highest Court.

The future of the abortion controversy is uncertain. The moral and philosophical issues surrounding abortion still sharply divide this country. One thing that is certain, however, is that the Supreme Court has to some degree elevated this issue with its controversial decisions and lawless approach to the question. Although Planned Parenthood and other pro-choice organizations have won some of the legal battles over abortion (though poor women have lost the war), we live in a more conservative world than we probably would without *Roe*. To some extent the great influence that the Religious Right and the legacy of Ronald Reagan has had on our current politics grew out of the opposition to the Court's abortion decisions. For those on the left who are strongly pro-choice and pro-women's rights in general, the question is whether the limited right to abortion the Court has protected has been on balance worth the costs. How one answers that question does not depend on an interpretation of legal text, history, or prior cases. It depends on one's values and politics. The same can be said about the question whether the United States Constitution protects a woman's right to terminate her pregnancy, and if so, in what ways. There is simply no way to predict what will happen to this issue in the Supreme Court without knowing who will serve on the Court in the future and what values they possess—and that involves predicting which Justices will be appointed, not examining the law of the Constitution.

CHAPTER 6

Guns

Eighty-six percent of the gun deaths of children under the age of 14 internationally are right here in the United States of America. It is madness.

—Congresswoman Nita Lowey

Taking my gun away because I might shoot someone is like cutting my tongue out because I might yell "Fire!" in a crowded theater.

—Peter Venetoklis

OVERVIEW

The Second Amendment to the United States Constitution provides that: "A well-regulated Militia, being necessary to the security of a Free State, the right of the people to keep and bear Arms, shall not be infringed." From 1788, when the Amendment was ratified, until 2008, the Supreme Court *never* ruled in favor of a plaintiff asserting a Second Amendment claim, and virtually all lower federal courts assumed that the Second Amendment did not apply to individuals asserting the right to own guns for self-defense or hunting, but only protected the right of the people to own guns for *militia* purposes. Traditionally, militias were composed of able-bodied men who were not serving in the military but who could be called to military service in case of emergency or invasion. There is virtually no official use of state militias today.

In 2008, the Supreme Court decided the landmark case of *District of Columbia v. Heller.*[1] By a bitterly contested 5–4 vote, the Court held that a District of Columbia law prohibiting all handguns violated the Second Amendment. Because the law at issue was not a state law but a law of the District of Columbia (which is essentially federal territory), the Court in *Heller* did not address whether the Second Amendment also limited state laws regulating gun possession. Two years later, the Court, again by a 5–4 vote, held that it did.[2] Although for the first time in history the Court in these two cases held that the Second Amendment protects an individual right to own guns, it also suggested that many traditional restrictions on that right, such as prohibiting gun ownership by certain people (felons, minors, and the mentally ill), and in certain places (government buildings, hospitals, etc.), were constitutional.

Our societal debate over the constitutionality, as well as the wisdom, of gun control legislation is heated and by no means settled by the Court's recent decisions. It is not the purpose of this chapter to provide a detailed summary of the policy arguments for and against gun control, but rather to explain how the Supreme Court's treatment of the Second Amendment supports this book's central theme—that the Supreme Court does not act like a court and its Justices do not decide cases like judges.

THE TEXTUAL ISSUES WITH THE SECOND AMENDMENT

A judge acting in good faith to interpret a disputed constitutional provision should start with the language of that provision. In all fairness to the Court, both the majority and dissenting opinions in *Heller* spent considerable time debating what the words of the Amendment mean. In order to place that debate in a proper context, here again is the text of the Second Amendment: "A well-regulated Militia, being necessary to the security of a Free State, the right of the people to keep and bear Arms, shall not be infringed."

To apply this constitutional provision to a state or federal law regulating or prohibiting guns, we would likely have to answer the following questions:

1. Does the Second Amendment protect only *militia-related* use of guns or does it protect the right to own guns for personal purposes such as self-defense and hunting?
2. Assuming the amendment protects more than the right to bear arms for militia purposes, what does the phrase *the*

right of the people mean? Does it mean the amendment protects a *group* right or can *individuals* also assert it?
3. What does the phrase *keep and bear arms* mean? Are those
two different ideas or just one?
4. What kinds of *arms* are protected? For example, are semiau-
tomatic weapons, which were unknown to the framers, protected? How about small handguns that can be easily hidden
(also unknown to the framers)?
5. Assuming the amendment protects a personal right to own
different kinds of guns, what does the phrase *shall not
be infringed* mean? Do stringent licensing requirements
"infringe" the right? How about laws prohibiting the possession of guns in public places or laws forbidding concealed
weapons?

Before turning to how the Supreme Court has dealt with these
questions, it is important to recognize that all of these issues raise,
not only difficult interpretative questions, but enormously complex
policy issues. Some cities, like Chicago and the District of Columbia,
would like to ban all handguns, believing that doing so reduces crime.
Other cities, like those in the Deep South and the West, feel differently
and have even flirted with laws *requiring* people to own guns.[3]

Although the decision whether to have rules and regulations concerning guns in the first instance is made by city councils, state legislatures, and the Congress, a robust reading of the Second Amendment
could potentially transfer to federal judges a veto power over all such
laws. In light of the fact that, as of 2009, our population of 307 million people owned approximately 300 million guns, and in light of
how strongly so many people feel about this important and difficult question (from 1990 through 2010 more than $24 million was
spent by lobbying groups on both sides of this issue on candidates for
federal elections),[4] the validity and wisdom of gun control legislation is likely to divide our courts, our legislatures, and our people for
years to come.

THE COURT AND GUNS

United States v. Miller

The National Firearms Act of 1934 placed substantial taxes and registration requirements on certain kinds of firearms such as short-
barreled shotguns and machine guns. In *United States v. Miller,*[5]

decided in 1939, two men were charged with moving unregistered shotguns across state lines in violation of the federal law.[6] The lower court dismissed the case on Second Amendment grounds without providing any explanation for its decision.[7] The government appealed but the defendants did not appear in the Supreme Court, and thus there were no briefs arguing their side of the case.[8] Given the defendants' failure to appear, it is unclear why the Supreme Court didn't just reverse the lower court decision and reinstate the indictment on the grounds that the defendants were absent. Nevertheless, the Court issued an opinion interpreting the "militia" language of the Second Amendment for the first time in the Court's history. As might be expected, given the lack of a true adversarial process, the Court's decision was short and to the point.[9] The thrust of its opinion came in the following paragraph:

> In the absence of any evidence tending to show that possession or use of a "shotgun having a barrel of less than eighteen inches in length" at this time has some reasonable relationship to the preservation or efficiency of a well-regulated militia, we cannot say that the *Second Amendment* guarantees the right to keep and bear such an instrument. Certainly it is not within judicial notice that this weapon is any part of the ordinary military equipment or that its use could contribute to the common defense.[10]

The Court then stated that it could not "accept the conclusion of the court below," and remanded the case for "further proceedings."[11]

The meaning of *Miller* has been debated by judges and academics since 1939. The opinion could have meant that the Second Amendment only protects those "arms" that bear a "reasonable relationship to the preservation or efficiency of a well-regulated militia." If this were the meaning of the case, then weapons, such as handguns, with little military utility, would not be covered by the amendment, but weapons with a military use would be subject to constitutional protections.

Miller could also mean, however, that the Second Amendment simply has no relevance when the right asserted has no connection to preserving a militia. Thus, regardless of the weapon at issue, an individual asserting a right to own guns for hunting or self-defense would not be able to rely on the Second Amendment. From 1939 to

2001, virtually every lower federal court interpreted *Miller* this way believing that the Second Amendment did not protect the use of a gun for nonmilitia purposes.[12] When this issue finally was decided by the Supreme Court in *Heller,* however, it reached a different conclusion.

District of Columbia v. Heller

Dick Heller is a security guard at a federal building in Washington, D.C., and a libertarian political activist.[13] He wanted to keep a handgun in his home for his personal self-defense but a 1976 law essentially prohibited the possession of such guns and also required that all other guns kept in the house be either unloaded or bound by a trigger lock.[14] Heller filed suit in federal court in the District of Columbia with the help of several conservative think tanks such as the Cato Institute and the Institute for Justice.[15] The lower court ruled for the city, but the Court of Appeals, in a divided opinion, reversed and held for Heller. The Supreme Court handed down its 5–4 opinion overturning the city's guns laws on June 26, 2008, more than 30 years after the law was first adopted.

Justice Scalia wrote the majority opinion on behalf of Justices Alito, Roberts, Thomas, and Kennedy (the conservative wing of the Court). Justices Stevens and Breyer both wrote dissenting opinions joined by Justices Souter and Ginsburg (the moderate wing). Scalia's opinion was 64 pages long, and Steven's response was 46 pages. Predictably, the five conservative Justices found in the Second Amendment a personal right to own guns for self-defense and recreational purposes while the four moderate Justices did not. Ironically, all the Justices who were in the majority (except for Justice Kennedy) usually argue against judicial enforcement of rights that are not expressly and unambiguously expressed in the Constitution (such as abortion and gay rights), while the four dissenting Justices often argue in favor of such rights (such as abortion and gay rights). In addition, the five Justices in the majority often argue in favor of providing cities and states significant autonomy over controversial subjects whereas the four Justices in the dissent often argue against such autonomy. In other words, at least eight of the Justices in this case advocated a result at odds with their normal views on constitutional interpretation.[16] This discrepancy suggests that the Justices were acting more as policy makers reviewing laws they either favored or didn't favor than judges interpreting legal text and prior case law. Moreover, the majority in *Heller*, like the majority in *Roe v. Wade*, dictated a set of rules that sound much more like the work of a legislature than the work of judges.[17]

The first important issue the *Heller* Court had to decide was the relationship between the opening words of the Second Amendment: "A well-regulated Militia, being necessary to the security of a free State," and the closing words: "the right of the people to keep and bear Arms, shall not be infringed." Justice Scalia said that "The Second Amendment is *naturally* divided into two parts: its prefatory clause and its operative clause. The former does not limit the latter grammatically, but rather announces a purpose."[18] Scalia's use of the word *naturally* is astonishing given that the Second Amendment is the *only* section of the Bill of Rights that has both a prefatory and an operative clause.

The Court summed up the opposing views as follows:

> The two sides in this case have set out very different interpretations of the Amendment. Petitioners and today's dissenting Justices believe that it protects only the right to possess and carry a firearm in connection with militia service. . . . Respondent argues that it protects an individual right to possess a firearm unconnected with service in a militia, and to use that arm for traditionally lawful purposes, such as self-defense within the home.[19]

Both Justice Scalia for the majority and Justice Stevens for the defense agreed that the dominant concern of the people who ratified the Second Amendment was to prevent Congress from eliminating local militia by taking away weapons from the able-bodied men who composed the militia.[20] In other words, at the time of the founding, there was a great worry that the national government would act tyrannically by disarming the state militias. There was also a great fear of the threat posed by standing armies, and the Founding Fathers believed that state militias could secure freedom and prevent tyranny in a way standing armies could not.

The issue that divided the Justices in *Heller*, therefore, was not the central purpose of the Second Amendment. The Justices agreed it was to protect state militias. The fighting concerned whether that was the *only* purpose. Justice Scalia argued that most people at the time of the ratification of the Second Amendment believed they had the right to own guns for self-defense and hunting, that these rights preexisted the Second Amendment, and that the Amendment was meant to reflect those other purposes. He relied on an array of historical sources for this argument including pre- and postconstitutional treatises and laws, state Constitutions enacted both before and after the National Constitution, letters from important founders, and case law dating from before and after the Civil War.[21] He also argued that the phrase *to keep and bear arms* was not limited to the military use of those arms but other uses such as self-defense and hunting, and that the phrase *right of the people* in the Second Amendment referred to an individual right, not the rights of a group of people or the people acting collectively.[22] Thus, Justice Scalia and the other four Justices in the majority interpreted the Second Amendment to provide a judicially enforceable constitutional right for individuals to own guns for purposes much broader than military service.

Justice Stevens, however, looked at the same historical materials and came to opposite conclusions. He concluded that the Second Amendment "is most naturally read to secure to the people a right to use and possess arms in conjunction with service in a well-regulated militia. So far as appears, no more than that was contemplated by its drafters or is encompassed within its terms."[23] The history of the ratification of the Second Amendment demonstrated, at least to Stevens and the three Justices who joined his dissent, that the people were exclusively concerned with the threat of standing armies and were interested in preserving the right of the people to form local militias that could not be disarmed. They were not trying to protect a person's right to hunt or own a gun for personal self-defense.[24] Stevens also argued that the phrase *to keep and bear arms* had a distinctly military meaning supporting his interpretation of the amendment as applying only to militia purposes. He also believed that the phrase *right of the people* referred to a group right based in the militia and not a personal right.[25] For Justice Stevens, the Second Amendment's right was limited to preventing the federal government from disarming state militias and nothing more. So read, the Second Amendment would be a virtual irrelevancy today.

The truth is that neither Justice Scalia nor Justice Stevens is an historian. The overwhelming impression generated by slogging through the historical analysis in the two opinions is that the sources relied upon by the two Justices are so vague and indeterminate that both of the Justices' conclusions are unpersuasive, and that any reliance on history to generate a result in this case is obviously result-oriented.

Not surprisingly, scholars are also divided on what the history and text of the Second Amendment reflects. One legal scholar who has studied the history of the amendment has called Justice Scalia's historical analysis "disingenuous and unprincipled," as well as "objectively untenable."[26] In addition, as this scholar notes, conservative and well-respected Court of Appeals Judges Richard Posner and Harvie Wilkinson have "savaged" Scalia's opinion as "results-oriented historical fiction."[27] These experts believe that the Second Amendment was discussed primarily in the context of the virtues of having local militias and the dangers of having a standing and professional army. Any notion that the Second Amendment, as a historical matter, was intended to protect the right to own guns for personal self-defense in the home or for recreational purposes is fanciful.[28]

On the other hand, there are respectable scholars who favor Justice Scalia's historical interpretations over those articulated by Justice Stevens. For example, historian Robert Churchill has written eloquently about the link between the Second Amendment and a broad individual right to own guns.[29] Moreover, prominent legal scholars Eugene Volokh and Nelson Lund have made strong cases for historical conclusions similar to those reached by Justice Scalia.[30]

Leaving aside who has the better historical argument, the important point is that few if any Justices or scholars with strong views about gun control one way or the other have changed their mind based on the historical record. In other words, because the text of the amendment is subject to reasonable disagreement over whether it applies only to the militia or to other situations, Justices and legal scholars who look to history as a guide not surprisingly often find exactly what they were looking for. Therefore, as is the case with most litigated constitutional issues, the meaning of the Second Amendment cannot be separated from the public policy issues implicated by the Constitution's text. When resolving those kinds of issues, as the Court purported to do in *Heller,* the Justices care *much more* about the real-life consequences of their decisions than the best reading of text, history, and prior case law. This explains how the Court could have read the Second Amendment one way for so long (as not protecting an individual right to own guns) and then changed its mind so abruptly when there were five votes for a different interpretation.

The Justices in *Heller* not only disagreed about the reading of the Second Amendment, but also about the underlying public policy issues implicated by the case. The District of Columbia law challenged by Dick Heller essentially prohibited the possession of handguns and required that all guns kept in the house be either unloaded or bound with a trigger lock. The majority held that these requirements were unconstitutional for the following reasons:

> [T]he inherent right of self-defense has been central to the Second Amendment right. The handgun ban amounts to a prohibition of an entire class of "arms" that is overwhelmingly chosen by American society for that lawful purpose. The prohibition extends, moreover, to the home, where the need for defense of self, family, and property is most acute. Under any of the standards of scrutiny that we have applied to enumerated constitutional rights, banning from the home the most preferred firearm in the nation to keep and use for protection of one's home and family would fail constitutional muster.
>
> We must also address the District's requirement (as applied to respondent's handgun) that firearms in the home be rendered and kept inoperable at all times. This makes it impossible for citizens to use them for the core lawful purpose of self-defense and is hence unconstitutional.[31]

Justice Breyer's opposing argument in dissent contended that, even assuming the Second Amendment protects an individual right to own guns, the District of Columbia had constitutionally sufficient reasons for banning handguns and requiring that all guns kept in the home be unloaded or bound by a trigger lock. To truly absorb the power of this argument, it is necessary to provide lengthy quotes from Justice Breyer's dissent, joined by three other Justices. He began by summarizing the evidence that the committee that proposed the law gave to the entire D.C. City Council when the council approved the law in 1976. According to Justice Breyer:

> [T]he committee observed that there were 285 murders in the District during 1974—a record number. The committee also stated that, "[c]ontrary to popular opinion on the subject, firearms are more frequently involved in deaths and violence among relatives and friends than in premeditated criminal activities." Citing an article from the American Journal of Psychiatry, the committee reported that "[m]ost murders are committed by previously law-abiding citizens, in situations where spontaneous

violence is generated by anger, passion or intoxication, and where the killer and victim are acquainted. Twenty-five percent of these murders," the committee informed the Council, "occur within families."

The committee report furthermore presented statistics strongly correlating handguns with crime. Of the 285 murders in the District in 1974, 155 were committed with handguns. This did not appear to be an aberration, as the report revealed that "handguns [had been] used in roughly 54% of all murders" (and 87% of murders of law enforcement officers) nationwide over the preceding several years. Nor were handguns only linked to murders, as statistics showed that they were used in roughly 60% of robberies and 26% of assaults.

In the absence of adequate federal gun legislation, the committee concluded, it "becomes necessary for local governments to act to protect their citizens, and certainly the District of Columbia as the only totally urban state like jurisdiction should be strong in its approach." It recommended that the Council adopt a restriction on handgun registration to reflect "a legislative decision that, at this point in time and due to the gun-control tragedies and horrors enumerated previously," in the committee report, "pistols . . . are no longer justified in this jurisdiction."[32]

Justice Breyer also summarized the evidence that was before the Supreme Court in 2008 when it heard the case. Again, to fully appreciate the stakes of this controversy and the nature of the Court's decision, significant excerpts from Justice Breyer's dissent must be provided:

Handguns are involved in a majority of firearm deaths and injuries in the United States. From 1993 to 1997, 81% of firearm-homicide victims were killed by handgun. . . . And among children under the age of 20, handguns account for approximately 70% of all unintentional firearm-related injuries and deaths. In particular, 70% of all firearm-related teenage suicides in 1996 involved a handgun.

Handguns also appear to be a very popular weapon among criminals. In a 1997 survey of inmates who were armed during the crime for which they were incarcerated, 83.2% of state inmates and 86.7% of federal inmates said that they were armed

with a handgun. . . . Department of Justice studies have concluded that stolen handguns in particular are an important
source of weapons for both adult and juvenile offenders.

Statistics further suggest that urban areas, such as the District,
have different experiences with gun-related death, injury, and
crime than do less densely populated rural areas. A dispropor-
tionate amount of violent and property crimes occur in urban
areas, and urban criminals are more likely than other offenders
to use a firearm during the commission of a violent crime. Ho-
micide appears to be a much greater issue in urban areas. . . . [A]
study of firearm injuries to children and adolescents in Pennsylvania between 1987 and 2000 showed an injury rate in urban
counties 10 times higher than in nonurban counties.[33]

Relying on these reports, statistics, and findings, Justice Breyer
argued that the city law at issue satisfied constitutional muster because it was a proportionate response to the problems of urban violence and serious crime. He also argued that the law should be upheld
because it was tailored to the one class of weapons (handguns) that
posed the greatest threat to people living in the district; because the
primary interest protected by the Second Amendment was the preservation of the militia not personal self-defense; and because there
was no lesser way of ridding the city of the numerous dangers posed
by handguns.[34]

Justice Scalia's response to these arguments was brief (especially
compared to the amount of time he spent discussing the history of
the Second Amendment). First, he criticized Justice Breyer's balancing of the relative merits of the law compared to the importance of
the right at issue. For Justice Scalia, "[t]he very enumeration of the
right takes out of the hands of government . . . the power to decide on
a case-by-case basis whether the right is *really worth* insisting upon.
A constitutional guarantee subject to future judges' assessments of
its usefulness is no constitutional guarantee at all."[35] In other words,
Justice Scalia argued that the Second Amendment's protections did
not allow for exceptions to the right to own guns articulated by
judges on a "case-by-case basis."

Justice Breyer's response to Scalia, however, shows the utter lack
of transparency in Scalia's argument. Breyer pointed out that the majority opinion, with no explanation whatsoever, carved out the following exceptions to the right to own guns: laws prohibiting the

"possession of firearms by felons . . . [and] the mentally ill, [or] laws forbidding the carrying of firearms in sensitive places such as schools and government buildings, [or laws imposing] conditions and qualifications attached to the commercial sale of arms."[36] Justice Breyer persuasively argued that the majority never explained why these exceptions were constitutional but the city's decision to eliminate one kind of firearms (handguns) was not. The most Scalia offered in rebuttal was that handguns are the types of weapons most commonly used for self-defense in the home, but Justice Breyer responded by arguing that the primary purpose of the Second Amendment was emphatically not self-defense in the home but the preservation of the militia; that there were laws at the time of the founding limiting what arms could be kept and used in the home, and that, in any event, the Founding Fathers could not possibly have envisioned the relationship between small but powerful handguns and urban crime and violence that exists today.[37]

Justice Breyer was not arguing that prohibiting all handguns and requiring guns in the home to be unlocked is the best way to combat urban crime and violence. Rather, he was arguing that the city council should have been allowed to reach that conclusion without undue interference from the Court. This point deserves emphasis. The five conservative Justices held in *Heller* that towns, cities, and states across the country, from Boston to Los Angeles to Chicago to rural areas and small towns in between, were constitutionally precluded from banning handguns regardless of how strongly the elected officials in those communities believed that such guns posed a serious threat to life and property within their jurisdiction. Moreover, as Justice Breyer also pointed out, the *Heller* decision would now, for the first time in our history, require federal judges to review and possibly second guess different kinds of restrictions on guns in a diverse array of communities.[38]

Justice Scalia responded to these concerns by analogizing to the First Amendment's protections for speech and arguing that the Constitution sometimes takes decisions away from elected officials.[39] But, there is common agreement that the First Amendment was designed to protect most forms of speech from governmental censorship, and there is a relatively long history of judicial protection for people wishing to engage in their constitutionally protected right to freedom of speech. Moreover, virtually everyone today agrees that the First Amendment gives at least serious protection to freedom of speech, and no one argues that the history of that amendment reveals otherwise. Before the *Heller* decision in 2008, however, the Supreme Court had *never* found that the Second Amendment protected an individual right to own a gun, and many, if not most, academics and historians believe that the history of the Second Amendment does not justify judicial interference with democratically imposed restrictions on guns.[40] Moreover, the text of the First Amendment, that Congress "shall make no law abridging the freedom of speech," unequivocally and unambiguously protects "speech" without exception. The text of the Second Amendment, with its emphasis on the "militia," is much more equivocal. Justice Scalia's analogy to the First Amendment to support judicial enforcement of the Second Amendment is simply unpersuasive.

Finally, there is a great irony arising from Justice Scalia's *Heller* opinion that supports this book's thesis that, whatever the Supreme Court is doing when it decides constitutional law cases, it is not acting like judges interpreting prior positive law. There have been no more vocal critics of the Court's abortion jurisprudence than Justices Scalia and Thomas. They have repeatedly argued that the Court should refrain from reviewing state and federal restrictions on abortion because a woman's right to terminate her pregnancy is not mentioned in the Constitution, has not been historically protected, and is an issue better left to the people and their elected representatives.[41] As conservative Judge Harvie Wilkinson has eloquently pointed out, however, the same criticisms apply to the Court's decision in *Heller* written by Justice Scalia and joined by Justice Thomas (and the rest of the conservatives all of whom but Kennedy would not find a right to an abortion in the Constitution).[42]

Judge Wilkinson makes the following four points about both *Roe* and *Heller*:

1. Both decisions reflect the absence of a commitment to reading the text of the Constitution seriously;
2. Both decisions required judges to "fine-tune" complex legislative judgments that will require years of litigation;
3. Both decisions fail to show respect for state and federal legislative judgments; and
4. Both decisions reject the idea that the federal government should leave contested value judgments on difficult questions to the states.[43]

The American people feel strongly, both pro and con, on the issues of abortion and gun control. Although the Constitution does not mention abortion at all and does refer to guns, the most plausible reading of the Second Amendment's text is that it protects guns *only* to the extent that a militia is involved. In any event, the ambiguity of the text should counsel judicial deference to elected policy makers. The Supreme Court did not find a right to abortion in the Constitution until 1973, and did not find an individual right to own guns in the Constitution until 2008. When discussing *Roe,* the conservatives claim that the liberals are engaging in judicial activism, and when critiquing *Heller* the liberals argue that the conservatives are engaging in judicial activism. The truth is that neither side can claim the moral or interpretative high ground. All we can say with any certainty is that the Justices in the majority in *Heller,* like the Justices in the majority in *Roe,* cared more about the right to own guns and the right to have abortions than fidelity to any coherent system of constitutional interpretation. The *only* honest way to reconcile the cases is that the Justices who decided them were not judges doing their best to interpret text, tradition, history, and precedent, but men and women sitting on an ultimate veto council who used text, tradition, history, and precedent to justify policy decisions made on other grounds. Justice Scalia, himself, has argued against such an unfortunate approach to constitutional law. Commenting on the national antiabortion protests that take place in Washington every year outside the Supreme Court building, he criticized the Court's opinions in abortion cases as follows:

> As long as this Court thought (and the people thought) that we Justices were doing essentially lawyers' work up here—reading text and discerning our society's traditional understanding of that text—the public pretty much left us alone. Texts and traditions are facts to study, not convictions to demonstrate about. But if in reality our process of constitutional adjudication consists primarily of making *value judgments* . . . then a free and intelligent people's attitude towards us can be expected to be (*ought* to be) quite different. The people know that their value judgments are quite as good as those taught in any law school—maybe better. If, indeed, the "liberties" protected by the Constitution are, as the Court says, undefined and unbounded, then the people *should* demonstrate, to protest that

we do not implement *their* values instead of *ours*. . . . Value judgments, after all, should be voted on, not dictated.[44]

Exactly so, Justice Scalia. It is the people and their elected representatives who should set gun policy (and abortion policy) in this country, not the unelected and unaccountable Supreme Court of the United States.

CHAPTER 7

Affirmative Action

[F]reedom is not enough. You do not wipe away the scars of centuries by saying: Now you are free to go where you want, and do as you desire, and choose the leaders you please. You do not take a person who, for years, has been hobbled by chains and liberate him, bring him up to the starting line of a race and then say, "you are free to compete with all the others," and still justly believe that you have been completely fair. Thus it is not enough just to open the gates of opportunity. All our citizens must have the ability to walk through those gates. This is the next and the more profound stage of the battle for civil rights. We seek not just freedom but opportunity. We seek not just legal equity but human ability, not just equality as a right and a theory but equality as a fact and equality as a result.

—Lyndon Johnson

OVERVIEW

The issue of race has sharply divided the American people since before the Constitution was adopted. Our Founding Fathers compromised on the issue of slavery; the Civil War was fought at least partly over race; the Thirteenth, Fourteenth, and Fifteenth Amendments were enacted to deal with race; and we have been wrestling with the consequences of our racial past for most of the 20th and early 21st centuries. Whereas for most of our country's history we fought over whether people of color *deserved* equal rights in society and under the law, now, for the most part, we argue over the best way to *achieve* that equality. The debate over affirmative action is one of the battlefields on which these arguments are now being fought.

After the Civil War, the Supreme Court interpreted the Reconstruction Amendments to prohibit Congress from ending racial discrimination in hotels, restaurants, and other places of public accommodations, while at the same time reading the same amendments to allow states to require racial segregation in those places. The effects of these two lines of decisions led to the Jim Crow South and formal legalized discrimination against blacks for almost 90 years. When the Supreme Court finally decided in 1954 in *Brown v. Board of Education* that legally segregated schools violated the Equal Protection Clause of the Fourteenth Amendment, the damage the Court's prior decisions had caused was overwhelming. Even 10 years after *Brown,* the public schools of the South were still overwhelmingly segregated. In 1963, for example, virtually no children in 12 Southern states attended public schools with children of another race.[1] Only after Congress passed the Civil Rights Act of 1964, and conditioned federal grant money to the states on their taking measures to desegregate their schools, was some progress finally made.[2]

During the 1960s and 1970s, most public schools stopped taking formal discriminatory measures but residential housing patterns as well as governmental subsidization of private schools through tax breaks and direct subsidies kept public schools heavily segregated. Because there is a strong correlation between education and earning potential,[3] and because segregated schools offered racial minorities inferior educational opportunities, affirmative action programs began to be adopted by universities, state and local governments, and the federal government.[4] These programs generated significant controversy, both in the courts and in the voting booths, and are still being debated today.

Although there are different varieties of *affirmative action* programs, for our purposes the phrase refers to the use of racial, gender, or ethnic preferences by a public institution to determine who receives a governmental benefit. This chapter begins by providing a context within which to understand how affirmative action began, moves on to a brief history and description of affirmative action programs, and then concludes with a discussion of the Supreme Court's response to these state and federal efforts to help minorities overcome the inequalities generated by America's racist past.

THE CONTEXT

Legally sanctioned racial preferences for whites were the norm in this country from 1788 until at least 1964. In addition to slavery and Jim Crow (legalized segregation), numerous governmental programs and officially sanctioned private practices led directly to many of the serious racial problems we confront today. For example, the Social Security Act of 1935 gave millions of Americans retirement and disability benefits but excluded from the act's coverage domestic workers and agricultural servants, most of whom were people of color.[5] The 1935 Wagner Act granted people the right to form unions and engage in collective bargaining, which increased salaries and benefits for millions of workers, but the act allowed unions to exclude nonwhites, which many did until the 1970s.[6] And, perhaps most important, around the same time as these New Deal programs were created, the federal government created the Federal Housing Administration, which set up a neighborhood appraisal system linking the ability to secure mortgages directly to race. Mixed-race neighborhoods were usually considered too risky for their residents to qualify for these mortgages and resulted in the infamous practice of "redlining."[7] Between 1934 and 1962, the federal government spent approximately $120 billion backing home loans but more than 98 percent of the money went to white families.[8] In Northern California alone, between 1946 and 1960, almost 350,000 new homes were built with the support of federally backed mortgages and less than 100 of those homes went to African American families.[9]

All of these practices led to widespread segregation of whites and blacks in housing and schools. As late as 1993, according to the United States Census, approximately 85 percent of suburban whites lived in neighborhoods in which blacks constituted less than 1 percent of the population.[10] To make matters even more unequal, these long-standing housing and economic disparities allowed whites to pass on much more wealth to their children than blacks could bequeath to theirs. These intergenerational transfers allowed whites to invest and accumulate more wealth, increasing the economic separation between whites and blacks.[11] These conditions of inequality did not occur naturally but were the result of official laws, policies, and programs created and administered by state and federal governments.

The point of this history is not to argue in favor of affirmative action programs as a policy matter. There are many legitimate arguments that such programs may cause more problems than they solve. The point is to put into context the strong judicial scrutiny of affirmative action programs that are voluntarily adopted by the same state and federal governments that for most of this country's history favored whites under the law. In other words, the same courts that allowed the government to officially discriminate *against* blacks for almost 180 years have now been called upon to review programs that *favor* blacks. Before the judicial reaction to such programs can be examined, however, it is necessary to briefly outline the development of affirmative action.

A BRIEF HISTORY

The first time the phrase *affirmative action* was used by an American political figure was in 1961 when President John F. Kennedy insisted that companies that contracted with the federal government end all discrimination based on race, creed, color, or national origin.[12] This demand, inserted into Executive Order 10925, was not an affirmative action measure as we think of that phrase today. Rather, it required color-blind employment decisions in all areas of employment including recruitment, promotion, demotion, rates of pay, and so on.[13] The passage of the antidiscrimination provisions of the Civil Rights Act of 1964, as well as subsequent executive orders signed by President Johnson, further reflected the federal government's efforts to prevent racially discriminatory employment practices. None of these measures, however, suggested that employers could or should use racial preferences to promote racial equality. In fact, because these federal laws appeared to mandate color-blind policies, many people suggested that they not only didn't allow such preferences but forbade them altogether.[14]

Although by the mid-1960s the Johnson administration experimented with a few racially defined hiring goals in the construction industry, it was Richard Nixon's administration, through his Philadelphia Plan, which actually adopted a true affirmative action program. Prior to this plan, the federal government had imposed race-based measures only to redress specific discriminatory decisions by employers and the relief only went to those personally discriminated against. The Philadelphia Plan, however, required specific targets of minority employees for companies bidding on federal projects in the Philadelphia metropolitan area.[15] It may be a little-known fact of American history that Richard Nixon, with all of his conservative policies, was a significant force in furthering affirmative action plans by the federal government.

Shortly after the Philadelphia Plan was implemented, the Executive Branch, again under President Nixon, began to require private employers to implement goals and timetables for minority hiring and promotion.[16] At the same time, the Equal Employment Opportunity Commission (EEOC) began pressuring major American companies such as IBM and Sears to implement racial preferences in their hiring policies. As the early 1970s went on, numerous advocacy groups started to apply pressure, with boycotts and other measures, to strongly encourage private companies to adopt voluntary affirmative action programs.[17] These measures were taken to try to redress huge disparities in the economic situations of whites and blacks, whites and other people of color, and men and women, caused by years of overt, legal, and formalized racial and sexual discrimination. Here are just a few examples of these disparities:

1. As of 1970, Alabama had *never* employed a black state trooper;
2. Prior to 1974, Kaiser Aluminum would only hire people with prior craft experience to work at its plant in Louisiana. Because blacks had been traditionally excluded from the craft unions, only 5 of the 273 workers at the plant were black;
3. In 1979, women represented only 4 percent of the San Francisco Police Department; and
4. As late as 1987, there were *no* Asians or women in the San Francisco Fire Department.[18]

These inequalities existed throughout the country and in most major industries. For most of our country's history, people of color and women were legally excluded from the same business opportunities as white males. The modest affirmative action plans of the 1970s and 1980s constituted an effort to provide more equality between white males and everyone else after centuries of inequality.

While all of this was happening in the business world, colleges and universities also began using racial preferences in their admissions decisions. In 1970, only 7.8 percent of college students were black.[19] Because of the low numbers of people of color and women receiving a college education, the U.S. Department of Health, Education, and Welfare (again under Nixon) issued directives requiring colleges and universities receiving federal funds (virtually all schools) to adopt goals and timetables to maximize educational opportunities for minorities and women.[20] The government actually threatened several elite schools such as Columbia, Harvard, and Michigan that it would withhold federal funds if the adoption of affirmative action plans did not commence quickly.[21] Moreover, many schools across the country voluntarily began actively recruiting people of color and changing their admissions criteria to admit more minority students. These practices became quite controversial, eventually resulting in state constitutional amendments outlawing affirmative action and United States Supreme Court decisions evaluating both state and federal affirmative action programs.

THE SUPREME COURT AND AFFIRMATIVE ACTION

The Medical School at the University of California at Davis opened in 1968 with a first-year class of 50 students.[22] When the school began, there was no affirmative action program for disadvantaged or minority students, and the first class had *no* blacks, Mexican Americans, or American Indians. Three years later, the faculty devised a special admissions program to increase the representation of "disadvantaged" students in each medical school class. This program consisted of a separate admissions system operating alongside the regular process and utilized different criteria for admission.[23] When the class size was 50, the quota for special applicants was 8, and when the class size doubled to 100 in 1974, the quota was raised to 16.

From 1971–1974, the special program resulted in the admission of 21 black students, 30 Mexican Americans, and 12 Asians. Although disadvantaged whites applied to the special program, no white candidate was given an offer through that process. In 1974, the special committee explicitly considered only "disadvantaged" special applicants who were members of one of the designated minority groups (blacks, Chicanos, Asians, and American Indians).[24]

Allan Bakke, a white male, applied to the Davis Medical School in both 1973 and 1974. His applications were considered under the general admissions program, and he received an interview in both years but he did not receive an offer. In both years, applicants were admitted under the special admissions program with grade point averages, test scores, and other benchmarks significantly lower than Bakke's.[25]

After his second rejection, Bakke filed a lawsuit in California State Court arguing that the special admissions program operated by the medical school violated state and federal statutes and the Equal Protection Clause of the Fourteenth Amendment to the United States Constitution on the grounds that the program excluded him from the school on the basis of his race. He won in the California courts, and the school appealed to the United States Supreme Court, which issued its landmark decision in 1978.

One of the most interesting aspects of the *Bakke* decision that many people don't know is that, as a technical matter, the important part of the opinion was joined by only one Supreme Court Justice—Lewis F. Powell Jr. The decision came down in a 4–4–1 split on the question whether the medical school's special admission program was unconstitutional. Four conservative Justices did not even discuss the constitutional question because they concluded that the special admissions program violated a federal statute requiring all universities receiving federal funds to not discriminate on the basis of race. Four more liberal Justices disagreed and wrote an opinion saying that the special admission program did not violate any federal law or the Constitution, and therefore the admissions program with its racial preferences was completely legal. Justice Powell broke this 4–4 tie on the validity of the program by concluding that the special admissions program violated both the statute and the Constitution (for the same reasons). His opinion on the constitutional validity of the preferences, however, wasn't joined by *any* other Justice. Nonetheless, for many years the *Bakke* decision was considered the law of the land and, eventually, a majority of the Court did adopt Justice Powell's reasoning in most part.

So what did Justice Powell say about the constitutionality of the quota system used by the Davis Medical School? Bakke sought a decision saying race could *never* be used as a factor in a public school's admissions process whereas the medical school wanted free reign to use race to admit its students. Justice Powell, in typical manner because he was the swing vote on the Court for much of his career, gave a little to both sides and took a little from both sides.

The first issue Justice Powell had to address was what legal standards or level of review the Court would give to the challenged state program. Generally speaking, when the government treats two groups differently, it is only required to have a rational basis for the difference that is reasonably related to a legitimate governmental interest. For example, when the government makes distinctions between minors and adults (drinking ages), or seniors and nonseniors (mandatory retirement ages), or veterans and nonveterans (veteran preference programs), the Court reviews the distinctions only to determine if the government has a rational basis for treating the people differently (a test the government usually, though not always, can meet). However, when the government makes distinctions based on a few disfavored criteria, the Court requires a far greater justification for the differing treatment than simple reasonableness. For example, if the government treats people differently based on race or national origin, it must have a compelling (as opposed to legitimate) justification for the distinction and the law must be narrowly tailored (as opposed to rationally related) to further that compelling interest (a test the government almost always fails to meet). There are many reasons for this heightened level of scrutiny but two of the most important are that the government should not penalize people for a trait they cannot alter, and often the groups that suffer such disadvantages are minorities who do not have the same ability to affect the democratic process as majorities. The essential point is that the level of review the Court gives is tied closely to the chances the law will be declared valid or invalid by the Court and, generally speaking, racial distinctions are given the highest level of scrutiny by the Court.

The point of dispute in the *Bakke* case, and an issue that conservative and liberal Justices are still fighting over today, is what level of review or scrutiny the Court should give to racial distinctions that are intended to *help,* as opposed to *hurt,* traditionally disadvantaged groups such as African Americans. Some Justices believe that the Equal Protection Clause requires that the strictest level of review should be applied to all racial classifications used by the government regardless of whether the government's intent is to help or hurt minorities. To these Justices, the Constitution is color-blind and forbids all official uses of race absent the most compelling of justifications. Other Justices disagree and point out that the United States formally discriminated on the basis of race for most of its history, and there is no way to provide the "equal protection of the law" to people who suffered under that regime without using race-based methods to make up for the ills that were done. Moreover, these Justices argue that whites don't need the Court to protect them from discrimination in the same way that blacks do because whites have a greater ability to protect themselves through democratic processes.

Justice Powell decided to adopt the strict and hard-to-satisfy compelling interest level of review for all racial classifications, even those intended to help minority groups. Justice Powell argued that (1) the Equal Protection Clause is worded generally, and the concept of equality of the races should be applied equally to people of all races (including whites); (2) sometimes racial preferences meant to help minority groups actually hurt them by, for example, stigmatizing the group; (3) who is a member of a majority or a minority group may vary from time to time and place to place and any legal rule that takes account of such temporary arrangements is unlikely to adequately serve the purposes of the Equal Protection Clause; and (4) it may be unfair to penalize people living in the present day for the sins of the past.[26]

Justice Powell's opinion reads as if he believed it was a relatively easy decision to apply strict scrutiny to the minority preference program at issue in the case even though the program was adopted by the majority group (whites) to help minorities. The truth, however, is that the issue is far from clear. Although Justice Powell is correct that the Equal Protection Clause is worded generally and promises equality for all, the hard issue is whether it is possible to provide that equality to people who have historically been subject to legal discriminatory measures adopted by the government. Moreover, although racial preferences meant to help minority groups may actually hurt them by stigmatizing them, it is questionable whether that possibility amounts to a constitutional reason for judges to strike down such programs, though it may be a good policy reason for legislators and others not to adopt such programs. Moreover, although who is a member of a majority or a minority group may vary at different times and in different places, the Court applies vague constitutional tests all the time and often has to draw difficult lines. Finally, although it may be unfair to penalize people living in the present for the sins of the past, someone is inevitably going to be penalized. Is it fair to suppress people under the law for generations and adopt official policies to keep them poor and uneducated and then one day simply declare that everyone will compete "equally?" That regime arguably punishes minorities unequally under the law.

The above discussion illustrates the complexity of the question of how much deference the Court should give to decisions by institutions like the Davis Medical School to adopt racial preferences to help African Americans and other minorities. Nevertheless, Justice Powell concluded that the Court must apply strict scrutiny to all governmental decisions based on race, which meant that Davis had the burden of demonstrating that its affirmative action program furthered a compelling governmental interest and was narrowly tailored to satisfy that interest. The selection of this level of review doomed the admissions program.

The medical school identified four interests that it claimed justified its decision to use racial preferences in its admissions program:

1. Reducing the historic deficit of minorities in medical schools and in the medical profession;
2. Countering the effects of societal discrimination;
3. Increasing the number of physicians who will practice in communities currently underserved; and
4. Obtaining the educational benefits that flow from an ethnically diverse student body.[27]

Justice Powell did not accept any of the first three interests as compelling enough to satisfy the Court's test. As to the first goal of bringing in more minorities to the medical profession, Justice Powell simply stated that "[p]referring members of any one group for no reason other than race or ethnic origin is discrimination for its own sake. This the Constitution forbids." Of course, the Constitution did not forbid such discrimination from 1788 to at least 1954 when many colleges and graduate schools only accepted whites. As Justice Marshall stated in his dissenting opinion in *Bakke,* "it must be remembered that, during most of the past 200 years, the Constitution as interpreted by this Court did not prohibit the most ingenious and pervasive forms of discrimination against the Negro. Now, when a State acts to remedy the effects of that legacy of discrimination, I cannot believe that this same Constitution stands as a barrier."[28] Nevertheless, starting with *Bakke* and continuing until today, the Court has held that racial quotas and preferences designed to do nothing more than increase the percentage of minorities in schools, public workplaces, and government settings are facially unconstitutional.

Justice Powell rejected the "countering the effects of societal discrimination" argument on the basis that the Court had "never approved a classification that aids persons perceived as members of relatively victimized groups at the expense of other innocent individuals *in the absence* of judicial, legislative, or administrative findings of constitutional or statutory violations."[29] In other words, Justice Powell believed that governmental institutions are not allowed to use racial preferences to cure general societal discrimination but are only allowed to use them if the specific institution itself had been guilty of distinct practices discriminating against racial groups.

The medical school also argued that, by graduating more minority doctors, poor and medically underserved communities would receive better health care. Justice Powell responded to this argument in less than two paragraphs by stating that the medical school did not meet its burden of proof of showing a strong enough connection between the racial preferences in its admissions program and the likelihood that doctors admitted in that program would actually serve such communities. It is still the law today that schools may not use racial preferences to increase the possibility that poor communities will be better served by doctors, lawyers, and other professionals.

The final purpose articulated by the medical school, that it needed to use racial preferences to ensure an ethnically diverse student body, was accepted by Justice Powell as a compelling enough purpose to satisfy the first part of the Court's strict scrutiny test. Justice Powell reached this conclusion for two reasons. First, he argued that "[a]cademic freedom, though not a specifically enumerated constitutional right, long has been viewed as a special concern of the First Amendment. The freedom of a university to make its own judgments as to education includes the selection of its student body."[30] Second, he stated that the "nation's future depends upon leaders trained through wide exposure to the ideas and mores of students as diverse as this Nation of many peoples. . . . An otherwise qualified medical student with a particular background—whether it be ethnic, geographic, culturally advantaged or disadvantaged—may bring to a professional school of medicine experiences, outlooks, and ideas that enrich the training of its student body and better equip its graduates to render with understanding their vital service to humanity."[31]

Thus, Justice Powell identified one interest, obtaining a diverse student body, as important enough to constitute a compelling governmental interest. The next question was whether the admissions program at the Davis Medical School was "narrowly tailored" enough to satisfy the compelling interest in a diverse student body. Justice Powell held that it was not.

Justice Powell believed that the medical school's compelling interest was in achieving a *generally diverse* student body not just a *racially and ethnically* diverse one, and its setting aside of 16 places for members of specific ethnic and racial groups was therefore unconstitutional. He said that the school's interest in diversity should encompass a broad array of qualifications and characteristics "of which racial or ethnic origin is but a single though important element. Petitioner's special admissions program, focused *solely* on ethnic diversity, would hinder rather than further attainment of genuine diversity."[32]

Not content with just voting to invalidate the school's admissions procedures, Justice Powell also argued that the interest in racial diversity, and diversity in general, would be better served by a different type of admissions program similar to the one in place at Harvard at the time *Bakke* was decided. The Harvard program took race into account on an individualized basis along with other diversity factors such as where the applicant was raised and any special skills the applicants possessed. Harvard did not use firm racial quotas. Justice Powell said that:

> In Harvard College admissions the Committee has not set target-quotas for the number of blacks, or of musicians, football players, physicists or Californians to be admitted in a given year. . . . But that awareness [of the necessity of including more than a token number of black students] does not mean that the Committee sets a minimum number of blacks or of people from west of the Mississippi who are to be admitted. It means only that in choosing among thousands of applicants who are not only "admissible" academically but have other strong qualities, the Committee, with a number of criteria in mind, pays some attention to distribution among many types and categories of students.[33]

The main distinction that Justice Powell thought was constitutionally required by the Equal Protection Clause of the Fourteenth

Amendment was that a public school may take race into account when deciding who to admit and who to reject as long as each applicant is reviewed on an individual basis and every applicant is, at least theoretically, able to compete for every seat in the class. Because the Davis Medical School set aside 16 seats for people of certain racial groups, Justice Powell believed that the program was not narrowly tailored enough to satisfy the compelling interest test and was therefore unconstitutional. Or to put it another way, the admissions committees at public colleges, universities, and graduate schools could use race as one factor when comparing individual candidates but they were not allowed to use racial quotas or strict numerical goals to admit a more diverse student body.

Four Supreme Court Justices believed that Justice Powell's decision was incorrect as a matter of constitutional law. Justice Marshall wrote the most compelling response. He began by detailing the tragic history of slavery and forced segregation of African Americans. He then made the following observations about the state of affairs between whites and black at the time that *Bakke* was decided:

> A Negro child today has a life expectancy which is shorter by more than five years than that of a white child. The Negro child's mother is over three times more likely to die of complications in childbirth, and the infant mortality rate for Negroes is nearly twice that for whites. The median income of the Negro family is only 60% that of the median of a white family, and the percentage of Negroes who live in families with incomes below the poverty line is nearly four times greater than that of whites.
>
> The relationship between those figures and the history of unequal treatment afforded to the Negro cannot be denied. At every point from birth to death, the impact of the past is reflected in the still disfavored position of the Negro.
>
> In light of the sorry history of discrimination and its devastating impact on the lives of Negroes, bringing the Negro into the mainstream of American life should be a state interest of the highest order. To fail to do so is to ensure that America will forever remain a divided society.[34]

Justice Marshall then recounted the history of the adoption of the Fourteenth Amendment. He argued it was enacted to help blacks achieve equality and pointed to laws passed in the wake of that amendment that gave special preferences to blacks. He argued that the Equal Protection Clause of the Fourteenth Amendment should not be interpreted by the Court to prohibit voluntary governmental measures designed to help blacks achieve greater equality in America. He concluded his dissent with the following observations about the role of the Supreme Court:

> I fear that we have come full circle. After the Civil War our Government started several "affirmative action" programs. This Court in the *Civil Rights Cases* and *Plessy v. Ferguson* destroyed the movement toward complete equality. For almost a century no action was taken, and this nonaction was with the tacit approval of the courts. Then we had *Brown v. Board of Education* and the Civil Rights Acts of Congress, followed by numerous affirmative-action programs. *Now,* we have this Court again stepping in, this time to stop affirmative-action programs of the type used by the University of California.[35]

Justice Blackmun, who also believed that the Davis admissions program was constitutional, suggested that the differences between the Harvard plan, where race was taken into account on an individual basis, and the Davis quota system, where race was used more formally, were not constitutionally significant. In both cases, governmental actors were taking race into account to remedy past discrimination, and the Constitution did not prefer one strategy over the other. And, in what became a famous passage, he said that "In order to get beyond racism, we must first take account of race. There is no other way. And in order to treat some persons equally, we must treat them differently. We cannot—we dare not—let the Equal Protection Clause perpetuate racial supremacy."[36]

Justice Brennan also took Justice Powell to task for his favoring of the Harvard program over the Davis program as a matter of constitutional law. This part of *Bakke* is important because the most recent Supreme Court case on the validity of racial preferences in higher education uncritically accepted Justice Powell's reasoning in *Bakke*. Justice Brennan agreed with Justice Blackmun that the difference between using race on an individualized basis and using a racial quota was not constitutionally significant, and he added these words:

> The "Harvard" program, as those employing it readily concede, openly and successfully employs a racial criterion for the pur-

pose of ensuring that some of the scarce places in institutions of higher education are allocated to disadvantaged minority students. That the Harvard approach does not also make public the extent of the preference and the precise workings of the system while the Davis program employs a specific, openly stated number, does not condemn the latter plan for purposes of Fourteenth Amendment adjudication. It may be that the Harvard plan is more acceptable to the public than is the Davis "quota." If it is, any State, including California, is free to adopt it in preference to a less acceptable alternative, just as it is generally free, as far as the Constitution is concerned, to abjure granting any racial preferences in its admissions program. But there is no basis for preferring a particular preference program simply because in achieving the same goals that the Davis Medical School is pursuing, it proceeds in a manner that is not immediately apparent to the public.[37]

The precise holdings of Justice Powell's opinion in *Bakke* were that (1) racial preferences used by the government to help minority groups would be subject to strict scrutiny; (2) racial quotas were constitutionally impermissible; but (3) not all uses of race in an admissions context were barred. Although Justice Powell's opinion was written by and joined by only one Justice, himself, it effectively became the law of the land. Thus, public universities all over the country began to model their admissions processes after the Harvard model described by Justice Powell. Race remained a significant factor in admissions but rigid quotas were abandoned, at least publicly. The result was that admissions committees applied different standards to people of color than to whites, but they did so behind closed doors to avoid the limitations set forth in Justice Powell's decision—a truly bizarre constitutional result.[38]

After the *Bakke* decision, the Supreme Court did not return to affirmative action in higher education for almost 25 years. During that time, however, the Court decided a number of other important affirmative action cases reviewing affirmative action programs adopted by local and state governments and even the federal government.

In 1980, in *Fullilove v. Klutznick*,[39] the Court upheld a federal law requiring that at least 10 percent of federal money given to states for local work projects be "set aside" for distribution to minority-owned contractors or subcontractors. Although there were a number of different opinions for the Court, five Justices appeared to hold that the standard of review of affirmative action programs enacted by the federal government would not be the strict standard suggested by Justice Powell in *Bakke,* but rather a lower intermediate level of scrutiny requiring an important, but not compelling governmental interest. The reason for this differing judicial treatment of federal and state laws was that the Fourteenth Amendment itself, which requires states to provide equal protection of the law to all people, also provides in Section 5 that *Congress* may enforce that requirement by "appropriate legislation." In other words, the Constitution gives Congress the power to enforce the provisions of the Fourteenth Amendment, and in this case *Congress believed* that the minority set-aside requirement was necessary to redress past violations *by the states* of the Equal Protection Clause. The Court said that "Congress, of course, may legislate without compiling the kind of 'record' appropriate with respect to judicial or administrative proceedings. Congress had before it, among other data, evidence of a long history of marked disparity in the percentage of public contracts awarded to minority business enterprises. This disparity was considered to result . . . from the existence and maintenance of barriers to competitive access which had their roots in racial and ethnic discrimination, and which continue today, even absent any intentional discrimination or other unlawful conduct. . . . Congress acted within its competence to determine that the problem was national in scope."[40]

Therefore, in the Court's first treatment of a federal, as opposed to state, affirmative action program, the Court showed significant deference to Congress's decision that racial preferences were needed to address the country's significant history of racial discrimination. The distinction the Court drew between state and federal affirmative action programs seemed to spring naturally from the authority given to Congress by the Fourteenth Amendment to enforce the requirements of the Equal Protection Clause. The debate over the appropriate level of judicial review of affirmative action programs, however, and thus their constitutional validity, was far from over.

In 1989, the Supreme Court issued an affirmative action decision in which the Court held that strict scrutiny would apply to all state programs containing racial preferences but again suggested that a different and easier-to-satisfy standard might apply to federal programs. In *City of Richmond v. J. A. Croson,*[41] the Court reviewed a contractor set-aside plan enacted by the City of Richmond, Virginia (the capital of the old Confederacy). The city had modeled this plan after the federal affirmative action program approved by the Court in *Fullilove*. It required that all contractors working for the city subcontract at least 30 percent of its business to minority firms. In applying the compelling interest test to Richmond's affirmative action plan, Justice O'Connor's opinion for the Court said that the Court was not revisiting its decision in *Fullilove* that less than strict scrutiny would apply to *congressionally* mandated racial preferences. Justice O'Connor wrote the following:

> Congress, unlike any State or political subdivision, has a specific constitutional mandate to enforce the dictates of the Fourteenth Amendment. The power to "enforce" may at times also include the power to define situations which Congress determines threaten principles of equality and to adopt prophylactic rules to deal with those situations. . . . The Civil War Amendments themselves worked a dramatic change in the balance between congressional and state power over matters of race. . . .
>
> That Congress may identify and redress the effects of society-wide discrimination does not mean that . . . the States and their political subdivisions are free to decide that such remedies are appropriate. . . . To hold otherwise would be to cede control over the content of the Equal Protection Clause to the 50 state legislatures and their myriad political subdivisions. The mere recitation of a benign or compensatory purpose for the use of a racial classification would essentially entitle the States to exercise the full power of Congress under § 5 of the Fourteenth Amendment and insulate any racial classification from judicial scrutiny under § 1. We believe that such a result would be contrary to the intentions of the Framers of the Fourteenth Amendment, who desired to place clear limits on the States' use of race as a criterion for legislative action, and to have the federal courts enforce those limitations.[42]

In light of the Court's assumption that Congress has more latitude to deal with racial inequalities than the states, the Court applied a strict level of review to Richmond's affirmative action plan, and found that it could not satisfy that review. The Court said Richmond did not present the requisite evidence to show that the city itself had engaged in racial discrimination in the handing out of city contracts, and its reliance on Congress's finding of nationwide discriminatory practices in the construction industry could not justify the racial preferences at issue. In addition, the Court also said that the required 30 percent set-aside was not adequately tied to the number of qualified minority firms wanting to do business with the city and, in any event, the definition of who was a minority, which included Eskimos, was constitutionally overbroad.

Justices Marshall, Brennan, and Blackmun filed bitter dissents arguing that the Court applied a much too strict standard of review to Richmond's affirmative action plan, and that the Court demanded far more proof than should have been necessary to support the plan. Justice Marshall argued that the history of racial discrimination in the construction industry across the country was well documented, and Congress just a few years earlier acted on that information in the federal set-aside law the Court approved in *Fullilove.* He also suggested that there was compelling statistical evidence that in Richmond itself minority firms had been traditionally shut out of city contracts. He concluded that the "new and restrictive tests it applies scuttle one city's effort to surmount its discriminatory past, and imperil those of dozens more localities. I . . . profoundly disagree with the cramped vision of the *Equal Protection Clause* which the majority offers today and with its application of that vision to Richmond, Virginia's, laudable set-aside plan. The battle against pernicious racial discrimination or its effects is nowhere near won."[43]

The Court's next affirmative action case would tilt in the opposite direction. In 1990, just one year after *Croson* was decided, a majority of the Court in *Metro Broadcasting v. FCC*[44] upheld a federal policy giving minority broadcasting firms preferences in the licensing of television and radio stations. The majority affirmed what several previous cases had suggested and explicitly applied a less demanding level of review to federal affirmative action programs than state programs. Instead of requiring that the government demonstrate that a racial classification be narrowly tailored to support a compelling governmental interest, the Court only required that the affirmative action plan be substantially related to an important governmental interest, a much easier test to satisfy.[45] The Court relied on its previous decision in *Fullilove* for the proposition that Congress has far more discretion to remedy racial discrimination than do local and state governments given Congress's express power to enforce the Fourteenth Amendment.

This lower level of review made all the difference to the outcome of the case. The government argued that minority participation in the ownership and management of radio and television stations was important and would lead to significantly more program diversity. Even though the government provided no evidence of specific prior discriminatory practices by the FCC, the Court deferred to the government's stated desire to remedy the societal conditions that led to the absence of significant minority participation in television and radio broadcasting. Thus, just one year after overturning Richmond's desire to remedy past discrimination in the construction industry by applying an almost impossible to meet burden of proof, the Supreme Court emphatically gave Congress and the federal government much more leeway to use racial preferences to assist minority groups. This deference to Congress, however, would not survive the personnel changes about to occur on the Court.

Over the next five years, Justices Brennan, Blackmun, and White would be replaced on the Court by Justices Breyer, Ginsburg, and Souter, but much more important, Justice Marshall, a staunch supporter of affirmative action, would be replaced by Justice Clarence Thomas, a strong opponent of affirmative action. By 1995, with four of the Justices in the *Metro Broadcasting* majority retired, a new Supreme Court was ready to change the law, and change the law it did.

The next time the Court reviewed a federal affirmative action program, *Adarand Constructors, Inc. v. Peña,*[46] the Court reversed course and held that strict scrutiny applied to all racial preferences, even those enacted by Congress. The issue in *Adarand* was the constitutionality of a federal program that gave financial incentives to contractors on government projects to hire minority and economically disadvantaged subcontractors.[47] The lower courts had not surprisingly upheld this affirmative action program under the lower level of scrutiny that the Court identified in its previous cases such as *Fullilove* and *Metro Broadcasting*. In other words, the lower courts followed the law.

Writing for a majority of the Court, that now included Justice Thomas, Justice O'Connor argued that the Court's cases prior to *Metro Broadcasting* established the principle that the level of review of state and federal racial preferences would be exactly the same—strict scrutiny.[48] That claim, of course, was simply false. No Supreme Court majority had ever reached that result.[49] To the extent that the Court had faced this issue directly, it had held exactly the opposite—that federal affirmative action programs like the one at issue in *Adarand* would be given more deference than state programs. This reality, however, stood in the way of what Justice O'Connor and the other Justices in the majority wanted to accomplish—the reversal of *Metro Broadcasting* for a reason other than simply the personnel on the Court had changed and the balance of power had shifted.

After distorting the Court's prior treatment of what level of re-view would be given to federal programs using racial preferences, Justice O'Connor said that "the Court took a surprising turn" in *Metro Broadcasting,* that *Metro Broadcasting* "departed from prior cases," and finally that *Metro Broadcasting* was "a significant depar-ture from much of what had come before it."[50] Based on those state-ments, the Court expressly overruled *Metro Broadcasting* and held, for the very first time, that *all* affirmative action plans, whether en-acted by the states or the federal government, would receive the high-est level of scrutiny from the United States Supreme Court.[51]

There are plausible arguments why *Metro Broadcasting* was in-correctly decided, and there may even be some reasonable grounds to suggest that the principles of *stare decisis* did not require it to be affirmed. However, there are no legitimate arguments that one of the reasons for not applying *stare decisis* to *Metro Broadcasting* was be-cause it was a "departure" from previous cases. As one noted com-mentator has observed, Justice O'Connor's treatment of the state of the law at the time of *Metro Broadcasting* was simply "dishonest."[52] Her reasoning was no better than the Court saying that it would not adhere to *Metro Broadcasting* because there were less than five Jus-tices who agreed to the decision. Had the Court given that mistaken fact as a justification for its decision, there would have been much outrage, even among those who supported the result. Saying that *Metro Broadcasting* was a significant departure from prior decisions is just as incorrect as saying that five Justices did not agree to its reasoning.[53]

The Court's incorrect statement of its prior case law in *Adarand* is an example of how the Court does not act like a court. The idea that the Court is bound to some degree to respect its prior cases is a fundamental aspect of its duty to make sure that similarly situated people are treated similarly, absent good reason for a change in the law. When the Court makes a mockery of prior doctrine, as Justice O'Connor did in *Adarand,* it acts outside its appropriate role as a court of law. Although we as a society may always be divided on the question of affirmative action, and what level of review should be applied to whom, we are not divided on the question of whether the Court should have to wrestle with its precedents in a meaningful and appropriate manner and then explain its decisions honestly. The Court simply failed to do this in *Adarand,* when it reversed a recent case because, and only because, the people on the Court had changed. Instead of transparently acknowledging that fact, the Court fabricated the history of the important question of what level of review would be given to federal affirmative programs.

Although the Supreme Court decided to apply strict scrutiny to the federal plan in *Adarand,* because the lower court had, not surprisingly, applied a lower level of review, the Court remanded the case for further factual findings in that court to determine whether the law could meet strict scrutiny. Lower courts are still struggling today with how to measure the large number of federal affirmative action programs against this rigorous standard. It would be eight years before the Supreme Court would return to the affirmative action question, and when it did so, the decision had a huge impact on public colleges and university across the country.

On the same day in 2003, the Court decided two companion cases involving the University of Michigan's affirmative action programs. The issue in *Grutter v. Bollinger*[54] was whether the University of Michigan Law School could employ racial preferences on an individualized basis in its admissions process to ensure that a "critical mass" of minority students attended the school. The issue in *Gratz v. Bollinger*[55] was whether the college at the University of Michigan could use race as a special "plus factor" in every minority's admissions application. In both cases, educational diversity was the only interest asserted by the university to be compelling. Four Justices, Scalia, Kennedy, Thomas, and Rehnquist, argued that racial preferences are *always* unconstitutional unless they are used to remedy specific instances of racial discrimination, and thus both the law school's plan and the college's plan violated the Fourteenth Amendment. Three Justices, Souter, Stevens, and Ginsburg, would have approved both programs. Two Justices, O'Connor and Breyer, believed that the law school's program was constitutional but the college's plan was not, and their votes dictated the results. Justice O'Connor wrote the majority opinion in the law school case while Justice Rehnquist wrote the majority opinion in the college's case. The two decisions, taken together, demonstrate how far away the Supreme Court of the United States has veered from acting like a court.

The law school admissions program allowed the admissions committee to review each applicant based on a host of factors including grades, test scores, and other reflections of the applicant's abilities. The admission policy also affirmed the school's long-standing commitment to diversity and especially "one particular type of diversity," that is, "racial and ethnic diversity with special reference to the inclusion of students from groups which have been historically discriminated against, like African-Americans, Hispanics and Native Americans, who without this commitment might not be represented in our student body in meaningful numbers."[56] The school admitted that its goal was to enroll a "critical mass" of minority students, and to "ensur[e] their ability to make unique contributions to the character of the Law School."[57] The school never indicated how many minority students were needed to constitute a "critical mass," nor did it ever shed light on how much weight ethnic diversity played in the consideration of individual applicants.

The college's admission program worked differently. Because of the large number of applicants to the University of Michigan's undergraduate school, individualized review of each applicant was not realistic. Therefore, each applicant received points based on high school grade point average, standardized test scores, the academic quality of an applicant's high school, in-state residency, alumni relationship, personal essay, personal achievement or leadership, and a miscellaneous category.[58] Up to 110 points could be assigned for academic performance, and up to 40 points could be assigned for the other, nonacademic factors. Michigan residents, for example, received 10 points, while children of alumni received 4. Counselors could also assign an outstanding essay up to 3 points and award up to 5 points for an applicant's personal achievement, leadership, or public service.[59] Most important for our purposes, an applicant automatically received a 20 point bonus if he or she possessed any one of the following "miscellaneous" factors: membership in an underrepresented minority group; attendance at a predominantly minority or disadvantaged high school; or recruitment for athletics.[60]

A majority of the Court reaffirmed *Croson* and *Adarand* and applied strict scrutiny to both admission programs. Moreover, a majority of the Court also reaffirmed Justice Powell's *Bakke* opinion that the only compelling interest sufficient to justify racial preferences in university admissions is the goal of attaining a diverse student body. The only question remaining in both cases was whether the admissions plans were "narrowly tailored" enough to satisfy the constitutional test. In what Justice Scalia critically referred to as the "*Grutter-Gratz* split double header,"[61] the Court upheld the law school's plan but invalidated the college's plan.

According to Justice O'Connor's opinions in both cases, the law school plan passed muster because race was used by the admissions committee on an individualized basis whereas the undergraduate program was unconstitutional because that admissions committee used race as an automatic "plus factor" for all protected minorities and did not conduct individualized (some might say subjective) review.[62] Justice O'Connor never explained why these differences in admissions programs, both of which employed racial classifications to further educational diversity, made a constitutional difference under the Fourteenth Amendment.

To the extent that the Court is going to look skeptically at racial preferences in public school admissions programs, the college's program seems more constitutional than the law school's. The discretion of the admission committee at the college level was tightly constrained and the public knew exactly how the racial factor played out in the admissions process. By contrast, the law school's use of race occurred behind closed doors and no one other than the committee itself knew how much weight race played in the process. Since the Court conceded that the goal of having a racially diverse student body was not only permissible but compelling, what is the constitutional problem with awarding a set number of points to minority students to reach that goal?[63] Moreover, under strict scrutiny, the government should only be allowed to use racial classifications when it does so openly, honestly, and consistently. To say that the college's transparent use of race was constitutionally defective whereas the law school's hidden use was permissible seems to turn the idea of strict scrutiny on its head.[64]

Justice O'Connor cited Justice Powell's *Bakke* opinion for the proposition that "outright racial balancing" and numerical quotas were prohibited by the Constitution.[65] But, the law school conceded that its goal was to enroll a "critical mass" of minority students.[66] In fact, the percentage of such students enrolled was often extremely close to the percentage who applied.[67] If the law school had said that it wanted 12 percent minorities or 18 percent minorities, in order to reach a "critical mass," that would be an unconstitutional quota according to Justice O'Connor. But the simple admission that there had to be a "critical mass" of minorities admitted every year somehow did not amount to such a quota. How can it be that the purposeful goal of enrolling a critical mass of minorities every year, no matter what, is not a quota or racial balancing, which Justice O'Connor says is "patently unconstitutional"? This is beyond all reason and strongly suggests that the Court is not providing the real basis for its decision and certainly that logical analysis of prior law (no racial balancing allowed) has nothing to do with the result in the case.

Finally, at the end of Justice O'Connor's opinion upholding the law school's racial preferences, she wrote that, "[w]e expect that 25 years from now, the use of racial preferences will no longer be necessary to further the interest approved today."[68] How does Justice O'Connor know what the state of racial affairs will be in this country in 25 years and what authorizes her to put a sunset provision on the holding of the case? A legislator voting for an unpopular piece of legislation might wish to place her vote in the context of a statement suggesting that a time may come when her vote will change or become unnecessary. But given the historical and political complexity of the affirmative action debate, for Justice O'Connor to suggest that she has some special awareness as to when race-based measures may no longer be necessary, and to identify that time 25 years in advance, is judicial hubris and an inappropriate and arbitrary exercise of judicial power. In fact, it is not "judicial" at all.

The holdings in *Grutter* and *Gratz* can be summarized as follows: public colleges and universities are allowed to take race into account when considering student applications but they must do so on an individualized basis without allocating a set "plus" factor for minority status. Moreover, strict numerical quotas are prohibited but more generalized goals such as wanting a "critical mass" of minorities are permissible. Interestingly, the Court's blessing to use race to foster diversity in colleges and graduate schools has been combined with a significant hostility to the programs in *Croson* and *Adarand* trying to diversify workplaces and construction projects. Why the Fourteenth Amendment would allow the use of race in one context but not another is a mystery except for possibly the value judgment, reached by the Court, that diversity is more important in the educational setting than the workplace. This, of course, is not a judicially defensible conclusion but a personal preference.

The most recent affirmative action case that the Court has decided, with Justice Alito having replaced Justice O'Connor, demonstrates that the Court's nonjudicial value judgments may soon displace affirmative action programs altogether. The issue in *Parents Involved in Community Schools v. Seattle School District No. 1*[69] was whether two school districts, one in Seattle and one in Louisville, could attack the serious problem of racially imbalanced public schools by using racial criteria in the assigning of some students to some schools. This issue of racially isolated public schools is a national one and the Court's decision in this case has had major effects on the country's schools. Because the context of this case is so important to understanding the seriousness of the Court's decision, it is necessary to briefly summarize why both Seattle and Louisville wanted to use limited racial balancing in their school systems.

Although Seattle never formally required segregated schools, long-standing housing patterns and school board transfer policies had resulted in mostly black public schools in the central and southeastern sections of the city while schools outside of those areas were virtually all white.[70] The problem was so serious that in 1969, the NAACP filed a lawsuit claiming that "of the 1,461 black students enrolled in the 12 senior high schools in Seattle, 1,151 (or 78.8%) attended 3 senior high schools, and 900 (61.6%) attended a single school, Garfield."[71] The lawsuit led the school district to significantly alter the way students were assigned to public schools by using busing, transfer policies, and other racially based measures to make a dent in the serious segregation problem. By 1980, the combination of measures had been so successful that the school board considered only one high school to be racially unbalanced and only by two students.[72]

This successful desegregation plan, however, provoked strong opposition from some parents who wanted their children to attend neighborhood schools, which resulted in a state constitutional amendment forbidding forced busing, which the Supreme Court struck down in 1982 at the request of the Seattle School Board.[73] During the 1980s, however, many white families left the school district while thousands of Asians moved in. By the end of the decade, the school board decided to abandon its busing policy and adopt new (and less racially stringent) measures to encourage whites to move back to the city while at the same time preventing a return to mostly segregated public schools.[74] After experimenting with various plans, in 1998 the school board adopted the plan that was at issue in the case. The goal of this plan was to make sure that the city's high schools were not racially imbalanced while at the same time giving students and their parents a significant choice in choosing which school the child would attend. Chief Justice Roberts described this plan as follows:

> Some schools are more popular than others. If too many students list the same school as their first choice, the district employs a series of "tiebreakers" to determine who will fill the open slots at the oversubscribed school. The first tiebreaker selects for admission students who have a sibling currently enrolled in the chosen school. The next tiebreaker depends upon the racial composition of the particular school and the race of the individual student. In the district's public schools approximately 41 percent of enrolled students are white; the remaining 59 percent, comprising all other racial groups, are classified by Seattle for assignment purposes as nonwhite. If an oversubscribed school is not within 10 percentage points of the district's overall white/nonwhite racial balance, it is what the district calls "integration positive," and the district employs a tiebreaker that selects for assignment students whose race "will serve to bring the school into balance." If it is still necessary to select students for the school after using the racial tiebreaker, the next tiebreaker is the geographic proximity of the school to the student's residence.[75]

In essence, Seattle's School Board wanted to accomplish two objectives: make sure its high schools were not segregated by race and maximize the individual choices of students and their parents. Because of a complex set of residential housing patterns and economic disparities, these goals sometimes conflicted and, when they did, the district would use limited racial balancing to ensure significant racial integration. The constitutionality of this racial balancing was the issue before the United States Supreme Court.

Unlike the Seattle School Board, the Jefferson County School Board in Louisville, Kentucky, long required segregated public schools as a matter of law. This intentional racial discrimination took many forms but was held unconstitutional in 1975.[76] After that lawsuit, Louisville began redrawing its attendance zones and employing mandatory busing in order to redress the racial imbalance in its public schools. These efforts were modified over the years to address changing housing patterns and other shifts in population and eventually the use of special magnet schools. In 2000, the district court dissolved the desegregation decree that had been in effect since 1975 finding that the board had in good faith tried to accomplish the goal of having desegregated public schools.[77]

Despite the dissolving of the injunction, the Jefferson County School Board was still committed to achieving racial balance in its schools despite housing patterns that made that goal difficult. The plan it used, which was challenged in the Supreme Court, required all schools in the district, other than magnet schools, to be between 15 percent and 50 percent black. Roughly 66 percent of the district's students are white and 34 percent are black.[78] The district tried to accommodate the wishes of the parents and students but at times had to refuse a request because of a school's racial imbalance. Interestingly, the precise details of Louisville's plans and how the racial balancing worked in individual cases cannot be gleaned from the record in the case, but the Supreme Court apparently did not find that fact troubling, though a true court would.[79]

Both the Seattle and the Louisville affirmative action plans were upheld by the lower courts.[80] In addition, prior to Justices Alito and Roberts replacing Justices Rehnquist and O'Connor, the Supreme Court had denied review in another case involving a similar plan that had also been approved by lower courts.[81] One can only surmise that the reason the Court changed its mind and decided to hear these two cases when it did was because, with Justice Alito's replacement of Justice O'Connor, the Court's conservatives knew they had five votes to overturn the plans.

Justice Roberts began his legal analysis for the majority of the Court by reaffirming that the Court would apply strict scrutiny to all racial classifications employed by state actors. Therefore, both Seattle and Louisville had to demonstrate that their desegregation plans promoted compelling governmental interests and the plans were narrowly tailored to further those interests. The only interests that would count as compelling, according to the Court, would be remedying previous racial segregation sanctioned by law and promoting a diverse student body. Neither Louisville nor Seattle could establish the first interest because Seattle had never required segregation under the law and Louisville had already been released by a court of law from complying with its history of segregation.

The majority also rejected the school boards' arguments that their interest in diverse student bodies justified the plans at issue. The Court characterized Seattle's and Louisville's interest in diversity as simply wanting racial diversity and using pure racial balancing to achieve that goal. The Court concluded that this interest in a specified number of white and nonwhite students was not a compelling interest and that the means used to achieve diversity—racial balancing—did not satisfy the "narrowly tailored" prong of the test.[82]

The majority in this case was made up of the five most conservative Justices: Roberts, Alito, Thomas, Scalia, and Kennedy. All but Kennedy agreed with the final section of the opinion, which is where the real basis for the decision is found. Justices Scalia and Thomas have always been strongly opposed to all affirmative action plans and both dissented in the *Grutter* case upholding such a plan. It now appears that Roberts and Alito feel the same way, which is why Justice Roberts concluded his opinion as follows:

> In *Brown v. Board of Education,* we held that segregation deprived black children of equal educational opportunities regardless of whether school facilities and other tangible factors were equal, because government classification and separation on grounds of race themselves denoted inferiority. It was not the inequality of the facilities but the fact of legally separating children on the basis of race on which the Court relied to find a constitutional violation in 1954. . . .
>
> What do the racial classifications at issue here do, if not accord differential treatment on the basis of race. . . . ? Before *Brown,* schoolchildren were told where they could and could not go to school based on the color of their skin. The school districts in these cases have not carried the heavy burden of demonstrating that we should allow this once again—even for very different reasons. . . . *The way to stop discrimination on the basis of race is to stop discriminating on the basis of race* [emphasis added].[83]

Justice Kennedy, who was the fifth vote to invalidate the desegregation plans, filed a separate concurrence specifically taking issue with this final section of the majority opinion. Kennedy said that Justice Roberts's opinion was "too dismissive of the legitimate interest government has in ensuring all people have equal opportunity regardless of their race. . . . [The] postulate that '[t]he way to stop discrimination on the basis of race is to stop discriminating on the basis of race,' is not sufficient to decide these cases. Fifty years of experience since *Brown v. Board of Education,* should teach us that the problem before us defies so easy a solution. . . . To the extent the plurality opinion suggests the Constitution mandates that state and local school authorities must accept the status quo of racial isolation in schools, it is, in my view, profoundly mistaken."[84] Justice Kennedy also stated that, although the goal of having a color blind society is a good one, "[i]n the real world, it is regrettable to say, it cannot be a universal constitutional principle."[85]

Justice Kennedy ended up voting to invalidate the affirmative action programs at issue because he believed there might have been other less racially inspired ways to achieve the goal of school integration than pure racial balancing. He was most disturbed by the idea that under the plans the government had to identify children as white or nonwhite and use that classification to provide a benefit (i.e., attendance at a desirable school). Justice Kennedy believed that the school districts should have tried other measures such as "strategic site selection of new schools; drawing attendance zones with general recognition of the demographics of neighborhoods; allocating resources for special programs; recruiting students and faculty in a targeted fashion; and tracking enrollments, performance, and other statistics by race. These mechanisms are race conscious but do not lead to different treatment based on a classification that tells each student he or she is to be defined by race, so it is unlikely any of them would demand strict scrutiny to be found permissible."[86] He concluded the following:

> This Nation has a moral and ethical obligation to fulfill its historic commitment to creating an integrated society that ensures equal opportunity for all of its children. A compelling interest exists in avoiding racial isolation, an interest that a school district, in its discretion and expertise, may choose to pursue. Likewise, a district may consider it a compelling interest to achieve a diverse student population. Race may be one component of that diversity, but other demographic factors, plus special talents and needs, should also be considered. What the government is not permitted to do, absent a showing of necessity not

made here, is to classify every student on the basis of race and to assign each of them to schools based on that classification. Crude measures of this sort threaten to reduce children to racial chits valued and traded according to one school's supply and another's demand.[87]

Justice Breyer wrote a long and bitter dissenting opinion on behalf of the four moderates who were on the Court (Breyer, Stevens, Souter, and Ginsburg). Many of his arguments are relevant to the entire debate over judicial review of affirmative action programs. These four Justices (and most likely Justices Kagan and Sotomayor who have since replaced Souter and Stevens) believe that the Fourteenth Amendment prohibits virtually all racial classifications designed to *hurt* minority groups but should be interpreted to permit a broad array of classifications designed to *help* minority groups. The true basis of *Brown v. Board of Education,* according to these four Justices, was that the system of "separate but equal" led to inferior schools for blacks and the segregated schools of today present many of the same risks. Thus, school districts are allowed to prevent that danger by using all necessary tools including racial balancing.[88]

Justice Breyer reviewed the history of school desegregation efforts at length to conclude that school districts have been traditionally allowed to use race-based measures to integrate their schools even when, contrary to the plurality's assertions, they were not constitutionally required to do so. He concluded that the desire to avoid racially isolated schools was a compelling governmental interest and using racial balancing was often the *only* way to further that interest.[89] And, in an emotional and poetic final section, he wrote the following:

> Finally, what of the hope and promise of *Brown?* For much of this Nation's history, the races remained divided. It was not long ago that people of different races drank from separate fountains, rode on separate buses, and studied in separate schools. In this Court's finest hour, *Brown v. Board of Education* challenged this history and helped to change it.
>
> Not everyone welcomed this Court's decision in *Brown.* . . . Today, almost 50 years later, attitudes toward race in this Nation have changed dramatically. Many parents, white and black alike, want their children to attend schools with children of dif-

ferent races. Indeed, the very school districts that once spurned integration now strive for it. The long history of their efforts reveals the complexities and difficulties they have faced. And in light of those challenges, they have asked us not to take from their hands the instruments they have used to rid their schools of racial segregation, instruments that they believe are needed to overcome the problems of cities divided by race and poverty. The plurality would decline their modest request. . . . The plurality is wrong to do so. The last half-century has witnessed great strides toward racial equality, but we have not yet realized the promise of *Brown*. To invalidate the plans under review is to threaten the promise of *Brown*. The plurality's position, I fear, would break that promise. This is a decision that the Court and the Nation will come to regret.[90]

The Justices in the majority in these cases believed that the government should never (for Justice Kennedy almost never) use racial classifications to dole out government benefits even if the motivation behind that decision is to help minority groups. On numerous occasions, Justices Thomas and Scalia (in the past joined by Chief Justice Rehnquist and Justice Powell) have strongly argued that such preferences threaten the ideal that a person's race should be irrelevant to governmental decisions, that such preferences taint the success of specific individuals, and that such preferences illegally harm whites who were not the perpetrators of the historical discrimination suffered by members of minority groups.[91] On the other side, Justices Breyer, Souter, Stevens, and Ginsburg (and in the past Justices Brennan, Blackmun, and Marshall) have argued that we still live in a society strongly impacted by racial discrimination and there is no way to make up for the hundreds of years of lawful discriminatory practices (and slavery) without using racial measures designed to combat that history.[92]

As a policy matter, the questions raised by affirmative action are complex and not easily answered by generalizations divorced from specific situations, geographic areas, and particular schools and industries. As a constitutional matter, a true court of law would begin with the text and history of the Fourteenth Amendment when trying to decide whether affirmative action programs are unconstitutional. The key question would be, does the text of the Equal Protection Clause either affirm or deny the validity of racial preferences? The only honest answer to this question would be that the text is inconclusive. One could certainly argue that whites are denied the "equal protection" of the laws when the government makes negative employment or schooling decisions affecting them solely on the basis of race. On the other hand, one could certainly argue that blacks are denied "equal protection" of the laws when, having suffered generations of legal discrimination leading to economic, social, and educational disadvantage they are told the government is not allowed to make up for those wrongs by providing blacks special treatment now. That today blacks earn less than whites, attend poorer schools, and are jailed far more often is not some historical accident but a result of a complicated array of factors including intentional systematic discrimination by whites who made governmental decisions. So, who has the better of this textual argument? There is no persuasive constitutional answer and for any member of the Court, liberal or conservative, to suggest there is such an answer is pure fantasy.

When the text of the Constitution is ambiguous, the Justices (at least the conservative ones) often talk the talk of resorting to the original understanding of the text at issue. However, the Supreme Court's conservatives have *never* discussed the original understanding of the Fourteenth Amendment in any serious way as it relates to affirmative action because, as several scholars have persuasively demonstrated, those who ratified the Fourteenth Amendment had no expectation that it would forbid racial preferences. There were many laws at the time containing those preferences and no one suggested they were unconstitutional.[93] Justices Thomas and Scalia have often advocated originalism as their preferred method of constitutional interpretation but neither Justice has any use for that doctrine when it leads to a result they don't favor such as approving affirmative action programs. In any event, a majority of the Supreme Court has never conducted a good faith analysis of the history of the Fourteenth Amendment when resolving affirmative action cases. This behavior is inconsistent with the idea that the Supreme Court is a court of law charged with applying and interpreting prior law.

Sometimes the conservatives on the Court emphasize overarching structural principles when resolving constitutional questions such as a strong belief in federalism and the right of local and state governments to structure their operations as they see fit. If these Justices really took these doctrines seriously, however, they would have to rethink their views on most affirmative action cases. For example, there is no greater example of a need to defer to local and state governments than the issues presented by *Parents Involved*. The problem of racial isolation in our country's public schools is a serious one and presents different issues depending on which region of the country we are talking about, the size and racial composition of the school district, local housing patterns, and so forth. For the Court's conservatives to suggest that there is a national ban on limited racial balancing to address these problems (in light of the vagueness of the text and the historical materials to the contrary) bespeaks of a great insensitivity to federalism issues and also shows that they care more about invalidating affirmative action programs than consistently applying a legal methodology that they claim to embrace.

I do not mean to suggest that the conservatives are the only members of the Court to not act like judges when it comes to affirmative action cases. There can be little question that the liberals' and moderates' views on this question are also molded by their own value judgments and life experiences. There would be nothing wrong with that if the Supreme Court were truly considered by the American people as an ultimate veto council. But, as long as the Justices portray themselves as judges, and the Court as a court, they should pay much more attention to the link between prior positive law and the issues they face than they currently do.

So, at the end of the day, should the Court uphold or invalidate affirmative action programs or does it depend on the nature, extent, and specifics of the program? Professor James Boyd White of the University of Michigan Law School has written one of the most eloquent and persuasive articles on this topic.[94] He begins with the historical reasons for the ratification of the post–Civil War Reconstruction Amendments and observes that they represented "an effort to address the greatest single social and political issue the nation has ever faced: human slavery and its consequences, particularly the denial of full citizenship to the descendants of slaves."[95] The framers of the amendments "anticipated serious and systematic state hostility to the newly freed slaves, for it is against this danger that the amendments were meant to guard. The amendments were in large part aimed at preventing the states from interfering with the process by which newly freed blacks, or those freed earlier, could become integrated into the nation as full citizens—autonomous, capable, independent."[96] Given that historical reality, Professor White argues that "it would be simply bizarre to use the Fourteenth Amendment to strike down reasonable state efforts to help African Americans achieve full autonomy and integration. The States would be doing just what the amendments wanted them to do—instead of the particularly odious kind of group warfare they had waged against African Americans for centuries, and that many of them were in fact to continue to wage in different guises for another century at least. 'Discrimination'—which sounds like a neutral term defining a generalized evil—in fact means something very different indeed when it refers to action by the white majority designed to increase their domination over blacks and when it refers to action by the same majority designed to reduce it."[97]

In arguing for the constitutional validity of affirmative action programs, especially for African Americans, Professor White does not suggest that the policy issues surrounding such programs are easily answered. His point is simply that the Court should not be second guessing the policy judgments of elected institutions on this issue:

> [Affirmative Action] programs are on the merits highly controversial and contested, and while I am strongly disposed to favor them, I also recognize that rational . . . arguments can be made against them. . . . My main point here is very different, *having to do with the attitude the Supreme Court* [emphasis added] . . . should take towards a state agency that has considered these matters, heard arguments both ways, and come to the conclusion that such a program is a wise and good thing. Given the aims of the Fourteenth Amendment and the shameful history of the nation—including state and federal courts—since that time, I think the Court has no business "strictly scrutinizing" reasonable state efforts to advance the purposes of the Civil War Amendments, but should instead be glad that the state has assumed the kind of responsibility it has and defer to its rational judgments.[98]

Professor White is correct that the policy arguments surrounding affirmative action are complex and reasonable people can disagree about the merits of such programs. But, when democratically elected institutions decide on their own to make up for prior and well-documented societal discrimination, when those institutions are by and large in the hands of the same racial group that historically used the law to oppress the minority, and when the dominant racial group still has the political clout to prevent the use of affirmative action, there is no legally justifiable reason for the Supreme Court to step in and prevent the kind of change deemed necessary by the majority to assist the minority. For better or worse the people of California, Michigan, and Nebraska, for example, have passed state constitutional amendments prohibiting the use of racial preferences.[99] In other words, the political process worked and whites could take care of themselves without the help of unelected judges. Conversely, when the public schools of other states, whether they are grade schools, high schools, colleges, or graduate schools, decide to overcome racial isolation through racial preferences, or when the Congress of the United States or our country's cities and states decide to give minority groups special access to public money to make up for past discriminatory decisions, on what legal basis should the Supreme Court step in and prevent those measures? Neither the text of the Fourteenth Amendment nor its history suggests a different answer. If the Supreme Court were truly a court, and its Justices really judges, it would review that prior positive law and come to the same conclusion.[100]

CHAPTER 8

Freedom of Religion

Total separation of church and state was considered the best safeguard for the health of each.

—Arthur Schlesinger

Probably, at the time of the adoption of the constitution and of the amendment to it, the general, if not the universal, sentiment in America was that Christianity ought to receive encouragement from the state, so far as was not incompatible with the private rights of conscience, and the freedom of religious worship. An attempt to level all religions, and to make it a matter of state policy to hold all in utter indifference, would have created universal disapprobation, if not universal indignation.

—Justice Joseph Story

OVERVIEW

The First Amendment provides that "Congress shall make no law respecting an Establishment of Religion or prohibiting the Free Exercise thereof."[1] The first section of this amendment, the Establishment Clause, prevents the government from *rewarding* religion too much, while the second section, the Free Exercise Clause, prohibits the government from *punishing* religion too much.

Although many people refer to the wall of separation between church and state, that phrase does not appear anywhere in the United States Constitution. Rather, the phrase was used by Thomas Jefferson in a letter he wrote in 1802.[2] The Court first cited the phrase in a case decided in 1947 that *allowed* the government to fund the transportation of children to private religious schools.[3] This case, decided almost halfway through the 20th century, marked the first time that the Supreme Court applied the religion clauses to the states and marked the beginning of the Court's tortured path through the interpretation of those clauses.

Most commentators and judges agree that the Establishment Clause means at least that the government is not allowed to "establish" a religion in the sense of officially declaring that we live in a "Christian" or "Judeo-Christian" country. There is also a general consensus that the Free Exercise Clause prohibits the government from taxing or penalizing one religion more than another or religion more than nonreligion. Aside from those paradigm cases, however, issues concerning the separation of church and state are difficult and polarizing among legal academics, judges, and the public at large. There are so many questions raised by the separation of church and state that a full presentation of the issues is well beyond the scope of this book. To support the themes presented herein, it is enough to detail two representative Establishment Clause problems that typify the difficulty the Supreme Court has had resolving religious issues and demonstrate that whatever the Court is doing in these cases, it is not acting like a court of law.

AID TO RELIGIOUS SCHOOLS

The Early Cases

Most state governments, as well as the federal government, provide significant educational assistance to public schools and to not-for-profit private schools. A difficult Establishment Clause question is whether the First Amendment allows the government to also provide aid to private religious schools. This is an immensely important issue for millions of Americans.

The first time the Court grappled with an Establishment Clause issue was a case in which a New Jersey law allowed a local school district to reimburse parents of children for the costs of transporting their children to private religious schools. The suit was brought by a local taxpayer who claimed that his tax dollars could not be used to fund religious schools. In *Everson v. Board of Education*,[4] Justice Black, writing for the majority, said the following about the

Establishment Clause in the Court's first major interpretation of the clause:

> The "establishment of religion" clause of the First Amendment means at least this: neither a state nor the Federal Government can set up a church. Neither can pass laws which aid one religion, aid all religions, or prefer one religion over another. . . . *No tax in any amount, large or small, can be levied to support any religious activities or institutions, whatever they may be called, or whatever form they may adopt to teach or practice religion* [emphasis added]. Neither a state nor the Federal Government can, openly or secretly, participate in the affairs of any religious organizations or groups, and vice versa. In the words of Jefferson, the clause against establishment of religion by law was intended to erect "a wall of separation between church and State."[5]

Given the strong wording of this paragraph, one would have expected the Court to say the plaintiffs' tax dollars could not be used to help parents transport children to private religious schools, but the Court reached a different result. Although the majority believed that New Jersey was not allowed to directly support religious schools, it also held that New Jersey was not prohibited from extending its public welfare benefits to such schools. Analogizing the transportation reimbursement program to fire and police services, which states can obviously provide to churches and church schools, the Court held New Jersey's legislation "does no more than provide a general program to help parents get their children, regardless of their religion, safely and expeditiously to and from accredited schools. The First Amendment has erected a wall between church and state. That wall must be kept high and impregnable. We could not approve the slightest breach. New Jersey has not breached it here."[6]

The dissent saw the issue quite differently. Justice Rutledge, writing for three other Justices, argued that no person's tax dollars can be used to support religious beliefs, and that there is a constitutionally significant difference between a fireman coming to the aid of a church that is on fire and the state defraying the expenses of church schools by paying for the transportation of their children to and from school.[7] He believed that the history of the Establishment Clause demonstrated conclusively that "the Amendment forbids any appropriation, large or small, from public funds to aid or support any and all religious exercises."[8] And, he argued that, because every child in the New Jersey district had the right to attend public schools, which were free, the independent choices of parents to send their children to private religious schools came with the corresponding obligation to forego all funding from the state for the education of their children.[9]

Justice Jackson also dissented arguing that the majority's rhetoric about the need for separating church and state was inconsistent with its holding. And he concluded that "the case which irresistibly comes to mind as the most fitting precedent is that of Julia who, according to Byron's reports, 'whispering 'I will ne'er consent,'—consented.'"[10]

A few years later, the Court decided *Board of Education v. Allen*,[11] upholding a New York law requiring that public schools lend textbooks to all schoolchildren, including students attending private religious schools. The Court approved the law noting that the books were, at least technically, provided to the children not the schools, and that the books had to be secular not religious.[12] Although conceding that the book program had an educational component that bus transportation did not, the Court said that there was no evidence that the religious schools were using the books for anything other than secular purposes, and that the state's interest in improving the educational opportunities of all children within the state was legitimate. Although the provision of the books to religious schools might have made their tuition more affordable, the Court said that was also true of the bus transportation program at issue in *Everson*.[13] The Court concluded that, absent evidence that the schools were using the books for religious indoctrination, the textbook program did not violate the Establishment Clause.

Interestingly, Justice Black, who wrote the Court's opinion in *Everson* upholding the reimbursement to parents of the costs of transporting their children to religious schools, filed a vehement dissent. He argued that providing books to children attending religious schools was constitutionally different than providing "streetcar fare for all school children, or a law providing midday lunches for . . . school children . . . or general laws to provide police and fire protection for buildings, including, of course, churches."[14] Justice Black believed that books were different because, although "secular," the books "realistically will in some way inevitably tend to propagate the religious views of the favored sect. Books are the most essential tool of education, since they contain the resources of knowledge which the educational process is designed to exploit."[15] Justice Black ended his dissent with this emotional statement:

> I still subscribe to the belief that tax raised funds cannot constitutionally be used to support religious schools, buy their school books, erect their buildings, pay their teachers, or pay any other of their maintenance expenses, even to the extent of one penny. The First Amendment's prohibition against governmental establishment of religion was written on the assumption that state aid to religion and religious schools generates discord, disharmony, hatred, and strife among our people, and that any government that supplies such aid is, to that extent, a tyranny. And I still believe that the only way to protect minority religious groups from majority groups in this country is to keep the wall of separation between church and state high and impregnable as the First and Fourteenth Amendments provide. The Court's affirmance here bodes nothing but evil to religious peace in this country.[16]

The policy issues raised by these cases are not easy. To some of the Justices, when a state allocates its money to the education of its children, such as providing transportation to and from school or providing textbooks free of charge, there is nothing wrong with the state extending those benefits to children in religious schools (as long as the benefits are extended equally to all). To other Justices, however, the state has no business defraying the costs of religious school education with taxpayer money and other than the provision of general noneducational social services provided to all, such as police and fire protection, the state has no business spending money on children in religious schools.

Beginning in 1971, the Court adopted a new approach to the issue of parochial school aid at first prohibiting almost all such aid and then slowly allowing more and more aid, and finally allowing almost all such aid, which is the current law. The twists and turns of these cases will show that text, history, and prior interpretations of the Establishment Clause had *virtually nothing* to do with how the Court approached this admittedly difficult issue. In other words, the Court's results in this area have little to do with legal interpretation but instead involve the Justices' personal value judgments about the separation of church and state.

The Middle Years

In 1971, in *Lemon v. Kurtzman*,[17] the Court wrestled with the constitutionality of a Rhode Island statute that supplemented the salaries of religious school teachers who taught nonreligious subjects, and the validity of a Pennsylvania law that reimbursed such schools for some of the costs (such as books and teachers' salaries) of providing nonreligious instruction. In trying to ascertain whether these laws constituted an impermissible "Establishment" of religion, the Court asked whether the laws had a secular legislative purpose; whether their effect was to advance or inhibit religion; and whether the laws fostered "excessive entanglement" between church and state.[18] The Court found that both laws had a secular legislative purpose (to improve education in the state) and did not answer the second question whether the laws advanced or inhibited religion. Instead, the Court struck down both programs because they caused "excessive entanglement" between church and state.[19] The Court said that, to be permissible, the salary supplements and other reimbursed costs would have to be applied only to teaching that was devoid of any religious influence, but the monitoring of the classes by public school officials to make sure that the assistance only went to secular instruction resulted in too much entanglement between church and state.[20] Of course, the same considerations could have been applied to the program in *Allen*, which paid for textbooks to children in parochial schools, but the Court believed that monitoring the use of textbooks to ensure they were used for nonreligious purposes was somehow constitutionally distinguishable from monitoring classes and teachers to make sure they were engaged only in secular teaching.[21] One would be hard pressed to find that slippery difference in the text or history of the Establishment Clause.

The Court in *Lemon* knew that its invalidating of the state aid could not readily be harmonized with the results in *Everson* and *Allen*, which is why it said that "[c]andor compels acknowledgment . . . that we can only dimly perceive the lines of demarcation in this extraordinarily sensitive area of constitutional law."[22] The Court also said that "the Constitution decrees that religion must be a private matter for the individual, the family, and the institutions of private choice, and that, while some involvement and entanglement are inevitable, lines must be drawn."[23] The Court assumed without discussing, of course, that it should draw those lines, not elected legislatures.

Justice White, who dissented in *Lemon,* began by stating that: "The issue [whether the aid violates the Establishment Clause] is fairly joined. It is precisely the kind of issue the Constitution contemplates this Court must ultimately decide. This is true although neither affirmance nor reversal of any of these cases follows automatically from the spare language of the First Amendment, from its history, or from the cases of this Court construing it, and even though reasonable men can very easily and sensibly differ over the import of that language."[24] He then argued that there was no evidence in the record that any of the money spent by the states went to religious instruction and, in fact, the trial court in the Rhode Island case specifically found that only secular education was furthered by the state money. Justice White also argued that the Court's opinion created an "insoluble paradox" for the states and religious schools: "The State cannot finance secular instruction if it permits religion to be taught in the same classroom; but if it exacts a promise that religion not be so taught—a promise the school and its teachers are quite willing and, on this record, able, to give—and enforces it, it is then entangled in the 'no entanglement' aspect of the Court's Establishment Clause jurisprudence."[25] Justice White believed that, absent direct evidence that state money was being used for religious instruction, there was nothing constitutionally impermissible about taxpayer money being used to defray the costs of secular education in private religious schools.

Another point made by Justice White in his dissent further demonstrates that the Court's cases in this area have little to do with a principled and good faith reading of prior positive law and everything to do with personal value judgments. On the same day that the Court decided *Lemon,* it ruled in *Tilton v. Richardson*[26] that the federal government could constitutionally give money to religious universities for the construction of new buildings as long as those buildings were not used for religious purposes.[27] The *Tilton* Court distinguished *Lemon* on the basis that the maturity of college students and the lack of religious permeation at the university level posed less risk that the aid would advance religion or foster excessive entanglement between church and state than similar aid to schools for young children. Justice White did not understand why the federal government could give substantial aid to religious colleges while state governments could not give similar aid to religious elementary and secondary schools. In neither case could the aid be used for religious purposes and in neither case was there any evidence that the aid had in fact been used for religious purposes. Justice White argued the following: "[w]hy the federal program in the *Tilton* case is not embroiled in the same difficulties [as the state programs in *Lemon*] is never adequately explained. Nor can I imagine the basis for finding college clerics more reliable in keeping promises than their counterparts in elementary and secondary schools."[28]

In the wake of the *Lemon* decision, a number of states tried to find new ways to circumvent the case and fund parochial schools. At first, the Court was quite hostile to these efforts but eventually, as the Court's personnel changed, the states got their way.

In 1973, just two years after *Lemon* was decided, the Court struck down a New York law authorizing direct grants to private schools for the maintenance and repair of buildings (for the ostensible purpose of keeping children safe), and providing partial tuition reimbursements and tax credits to parents of children attending religious schools.[29] The Court invalidated the law because New York did not put into place any system to ensure that the aid would not be used for religious purposes but, of course, any such monitoring would probably have invalidated the laws by causing "excessive entanglement" between church and state. In another case, the Court struck down a state statute reimbursing religious schools for the costs of complying with state-required testing requirements.[30] In both cases, Justice White dissented arguing that the states have a strong interest in helping all schools, including private religious schools, educate our nation's children. More important, Justice White described the true basis for the Court's decisions in this area:

> No one contends that he can discern from the sparse language of the Establishment Clause that a State is forbidden to aid religion in any manner whatsoever or, if it does not mean that, what kind of or how much aid is permissible. And one cannot seriously believe that the history of the First Amendment furnishes unequivocal answers to many of the fundamental issues of church state relations. In the end, the courts have fashioned answers to these questions as best they can, the language of the Constitution and its history having left them a wide range of choice among many alternatives. But decision has been unavoidable; and, in choosing, the courts necessarily have carved out what they deemed to be the most desirable *national policy* governing various aspects of church-state relationships [emphasis added].[31]

The point of this book, of course, is that Justice White's description of the Court's parochial school aid cases is true for all of the Court's constitutional jurisprudence. Whether the issue is abortion, affirmative action, gun control, or Congress's powers to regulate the economy, the Court has been doing nothing more and nothing less than carving out what the Justices believe is the "most desirable national policy governing" these questions. The formulation of this national policy should not be made by unelected, life-tenured federal judges, or if it should, only after a full public awareness that the Court is making political, not legal, choices.

In the mid- and late 1970s, the Court issued a pair of decisions demonstrating great hostility to parochial aid statutes generally and to the rule of law specifically. In *Meek v. Pittenger*[32] and *Wolman v. Walter,*[33] the Court reviewed Pennsylvania and Ohio statutes that (1) loaned not just textbooks but also film projectors, maps, globes, and other instructional materials and equipment to private schools, including religious schools; (2) authorized the provision of numerous secular services by the states on the premises of the private schools including guidance counseling, remedial instruction, and speech and hearing services; and (3) provided for diagnostic testing and field trip transportation for children attending religious schools off the premises of those schools.

In both cases the Court reaffirmed that states can loan textbooks to religious school students and specifically rejected the plaintiffs' request that the Court overturn the *Allen* decision.[34] In both cases, however, the Court also held that it was unconstitutional for the states to provide any other kinds of instructional materials or equipment to the religious schools or children attending those schools. The Court said that the provision of this kind of aid had the unlawful effect of advancing the religious mission of the schools because the religious and secular missions could not be separated.[35] Taken together, the decisions in *Allen, Meek,* and *Wolman* meant that it was constitutionally permissible for states to provide textbooks to private religious schools, but it was a violation of the Establishment Clause for the state to provide any other kind of instructional material. The Court itself recognized this absurdity by noting that there was a "tension" between the results in *Meek* and *Wolman* and *Allen* but said it would follow *Allen* as a matter of precedent while not extending it to other kinds of aid.[36] Thus, as of 1977, the Supreme Court of the United States had interpreted the First Amendment to allow the provision of books to religious schools, including atlases containing maps, but states could not provide maps themselves, even if they were identical to the maps contained in the atlases that were permissible. As Justice Powell said in his concurring opinion in *Wolman*, greatly understating the matter, "[o]ur decisions in this troubling area draw lines that often must seem arbitrary."[37]

The Court's resolution of the other issues raised by *Meek* and *Wolman* was just as troubling and "arbitrary." The Court invalidated (in addition to the providing of educational materials except for books) (1) remedial instruction, guidance counseling, and speech and hearing services provided by public employees *inside* private schools because the monitoring necessary to make sure religion did not affect those services would result in excessive entanglement between church and state; and (2) the public funding of field trips for children in private schools on the basis this funding unlawfully advanced religion and the monitoring of the private school teacher who led the field trip to make sure that no religious message was conveyed would also cause excessive entanglement between church and state.[38]

The Court upheld (in addition to the providing of textbooks) (1) state-funded testing and scoring services for children attending religious schools because there was no danger of religious content since the state prepared and graded the tests; (2) diagnostic testing for children in private schools because unlike teaching and counseling there was no danger of a religious message being conveyed by the public school employee when conducting diagnostic as opposed to remedial teaching; and (3) therapeutic and remedial educational services *off* the premises of the private schools by public school teachers because *off* the premises there was less danger of religious indoctrination.

The lines between permissible and impressible aid drawn by the Court in these decisions demonstrate how far afield the Court had moved from relying on traditional legal sources to decide, or for that matter, even explain the Court's decisions. After these cases, states could provide significant remedial and therapeutic services to children attending religious schools as long as those services were provided off the premises of the schools, and the states could provide books to children in religious schools (as well as bus transportation to and from school), but states could not pay for field trips, most educational services inside the private schools (even by the same public school employees who were allowed to provide those services off premises), and *any* educational equipment or materials other than books. Whatever one thinks of these lines as a policy matter, there is no plausible argument that they derive from any reasonable reading of the text or history of the Establishment Clause.

Over the next few years, as membership on the Court began to change, the Court went back and forth approving some aid to religious schools and disapproving other kinds of aid. In two cases decided the same day in 1985, *Aguilar v. Felton*[39] and *School District of Grand Rapids v. Ball*,[40] the Court invalidated state and federal programs authorizing public school teachers to teach remedial, secular subjects in private school classrooms and also invalidated the reimbursement of private schools for having their own teachers teach secular subjects after hours in the private schools. Under the state programs, there was no monitoring of the teachers to make sure there was no religious content to the classes and thus the Court said those programs unlawfully advanced religion (even though there was no evidence of any religious indoctrination). The federal program did require the monitoring of the public school teachers in the private school classrooms and the Court held that the monitoring fostered excessive entanglement between church and state.

During this same period, however, the Court approved a Minnesota statute that provided a tax deduction for tuition and other educational expenses for parents of children attending private schools including religious schools.[41] Even though 95 percent of the aid went to parents of children attending religious schools, the Court said the program did not unlawfully advance religion because the aid was technically available to all parents, and because the aid went to the parents not the schools. Of course, the aid was really not available to parents of children in public schools (who had no expenses) and virtually all the parents who received the aid had children in private, religious schools. Therefore, the dissenting opinion argued that the Minnesota program was designed to and had the effect of making religious schools more affordable at the expense of the public schools and thus violated the Establishment Clause.[42]

A Dramatic Change

Twelve years after the Court ruled that it was unconstitutional for public school employees to teach secular subjects to religious school children inside the halls of those schools, a differently constituted Supreme Court reversed course. In *Agostini v. Felton,* the Court upheld the same federal program (allowing public school teachers to enter private school classrooms and provide remedial education) that it had invalidated earlier.[43] In summarizing the Court's previous decisions (*Felton* and *Ball*), Justice O'Connor noted that there were three primary reasons the Court had held that public school teachers could not teach inside the religious schools: (1) the teachers might consciously or unconsciously insert religious teaching into the courses as the teachers were physically inside the religious schools; (2) the use of public school teachers inside religious schools caused an unconstitutional symbolic union of church and state; and (3) assisting the secular mission of the religious schools has the effect of supporting the religious mission because the two missions could not be separated.[44] After setting forth those prior rationales, Justice O'Connor then went to great lengths to try and explain why all of those rationales were no longer persuasive and had been changed by later cases. Her discussion, however, as Justice Souter demonstrated in dissent, was simply not persuasive. What had changed was not "legal doctrine," but the composition of the Court.

As hard as the Court tried to hide the truth, its unpersuasive attempts to show why the law had changed demonstrates that what the Court was really doing in *Agostini* was reversing prior cases because now it had the votes and power to do so. In 1985, there were five Justices who believed that public school teachers should not be allowed to provide remedial, secular education inside the halls of religious schools because doing so was an unconstitutional "Establishment" of religion. Twelve years later, in 1997, with conservative Justice Thomas replacing liberal Justice Marshall, and Justice Kennedy replacing Justice Powell, there were now five Justices who believed that states could provide significant assistance to religious schools, both inside and outside their halls, without violating the Establishment Clause. This change did not come about because of recent discoveries about the history of the Establishment Clause or because of a slow and steady change in core legal doctrine. The change in law came about because the opinions and values of five Supreme Court Justices about the proper relationship between church and state had dramatically changed.

The Court's personnel changes also made inevitable two other major shifts in the law of the Establishment Clause as it applies to aid given to religious schools. First, after the Court had changed its mind and allowed the funding of public school teachers in private religious schools, the Court turned its attention to the baffling distinction it previously made between books and all other educational assistance to religious schools. In *Mitchell v. Helms*,[45] the Court explicitly overruled *Meek* and *Wolman* and upheld a federal program that provided a variety of educational materials and equipment to public and private schools including religious schools. Justice Thomas, who wrote the principal opinion, said there was nothing constitutionally problematic with providing even significant aid to the secular mission of religious schools and, instead of asking whether that aid furthers the religious mission of the school, Justice Thomas asked whether the government was responsible for any religious indoctrination that may occur within the school. His answer was no because "[i]f the religious, irreligious, and areligious are all alike eligible for governmental aid, no one would conclude that any indoctrination that any particular recipient conducts has been done at the behest of the government."[46] Justice Thomas went on to hold that the government may provide as much aid as it likes to religious schools as long as the aid is secular in nature and is available to all schools on a nonreligious basis. Justice Thomas's opinion did not require that the aid be monitored nor did it matter how much of the secular mission of the religious school was subsidized by taxpayer money.[47] Nor did it matter whether the aid went to the parents, the children, or directly to the schools. In brief, the Court reversed more than 20 years of Supreme Court decisions in this area and basically authorized the use of taxpayer money to provide significant assistance to religious schools as long as the aid was secular in nature and provided to nonreligious schools as well.

Once the Court allowed public school teachers to provide educational services inside the religious schools, and also allowed the provision of educational assistance other than just books, the last step in the abandonment of any real Establishment Clause limit on aid to religious schools occurred in 2002. In *Zelman v. Simmons-Harris*,[48] the Court upheld the use of vouchers to help children pay for the tuition costs of pervasively religious private schools. Even though well over 90 percent of the money went to parents of children attending religious schools, the fact that the aid was technically available to parents of children attending nonreligious schools led the Court majority to uphold the program.[49] The Court concluded that the program was designed to and actually led to more parental choice about where to send children to school, and the Establishment Clause of the First Amendment does not prevent the state from making religious schools more affordable and more desirable as long as comparable aid is also available to nonreligious schools.

Whether or not state and federal governments should provide assistance to religious schools is a difficult and complex question. On the one hand, the state has a legitimate interest in improving the educational opportunities of all students in our schools. On the other hand, nonreligious taxpayers have a legitimate complaint when their money is being used to support religious schools and their religious mission. There are a large number of other competing considerations such as will assisting private schools hurt the public schools or will such aid make public schools work harder and become more competitive? There are no easy answers to these questions. What is clear, however, is that the Court's gyrations in this area—from allowing very little aid in the 1970s and 1980s, to allowing slightly more aid in the 1990s, to the Court's present stance of allowing almost any kind of aid in any amount—are not based in constitutional law. There is nothing in the text or history of the Establishment Clause to suggest what level of aid, if any, the government can give to religious schools. Although the Court framed its decisions in the language of legal phrases like *excessive entanglement, symbolic union,* and *laws which advance religion,* the truth is that some Justices simply have more separationist instincts and values than other Justices. Justices Stevens, Marshall, and Souter, for example, believed that the government should not be allowed to support the educational mission of religious schools with taxpayer money because such aid, even if generally available, directly furthers the religious mission of those schools. Justices Thomas and Scalia, on the other hand, believe that the government is allowed to help religious schools as much as it wants to as long as the aid is defined without regard to religion. *Neither side has the better of the argument when it comes to interpreting the text and history of the Constitution.* All we can accurately say about the Court's decisions in this area is that they are based much more on the Justices' sense of the appropriate place of religion in public life, and on the Justices' personal value judgments, than on a good faith reading of prior positive law.

RELIGIOUS SYMBOLS ON GOVERNMENTAL PROPERTY

One of the most divisive constitutional law issues the Court has faced involves the constitutionality of religious symbols on governmental property. In public buildings, public parks, and other governmental buildings across America, one can find crosses, Ten Commandments monuments, Christmas displays, and other religious symbols. As of this writing, the Justices on the Supreme Court are hopelessly divided on the constitutionality of these displays. The more liberal Justices believe that virtually any religious symbol on governmental property violates the Establishment Clause because it places official approval behind one particular religion (almost always Christianity or Judaism) and makes nonadherents feel like political outsiders. The more conservative Justices would allow almost any religious symbol on governmental property as long as no one is officially coerced to honor that symbol. These Justices believe that the government is allowed to accommodate those citizens who wish to acknowledge that we live in a religious society and nonadherents should tolerate these noncoercive religious gestures. The more moderate Justices, whose votes dictate the results in these cases, would allow religious symbols in some cases but not others depending on the specific context and history of the display in question. Due partly to the differing views of the Justices, as well as the emotional nature of this issue, the only statement one can make about this area of the law is that "the law" has very little to do with how the Supreme Court has decided these cases.

The first time the Court dealt with this issue was in 1980 in *Stone v. Graham*,[50] when the Justices reviewed a Kentucky law requiring that a copy of the Ten Commandments, paid for with private money, be posted in all public school classrooms. The legislature required the following disclaimer to be placed at the bottom of each display: "The secular application of the Ten Commandments is clearly seen in its adoption as the fundamental legal code of Western Civilization and the Common Law of the United States."[51] Although Kentucky argued that this disclaimer demonstrated the secular purpose behind the requirement, the Court disagreed and held that the law violated the Establishment Clause. In a brief (three-page) opinion, the Court held that the:

[p]reeminent purpose for posting the Ten Commandments on schoolroom walls is plainly religious in nature. *The Ten Commandments are undeniably a sacred text in the Jewish and Christian faiths, and no legislative recitation of a supposed secular purpose can blind us to that fact* [emphasis added]. The Commandments do not confine themselves to arguably secular

matters, such as honoring one's parents, killing or murder, adultery, stealing, false witness, and covetousness. Rather, the first part of the Commandments concerns the religious duties of believers: worshipping the Lord God alone, avoiding idolatry, not using the Lord's name in vain, and observing the Sabbath Day. . . .

Posting of religious texts on the wall serves no such educational function. If the posted copies of the Ten Commandments are to have any effect at all, it will be to induce the schoolchildren to read, meditate upon, perhaps to venerate and obey, the Commandments. However desirable this might be as a matter of private devotion, it is not a permissible state objective under the Establishment Clause.[52]

Although three Justices dissented from this holding, the Court's reasoning was at least clear and could be applied to similar cases in a consistent way. *Stone v. Graham* would be the last religious symbol case the Court would decide in that manner.

In 1984, with Justice O'Connor now on the bench having replaced Justice Stewart, the Court decided its next religious symbol case. The issue in *Lynch v. Donnelly*[53] was the constitutionality of a government-funded Christmas display located in a private park in Pawtucket, Rhode Island. The display contained a Santa Claus house, reindeer pulling Santa's sleigh, candy-striped poles, a Christmas tree, Christmas carolers, a talking wishing well, a large banner that said "SEASON'S GREETINGS," and, most important, a crèche containing the figures of Mary and Joseph depicting the birth of Jesus Christ.[54] The crèche was acquired by the city in 1973 for a cost of $1,365, and erecting and dismantling the crèche every Christmas cost the city about $20 per year.[55]

Residents of Pawtucket as well as members of the Rhode Island affiliate of the ACLU sued the city claiming that the inclusion of the crèche in the display violated the Establishment Clause. The trial court agreed finding that the city had "tried to endorse and promulgate religious beliefs," because the "erection of the crèche has the real and substantial effect of affiliating the City with the Christian beliefs that the crèche represents." This "appearance of official sponsorship," the court said, "confers more than a remote and incidental benefit on Christianity."[56] The court permanently enjoined the city from including the crèche in the display, and the Court of Appeals affirmed that decision. By a divided and fractured 5–4 vote, the Supreme Court reversed and held that the publicly owned crèche display did not violate the Establishment Clause.

Chief Justice Burger wrote the principal opinion for the Court joined by Justices Rehnquist, White, Powell, and O'Connor, although Justice O'Connor wrote a separate concurring opinion that would end up being more important for later cases. Justice Burger's opinion can be distilled to his belief that there "is an unbroken history of official acknowledgment by all three branches of government of the role of religion in American life from at least 1789."[57] He said that "our history is replete with official references to the value and invocation of Divine guidance in deliberations and pronouncements of the Founding Fathers and contemporary leaders. Beginning in the early colonial period long before Independence, a day of Thanksgiving was celebrated as a religious holiday . . . [and] President Washington and his successors proclaimed Thanksgiving, with all its religious overtones, a day of national celebration."[58] Justice Burger went on to note that it has long been the practice that federal employees receive Thanksgiving and Christmas off, that there are paid chaplains for the United States Senate, the House of Representatives, and the military services, and that other official acknowledgments of the significance of religion to our country are found in the prescribed national motto "In God We Trust," which is on our coins and in the language "One nation under God," as part of the Pledge of Allegiance.[59] Finally, Justice Burger noted that the National Gallery in Washington, maintained with government support, has long exhibited paintings with religious messages, that Congress has authorized the president to proclaim a National Day of Prayer each year, and that presidential proclamations have also been issued to commemorate Jewish Heritage Week and the Jewish High Holy Days.[60]

Having recited what he argued was overwhelming evidence of governmental accommodation of religious beliefs, Justice Burger found that the trial court had erred by assuming that the inclusion of the crèche in the Christmas display had no secular purpose and therefore violated the Establishment Clause. He pointed out that the crèche was a small part of an overall display of the holiday season, and that there was "insufficient evidence to establish that the inclusion of the crèche is a purposeful or surreptitious effort to express some kind of subtle governmental advocacy of a particular religious message. . . . The city, like the Congresses and Presidents . . . has principally taken note of a significant historical religious event long celebrated in the Western World."[61] In response to the argument that the display unconstitutionally promoted one religion (i.e., Christianity), Justice Burger responded that "whatever benefit there is to one faith or religion or to all religions, is indirect, remote, and incidental; display of the crèche is no more an advancement or endorsement of religion than the Congressional and Executive recognition of the origins of the Holiday itself . . . or the exhibition of literally hundreds of religious paintings in governmentally supported museums."[62]

Justice Brennan, dissenting along with Justices Blackmun, Marshall, and Stevens, saw this case differently. For Justice Brennan, there was a significant legal difference between governmental acknowledgment of Christmas as a holiday season with secular aspects such as "gift-giving, public festivities, and community spirit," and official governmental sponsorship of the "distinctively sectarian aspects of the holiday."[63] According to Justice Brennan, the crèche, unlike such secular figures as Santa Claus, reindeer, or carolers, is far more than a mere traditional symbol of Christmas because its purpose and effect

is to prompt the observer to experience a sense of simple awe and wonder appropriate to the contemplation of one of the central elements of Christian dogma—that God sent His Son into the world to be a Messiah. . . . To suggest, as the Court does, that such a symbol is merely "traditional," and therefore no different from Santa's house or reindeer is not only offensive to those for whom the crèche has profound significance but insulting to those who insist, for religious or personal reasons, that the story of Christ is in no sense a part of "history" nor an unavoidable element of our national heritage.[64]

Justice Blackmun filed a separate dissent agreeing with Justice Brennan but making an additional interesting argument. He suggested that the witnesses for the city at the trial and the Justices in the majority opinion defended the Christmas display by downplaying the religious message inherent in the crèche. To Justice Blackmun, "the crèche has been relegated to the role of a neutral harbinger of the holiday season, useful for commercial purposes but devoid of any inherent meaning and incapable of enhancing the religious tenor of a display of which it is an integral part. . . . The import of the Court's decision is to encourage use of the crèche in a municipally sponsored display, a setting where Christians feel constrained in acknowledging its symbolic meaning and non-Christians feel alienated by its presence. Surely, this is a misuse of a sacred symbol. Because I cannot join the Court in denying . . . the sacred message that is at the core of the crèche, I dissent."[65]

Justice O'Connor provided the deciding fifth vote in this case and announced a new approach to Establishment Clause cases that would affect how the Court would decide future church/state cases. Rather than ask whether the challenged governmental practice had a religious purpose or had the effect of unlawfully advancing religion, Justice O'Connor said that the Establishment Clause test should be whether the government's actual purpose is to *endorse* religion, and whether, irrespective of the government's actual purpose, the practice under review in fact conveys a message of *endorsement* of religion. An affirmative answer to either question would render the challenged practice unconstitutional.[66] The rationale for this new test was that "endorsement sends a message to nonadherents that they are outsiders, not full members of the political community, and an accompanying message to adherents that they are insiders, favored members of the political community. Disapproval sends the opposite message."[67]

Applying this test to the facts of *Lynch,* Justice O'Connor first said that the city did not intend to endorse religion through its display because the "purpose of including the crèche in the larger display was not promotion of the religious content of the crèche, but celebration of the public holiday through its traditional symbols. Celebration of public holidays, which have cultural significance even if they also have religious aspects, is a legitimate secular purpose."[68] Similarly, Pawtucket's display of the crèche did not have the effect of endorsing religion because the Christmas holiday "has very strong secular components and traditions. Government celebration of the holiday, which is extremely common, generally is not understood to endorse the religious content of the holiday, just as government celebration of Thanksgiving is not so understood. The crèche is a traditional symbol of the holiday that is very commonly displayed along with purely secular symbols, as it was in Pawtucket."[69] Thus, according to Justice O'Connor, the display did not unconstitutionally endorse Christianity any more than other governmental acknowledgments of religion (such as legislative prayers, "Under God" in the Pledge, etc.) that also do not have the purpose or effect of endorsing religion in violation of the Establishment Clause.

The issues raised by *Lynch* are not easy. One could argue that the crèche is obviously a religious symbol, that there is no reason the government would use it other than to promote one religion, Christianity, and that the Establishment Clause should be interpreted to forbid governmental use of sectarian symbols, especially ones that are identified with only one religion. On the other hand, one could also argue that *endorsing* or *approving* religion is not the same as unconstitutionally *establishing* a religion, and that there are many examples of governmental acknowledgments of religion dating back to our country's beginning. If the government is not allowed to acknowledge the role religion plays in our public life, then *In God We Trust* must be taken off our coins, the phrase *Under God* must be taken out of the Pledge of Allegiance, and nondenominational prayers must be discontinued at all legislative and other governmental meetings. Such rulings, it can be argued, would display an overt hostility to religion that the Constitution not only does not require but might actually forbid under the Free Exercise Clause. Those who believe in the latter approach would also argue that, absent governmental coercion, there is nothing wrong with the government recognizing the importance of religion generally and perhaps even the Judeo-Christian tradition specifically.

A third approach to this problem might be to allow the government to use some religious symbols but not others depending on the context, nature, and reasons for the symbols. This way to deal with the problem was embraced by the Supreme Court in 1989, and continues to this day. As we will see, however, this approach is legally defensible only if the distinctions between the cases are coherent and reasonable. Unfortunately, the Court's rules do not come close to meeting that standard.

Two religious displays were at issue in *County of Allegheny v. ACLU*.[70] The first was a crèche placed on the Grand Staircase of the Allegheny County Courthouse in downtown Pittsburgh. The crèche was a visual representation of the scene in the manger after the birth of Jesus, and included figures of the infant Jesus, Mary, and Joseph, farm animals, shepherds, and the Wise Men. The crèche stood by itself apart from any other holiday displays and served as the backdrop for the city's Christmas carol program where, during the month of December, various student groups and other musicians would sing holiday songs during the lunch hour. There was a sign next to the crèche noting that it was owned by the Holy Name Society, a Roman Catholic organization.[71]

The second display at issue was an 18-foot Chanukah menorah placed next to the city's 45-foot lighted Christmas tree, and alongside a sign that said, "During this holiday season, the city of Pittsburgh salutes liberty. Let these festive lights remind us that we are the keepers of the flame of liberty and our legacy of freedom."[72] The menorah was owned by Chabad, a Jewish group, but was stored, erected, and removed each year by the city.[73]

In deciding on the constitutionality of these two displays, the Court issued five different opinions with varying rationales and theories supporting the Justices' views on the Establishment Clause. When the smoke cleared, one majority believed that the display of the crèche was unconstitutional and ordered it removed while a different majority found the display of the menorah was constitutional and said it could stay.

Justice Blackmun, writing for the liberals on the Court as well as Justice O'Connor, believed the crèche to be unconstitutional applying the endorsement test set forth by Justice O'Connor in her concurring opinion in the *Lynch* case. The difference between *Lynch* and this case, according to Justice Blackmun, was that in *Lynch* the crèche was surrounded by a host of nonreligious symbols such as a Santa Claus, reindeer, and a talking wishing well, all of which detracted from the religious significance of the crèche and suggested the government was more concerned with celebrating the holiday season than any particular religion. The crèche in *County of Allegheny,* by contrast, stood by itself without any secular symbols nearby. According to Justice Blackmun, "*Lynch* teaches that government may celebrate Christmas in some manner and form, but not in a way that endorses Christian doctrine. Here, Allegheny County has transgressed this line. It has chosen to celebrate Christmas in a way that has the effect of endorsing a patently Christian message. . . . Under *Lynch,* and the rest of our cases, nothing more is required to demonstrate a violation of the Establishment Clause."[74] Justice Blackmun concluded that the crèche amounted to an unconstitutional endorsement of the Christian religion and had to be removed from the Allegheny County Courthouse.

Justice Blackmun, joined by Justice O'Connor and the four conservatives (Scalia, Kennedy, White, and Rehnquist in the result only), voted differently with regard to the menorah. Justices Blackmun's and O'Connor's reasons for upholding the menorah were, however, quite different than the conservatives' rationale. For Blackmun and O'Connor, the 18-foot menorah didn't violate the Establishment Clause because it was sitting next to a 45-foot Christmas tree and a sign saluting liberty. Finding that the Christmas tree was not a religious symbol, Justices Blackmun and O'Connor believed that a "reasonable observer" would believe that the city was endorsing the secular holiday season and not the religious holidays of Christmas and Chanukah.[75] Justice Blackmun argued that the menorah, while a religious symbol, also has secular components and that, if the city wanted a symbol of Chanukah it had no other alternative as an "18-foot dreidel would look out of place, and might be interpreted by some as mocking the celebration of Chanukah."[76]

Justice O'Connor didn't believe that it was relevant whether or not the city had an alternative secular symbol for Chanukah. For her, the overall context of the display with the Christmas tree, the menorah, and the sign celebrating liberty would be perceived by a reasonable observer as a "message of pluralism," and not an unconstitutional endorsement of religion.[77] Both Justices believed that the Establishment Clause issues in these cases called for "careful line drawing" and no clear, fixed rules can decide the validity of religious symbols on governmental property.

Justice Kennedy wrote an opinion for Justices Scalia, Rehnquist, and White that presented a scathing and blistering attack on the endorsement test that had been adopted by Justices Blackmun and O'Connor. Justice Kennedy suggested that the Establishment Clause is not violated unless the government actually coerces religious beliefs or practices or proselytizes on behalf of religion. He argued that there was no plausible argument in this case that "the government's power to coerce has been used to further the interests of Christianity or Judaism in any way. No one was compelled to observe or participate in any religious ceremony or activity. Neither the city nor the county contributed significant amounts of tax money to serve the cause of one religious faith. The crèche and the menorah are purely passive symbols of religious holidays. Passersby who disagree with the message conveyed by these displays are free to ignore them, or even to turn their backs, just as they are free to do when they disagree with any other form of government speech. There is [also] no realistic risk that the crèche and the menorah represent an effort to proselytize or are otherwise the first step down the road to an establishment of religion."[78]

Justice Kennedy described the endorsement test as being inconsistent with settled historical practices such as chaplains beginning legislative sessions with prayers, putting the phrase *In God We Trust* on our coins and the phrase *Under God* in the Pledge of Allegiance, as well as the Supreme Court beginning its arguments with the phrase *God Save This Honorable Court.* If the Establishment Clause is violated every time a nonadherent or atheist would feel like an outsider and not a full member of the "political community" Justice Kennedy argued, than "[e]ither the endorsement test must invalidate scores of traditional practices recognizing the place religion holds in our culture or it must be twisted and stretched to avoid inconsistency with practices we know to have been permitted in the past, while condemning similar practices with no greater endorsement effect simply by reason of their lack of historical antecedent. Neither result is acceptable."[79]

Not only is the endorsement test inconsistent with our history, according to Justice Kennedy, but it also "threatens to trivialize constitutional adjudication."[80] To apply it in the manner that Justices Blackmun and O'Connor advocate, Kennedy argued, courts will have to embrace "a jurisprudence of minutiae."[81] They will have to look at the size of the symbols, where they are placed relative to other symbols, what alternatives, if any, there were to the religious symbols, and the nature of the property on which the symbol is placed. The endorsement test, according to Justice Kennedy, "could provide workable guidance to the lower courts, if ever, only after this Court has decided a long series of holiday display cases, using little more than intuition and a tape measure. Deciding cases on the basis of such an unguided examination of marginalia is irreconcilable with the imperative of applying neutral principles in constitutional adjudication."[82] For Justice Kennedy, and the conservatives, using this approach to invalidate the crèche amounted to an "unjustified hostility toward religion, hostility inconsistent with our history and our precedents."[83]

Although Justice Kennedy suggested that, absent coercion or proselytization, the Establishment Clause would not be violated by religious symbols on governmental property, he did concede that the clause would forbid a city from erecting a "permanent . . . large Latin cross on the roof of city hall . . . because such an obtrusive year-round religious display would place the government's weight behind an obvious effort to proselytize on behalf of a particular religion," and that it would be unconstitutional if a city "displayed a Christian symbol during every major Christian holiday, but did not display the religious symbols of other faiths during other religious holidays."[84] These concessions allowed Justice Blackmun to fire back at Justice Kennedy for Kennedy's harsh criticisms of the endorsement test and its fact-specific inquiries:

> In order to define precisely what government could and could not do under Justice Kennedy's "proselytization" test, the Court would have to decide a series of cases with particular fact patterns that fall along the spectrum of government references to religion (from the permanent display of a cross atop city hall to a passing reference to divine Providence in an official address). If one wished to be "uncharitable" to Justice Kennedy, . . . one could say that his methodology requires counting the number of days during which the government displays Christian symbols and subtracting from this the number of days during which non-Christian symbols are displayed, divided by the number of different non-Christian religions represented in these displays, and then somehow factoring into this equation the prominence of the display's location and the degree to which each symbol possesses an inherently proselytizing quality. Justice Kennedy, of course, could defend his position by pointing to the inevitably fact-specific nature of the question whether a particular governmental practice signals the government's unconstitutional preference for a specific religious faith. But because Justice Kennedy's formulation of this essential Establishment Clause inquiry is no less fact-intensive than the "endorsement" formulation adopted by the Court, Justice Kennedy should be wary of accusing the Court's formulation as "using little more than intuition and a tape measure," lest he find his own formulation convicted on an identical charge.[85]

For Justices Blackmun and O'Connor, the Court has to look carefully at the religious display to determine if the government is "endorsing" religion whereas for Justices Kennedy, Rehnquist, White, and Scalia, the Court has to look at the display only to see if it is "coercing" or "proselytizing" religion. Obviously, far more displays will endorse than coerce religion. For the remaining three Justices, Brennan, Marshall, and Stevens, they would have invalidated both displays in this case as well as the crèche in the *Lynch* case. They advocated a "strong presumption against the public use of religious symbols,"[86] and argued that:

> such symbols will offend nonmembers of the faith being advertised as well as adherents who consider the particular advertisement disrespectful. Some devout Christians believe that the crèche should be placed only in reverential settings, such as a church or perhaps a private home; they do not countenance its use as an aid to commercialization of Christ's birthday. . . . In this very suit, members of the Jewish faith firmly opposed the use to which the menorah was put by the particular sect that sponsored the display at Pittsburgh's City-county Building. . . . Even though "[p]assersby who disagree with the message conveyed by these displays are free to ignore them, or even to turn their backs," [citing Justice Kennedy] displays of this kind inevitably have a greater tendency to emphasize sincere and deeply felt differences among individuals than to achieve an ecumenical goal. The Establishment Clause does not allow public bodies to foment such disagreement.[87]

In *County of Allegheny,* nine Supreme Court Justices wrestled with the issue of when religious symbols could be constitutionally placed on governmental property. Three (Brennan, Marshall, and Stevens) believed the appropriate answer was almost never; four (Kennedy, Rehnquist, Scalia, and Thomas) believed the right answer was almost always; and two (O'Connor and Blackmun) were in the middle with almost no way to predict how they would vote in future cases.

All nine Justices represent the best and the brightest of our legal system, all went to excellent law schools and had prestigious and important legal careers prior to the Supreme Court appointments. None were significantly better or worse than the others at legal interpretation or examining prior positive law. Before moving on to the end of our discussion of the validity of religious symbols on governmental property, we should pause and reflect on what this issue tells us about constitutional law. The reason these Justices disagree so vehemently on this issue *has nothing to do with their abilities as judges*

or lawyers. They have different views on the proper relationship between religion and public life, and they have different personal values
and experiences. They are not deciding these cases as judges but as
people. They may explain their decisions in legal language, and they
may pay lip service to prior cases (or not), but in the end no amount
of legal skill can provide a persuasive answer to this difficult issue.

Returning to the question at hand, it should come as no surprise
that, given the divisions on the Court, as well as the inherent elastic-
ity of the endorsement test that was technically the rule after these
cases, lower courts have ended up in complete confusion and disar-
ray when deciding these kinds of cases. They struggled with nativ-
ity scenes, references to God in state seals, crosses and menorahs on
state property, and, of course, Ten Commandments displays in courthouses, state capitols, and other governmental buildings, as well as
numerous other problems relating to religious symbols on governmental property.[88] To say that these cases were characterized by inconsistent rulings, long and bitter dissents in the courts of appeals,
and general confusion would be a vast understatement. One famous
judge wrestling with these issues quipped that the Supreme Court's
cases in this area required "scrutiny more commonly associated with
interior decorators than with the judiciary."[89]

In 2005, a full 16 years after *County of Allegheny,* and after numerous lower court judges had to struggle with the Court's decisions,
the Supreme Court had the opportunity to clean up the mess it had
made of this doctrine when it ruled on the same day on two Ten
Commandments displays on governmental property. Sadly, the Court
made matters even worse.[90]

In the summer and fall of 1999, two counties in rural Kentucky
decided to post large gold-framed copies of the Ten Commandments
in their courthouses. In McCreary County, the posting was accompanied by a ceremony attended by local clergy and members of the
American Legion. In Pulaski County, amidst reported controversy
over the display, the commandments were hung in a ceremony pre-
sided over by the county judge-executive, who called them "good
rules to live by" and who told the story of an astronaut who believed "there must be a divine God" after looking at Earth from the
moon.[91] The judge-executive was accompanied by the pastor of his
church, who called the commandments "a creed of ethics" and told
the press after the ceremony that displaying the commandments was
"one of the greatest things the judge could have done to close out

the millennium."[92] In both courthouses, the displays were visible to people who had to appear at the courthouse to register to vote, obtain driver's licenses, pay local taxes, and appear for other official business.[93]

After the ACLU filed suit against the displays, both counties, upon the advice of counsel, expanded the displays to include other documents such as the national motto "In God We Trust," and various other statements by former presidents referring to God and prayer. As the obvious purpose of these second displays were to show that religion and government often go hand in hand, the trial court enjoined them finding that the counties had acted with the impermissible purpose to endorse religion and that "[w]hile a display of some of these documents may not have the effect of endorsing religion in another context . . . they collectively have the overwhelming effect of endorsing religion," in this context because "the only unifying element among the documents is their reference to God, the Bible, or religion."[94]

After this judicial defeat, the counties, upon advice of new counsel, again changed the display this time to add framed copies of the Magna Carta, the Declaration of Independence, the Bill of Rights, the lyrics of the Star Spangled Banner, the Mayflower Compact, the National Motto, the Preamble to the Kentucky Constitution, and a picture of Lady Justice. The collection was called "The Foundations of American Law and Government Display" and each document came with a statement about its historical and legal significance. The comment on the Ten Commandments read:

> The Ten Commandments have profoundly influenced the formation of Western legal thought and the formation of our country. That influence is clearly seen in the Declaration of Independence, which declared that "We hold these truths to be self-evident, that all men are created equal, that they are endowed by their Creator with certain unalienable Rights, that among these are Life, Liberty, and the pursuit of Happiness." The Ten Commandments provide the moral background of the Declaration of Independence and the foundation of our legal tradition.[95]

In court, the counties then argued that the purpose behind the displays were educational not religious and that the displays as a whole were intended to "educate the citizens of the county regarding some of the documents that played a significant role in the foundation of our system of law and government."[96] The trial court disagreed and permanently enjoined the displays on the grounds that the second and third displays were "shams" and both counties' purpose in including the Ten Commandments with the other documents was to unlawfully endorse religion.[97] A divided panel of the Court of Appeals affirmed and the Supreme Court decide to hear the case titled *McCreary County v. ACLU*.[98]

This case ended up being decided the same day as another Ten Commandments case coming out of Austin, Texas, called *Van Orden v. Perry*.[99] The Texas State Capitol grounds run for 22 acres and contain 17 monuments and 21 historical markers commemorating the "people, ideals, and events that compose Texan identity."[100] The Ten Commandments display at issue stood 6 feet high and 3 feet wide and was located between the Capitol and the Supreme Court building. On the display were the Ten Commandments, an eagle grasping the American flag, an eye inside of a pyramid, and two small tablets with ancient script carved above the text of the Ten Commandments. The bottom of the monument had the inscription "PRESENTED TO THE PEOPLE AND YOUTH OF TEXAS BY THE FRATERNAL ORDER OF EAGLES OF TEXAS 1961."[101] The Eagles paid for the erecting of the monument (as they did throughout the country), and it was dedicated by two state legislators. On other parts of the Capitol grounds stood monuments and markers dedicated to, among others, "Heroes of the Alamo," "the Texas Rangers," "Texas Pioneer Women," "Pearl Harbor Veterans," and "Texas Peace Officers."[102]

The plaintiff, Thomas Van Orden, was a native Texan and a resident of Austin who at one time had been a licensed lawyer, having graduated from Southern Methodist Law School. He testified that, since 1995, he had viewed the Ten Commandments display during his visits to the Capitol grounds. Forty years after the monument's erection, he filed a lawsuit claiming that the monument violated the Establishment Clause. The trial court held that the monument did not violate the Constitution because the state had a valid secular purpose in recognizing and commending the Eagles for their efforts to reduce juvenile delinquency by donating the display. The court also said "that a reasonable observer, mindful of the history, purpose, and context, would not conclude that this passive monument conveyed the message that the State was seeking to endorse religion."[103] The

Court of Appeals affirmed the decision and the Supreme Court decided to hear the case.

Both cases involved Ten Commandments displays on government property donated by private organizations. Four Justices voted to allow both displays, four Justices voted to invalidate both displays, and one, Justice Breyer, believed the Kentucky display was unconstitutional and the Texas display constitutional. In the Texas case, seven of the nine Justices wrote separately and in the Kentucky case, three justices wrote opinions, adding up to 10 separate opinions in the two cases. The dizzying result was more confusion and chaos for the lower courts, future plaintiffs, defendants, the country, and probably, at this moment, the reader of this book.

Justices Rehnquist, Scalia, Kennedy, and Thomas would have upheld the displays in both Kentucky and Texas. They argued that American history is replete with official acknowledgments of religion generally and the Ten Commandments specifically. Justice Rehnquist's opinion for the other three pointed out that to see such displays:

We need only look within our own Courtroom. Since 1935, Moses has stood, holding two tablets that reveal portions of the Ten Commandments written in Hebrew, among other lawgivers in the south frieze. Representations of the Ten Commandments adorn the metal gates lining the north and south sides of the Courtroom as well as the doors leading into the Courtroom. Moses also sits on the exterior east facade of the building holding the Ten Commandments tablets. Similar acknowledgments can be seen throughout a visitor's tour of our Nation's Capital. For example, a large statue of Moses holding the Ten Commandments, alongside a statue of the Apostle Paul, has overlooked the rotunda of the Library of Congress' Jefferson Building since 1897. . . . A medallion with two tablets depicting the Ten Commandments decorates the floor of the National Archives. Inside the Department of Justice, a statue entitled "The Spirit of Law" has two tablets representing the Ten Commandments lying at its feet. In front of the Ronald Reagan Building is another sculpture that includes a depiction of the Ten Commandments. So too a 24-foot-tall sculpture, depicting, among other things, the Ten Commandments and a cross, stands outside the federal courthouse that houses both the Court of Appeals and the District Court for the District of Columbia. Moses is also prominently featured in the Chamber of the United States House of Representatives.[104]

For these four Justices, passive displays of the Ten Commandments, as well as other religious symbols, do not violate the Establishment Clause just because they are housed on governmental property. Although there may be limits to the use of such symbols, for example, the four Justices cited with approval the *Graham* case invalidating the placing of the Ten Commandments in public school classrooms, those limits were not reached in this case. Other than suggesting that classrooms were different because of the impressionable nature of schoolchildren, however, these Justices did not discuss at length the context or history of the Austin display. For them, it was enough that Texas "has treated its Capitol grounds monuments as representing the several strands in the State's political and legal history."[105] Rehnquist explained that: "The inclusion of the Ten Commandments monument in this group has a dual significance, partaking of both religion and government. We cannot say that Texas' display of this monument violates the Establishment Clause of the First Amendment."[106]

Justice Breyer agreed with these four but for very different reasons. Before discussing his key fifth vote, we have to summarize the views of the Justices who would have invalidated both displays. Justice Souter writing for O'Connor, Stevens, and Ginsburg (and joined by Breyer in the Kentucky case) seemed to articulate a strong presumption against religious symbols on governmental property while also recognizing that "under the Establishment Clause detail is key."[107] The Justices believed that the record in the Kentucky case amply supported the trial court's determination that the county had acted for an express religious purpose in placing the Ten Commandments displays in the courthouse and that the latest display, which also included a host of other secular documents, amounted to nothing more than a litigation position that did not dispel the original religious motive. Because religion was the primary motivating factor, these Justices held the display unconstitutional while also saying that "we have [no] occasion here to hold that a sacred text can never be integrated constitutionally into a governmental display on the subject of law, or American history. We do not forget . . . that our own courtroom frieze was deliberately designed in the exercise of governmental authority so as to include the figure of Moses holding tablets exhibiting a portion of the Hebrew text of the later, secularly phrased Commandments; in the company of 17 other lawgivers, most of them secular figures, there is no risk that Moses would strike an observer as evidence that the National Government was violating neutrality in religion."[108]

The Justices who joined Justice Souter's opinion in the Kentucky case, except for Justice Breyer, would also have invalidated the Ten Commandments display in Austin. Justice Souter summarized their beliefs as follows: "the simple realities [are] that the Ten Commandments constitute a religious statement, that their message is inherently religious, and that the purpose of singling them out in a display is clearly the same."[109] For these Justices, the fact that the display in Austin was on the same land as numerous nonreligious displays did not cure the problem because the other monuments and markers were not organized around a common theme (such as the theme of lawgivers on the walls of the Supreme Court where Moses appears with the Ten Commandments), and therefore it stood by itself as a government endorsement of religion. These Justices did discuss the context and history of the display in detail but reading their various opinions one gets the strong sense that they would be hostile to virtually any Ten Commandments display that was actually challenged in litigation. In fact, Justice Stevens, writing separately, again argued that there should be a strong presumption against the use of any religious symbols on governmental property.[110]

To recount, four Justices would have upheld both displays, four Justices would have invalidated both displays, and one, Justice Breyer, split the difference. Before finally turning to his key opinion, however, a word must be said about Justice O'Connor. In prior cases, she voted to affirm the crèche in Pawtucket, Rhode Island, that was surrounded by a Christmas tree, and other secular symbols as well as the menorah in Pittsburg surrounded by the Christmas tree and sign saluting liberty, while voting to invalidate the crèche in Pittsburg that stood by itself. In all three of those instances, she suggested that context was key and that the inclusion of secular symbols surrounding the religious symbol would go a long way in rendering a religious symbol on governmental property constitutional. Despite these prior cases, however, she surprisingly voted to overturn the Ten Commandments displays in both Kentucky and Austin. The notable aspect of her decisions was that she failed to explain why she voted the way she did. She wrote a short concurring opinion in the Kentucky case that did not mention the specific facts of that case at all and simply joined Justice Souter's dissenting opinion in the Austin case, which seemed inconsistent with Justice O'Connor's previous decision upholding a crèche and a menorah on governmental property. If Justice O'Connor were truly a judge concerned with the rule of law, she would have explained why she seemed to be taking a much more activist view of the Establishment Clause than she had ever taken before. The litigants before her, as well as the American people, deserved at least that much. But Justice O'Connor felt no such obligation, which provides evidence yet again that Supreme Court Justices do not act like judges.

Finally, we must turn to Justice Breyer because it is his opinion in the Austin case that emerged as the rule "of law" that lower courts must now follow. He began his analysis by saying that "[i]f the relation between government and religion is one of separation, but not of mutual hostility and suspicion, one will inevitably find difficult borderline cases. And in such cases, I see no test-related substitute for the exercise of legal judgment. . . . That judgment is not a personal judgment. Rather, as in all constitutional cases, it must reflect and remain faithful to the underlying purposes of the Clauses, and it must take account of context and consequences measured in light of those purposes."[111] The reader can decide, after reading the summary of Justice Breyer's opinion for the validity of the Austin display but against the Kentucky display, whether his judgment is "legal" or "personal."

Justice Breyer argued that sometimes the display of the Ten Commandments conveys a religious message and sometimes a secular message. He concluded that in the Texas case, the display was more about history than religion because it was donated by a private group to help combat juvenile delinquency, it was placed on the spacious grounds of the Texas Capitol surrounded by numerous nonreligious monuments and markers, and the overall context showed that the state intended the display to reflect moral ideals not religious principles.[112] The problem with these arguments, however, was that Justice Breyer also joined Justice Souter's opinion in the Kentucky case, which stated that Ten Commandments displays inevitably convey unmistakably religious statements dealing with religious obligations.[113] Souter's argument seems persuasive as the first four commandments on the Texas display were the following:

Thou shalt have no other gods before me.
Thou shalt not make to thyself any graven images.
Thou shalt not take the Name of the Lord thy God in vain.
Remember the Sabbath day, to keep it holy.[114]

It is hard to imagine any secular or nonreligious purpose behind the state wanting to promote those four ideals, none of which could ever constitutionally be made a part of American law. It is understandable why the conservatives were not bothered by that fact because they believe that the Establishment Clause is not violated unless the state coerces religious belief or actually adopts or establishes a religion. Justice Breyer, however, does not share that view as his vote in the Kentucky case demonstrates. That being the case, it is somewhat difficult to understand his vote in the Austin case.

Justice Breyer distinguished the *Graham* case on the basis that the Austin display was "not on the grounds of a public school, where, given the impressionability of the young, government must exercise particular care in separating church and state."[115] And, he distinguished the Kentucky case on the grounds that "the short (and stormy) history of the courthouse Commandments' displays demonstrates the substantially religious objectives of those who mounted them, and the effect of this readily apparent objective upon those who view them."[116] One could ask why the state has to be more careful not to endorse religion in classrooms than on the grounds of the state capitol where those who live in Texas must conduct official business. One could also ask why the motivation of those in Kentucky who wanted the displays is more constitutionally important than the fact that, by the time the case reached the Supreme Court, the displays contained numerous nonreligious symbols that placed the Ten Commandments in a secular and historical perspective much like the display in Texas. These questions, and many others that come to mind, were not answered or even discussed by Justice Breyer.

Perhaps the real reasons behind Justice Breyer's decision to uphold the Austin display are contained at the end of his opinion, where he stated the following:

As far as I can tell, 40 years passed in which the presence of this monument, legally speaking, went unchallenged (until the single legal objection raised by petitioner). And I am not aware of any evidence suggesting that this was due to a climate of intimidation. Hence, those 40 years suggest more strongly than can any set of formulaic tests that few individuals, whatever their system of beliefs, are likely to have understood the monument as amounting, in any significantly detrimental way, to a government effort to favor a particular religious sect, primarily to promote religion over nonreligion, to "engage in" any "religious practic[e]," to "compel" any "religious practic[e]," or to "work deterrence" of any "religious belief." Those 40 years suggest that the public visiting the capitol grounds has considered the religious aspect of the tablets' message as part of what is a broader moral and historical message reflective of a cultural heritage. . . .

This display has stood apparently uncontested for nearly two generations. That experience helps us understand that as a practical matter of degree this display is unlikely to prove divisive. And this matter of degree is, I believe, critical in a borderline case such as this one.

At the same time, to reach a contrary conclusion here, based primarily upon on the religious nature of the tablets' text would, I fear, lead the law to exhibit a hostility toward religion that has no place in our Establishment Clause traditions. Such a holding might well encourage disputes concerning the removal of longstanding depictions of the Ten Commandments from public buildings across the Nation. And it could thereby create the very kind of religiously based divisiveness that the Establishment Clause seeks to avoid.[117]

Justice Breyer appears to be saying that what most motivated him in this case was the fact that the monument had been on the capitol grounds for a long time (40 years), that no one had challenged it before, and that its removal might generate more litigation over the validity of other Ten Commandments displays all over the country (maybe even, God forbid, in the Supreme Court building itself)!

The best way to demonstrate the utterly "personal" and not "legal" nature of Justice Breyer's opinion is to imagine yourself a lower court judge having to decide whether a particular religious display violates the Establishment Clause under the rules set forth in the decisive opinion for the Court. Here are some of the relevant factors you would have to look at:

1. Where is the display housed? Is it in a primary school class-room, a capitol, a state university classroom, a courthouse, and so forth?
2. Does the display stand alone? What is it surrounded by and when and why were the other symbols added?
3. How long ago was the symbol placed on the property? Was it put there by the government or a private organization? Were there religious statements made when the symbol was first displayed?
4. Has the symbol ever been challenged in court prior to the instant case? Is the removal of the symbol likely to generate more controversial litigation?[118]

The discretion that this list of factors offers to lower court judges is vast, and the result will be, and in fact has already been, lower courts deciding these cases not under the law but under their own personal values. Lower courts are already divided over the validity of other Ten Commandments displays.[119] The expensive, divisive, and time-consuming litigation is unlikely to end until the Court provides more guidance on this issue.

The constitutionality of religious symbols on governmental prop-erty poses a difficult constitutional question. A good faith reading of the text of the Establishment Clause and its history as well as case law could lead either to a strong presumption for the validity of such symbols (the conservatives), the invalidity of such symbols (the moderates/liberals except Breyer), or maybe even some middle-of-the-road approach likely to make no one too angry and no one too happy. Although there is no clear constitutional answer to this issue, what we do know is that one could have predicted the votes of most of the Justices *without ever looking at any of the law relevant to these cases.* The Justices in this area of the law, as well as all the other areas of constitutional law that we have discussed, are simply exercising a veto power they have the authority to exercise. That these nine people have this authority does not make them judges in-terpreting the law. That would require that prior positive law play at least a meaningful role in generating results in constitutional cases, and no amount of legal jargon can obscure the fact that prior posi-tive law simply doesn't matter much when the Supreme Court de-cides on the constitutionality of religious symbols on governmental property.

CHAPTER 9

Proposals

John Marshall was wrong: it is emphatically the province and duty of the American people, not of the nine justices of the United States Supreme Court, to say what the Constitution is. A national reappraisal of the . . . court chosen by judicial roulette is crucial if American democracy is to meet the rising challenges of the twenty-first century.

—Pulitzer Prize winner James MacGregor Burns

If the constitutional decisions of the Supreme Court of the United States are based much more on subjective value judgments than preexisting law, why should the American people delegate fundamental policy questions to this particular political institution? The Justices have no special insights into the complexities of affirmative action, gun control, abortion, or how the national economy should be regulated, yet in all of those areas (and many others) they have not only exercised an important veto power but also set forth rules of conduct that all Americans, and their local and nationally elected leaders, must follow. In addition, the Justices' decisions at times stifle democratic debate, preclude local decision making, and take off the table legislative solutions favored by many Americans.

The Supreme Court's power should be reevaluated by taking into account two of the fundamental flaws in our current system of judicial review. First, all of the problems described in this book with the Court acting as a legislative veto council are heightened significantly by the Justices' life tenure. Our Supreme Court is the *only* court *in the world* staffed by judges who can serve as long as they see fit and whose decisions are not reviewed by other courts or any other democratic institution. The American people should pass a constitutional amendment abolishing life tenure and replacing it with fixed terms and a guaranteed salary for life. In a democracy, no governmental official, much less one with virtually unreviewable power, should serve for life.

Second, the American people should insist that the Supreme Court exercise the great power of judicial review only when it is necessary to enforce the constitutional principles expressly set forth in our Constitution. The only persuasive justification for allowing the Court to overturn the decisions of more accountable government officials is that "We the People" forbade such decisions either in the constitutional text or its amendments. Thus, unless the constitutional text or undisputed history behind that text forecloses a governmental decision, the Court should defer to the elected branches and the states.

In addition to these major proposals, there are other changes that should be made that would make the Court more transparent and more democratic. For example, the Court's oral arguments should be televised, and the confirmation hearings for the Justices should not be a week-long charade allowing the nominee to evade all difficult questions and pretend that he or she has no preexisting views on the important issues of the day. But, those improvements, though helpful, would not make a significant difference. To encourage the Court to act like a court, and the Justices to decide cases like judges, both life tenure and how the Court views its role in American society must be changed. Although these proposals are unlikely to be adopted in the near future, the conversation and debate over how to limit the power of the Supreme Court must begin somewhere. Maybe, just maybe, by adding more voices to the list of people urging the Court to act differently, progress can slowly be made.

ABOLISH LIFE TENURE

It is worth repeating that the United States is the only democracy in the world whose highest court has Judges with life tenure.[1] During the 20th century, many countries looked at the American system of judicial review and adopted similar mechanisms but *none* of those countries decided to give the judges of their highest court life tenure. Some countries such as France and Italy have fixed nonrenewable terms while others like Canada and Australia have mandatory retirement ages.[2] These and other countries decided that it is a serious mistake to give government officials great power and prestige and then let them serve as long as they see fit. Moreover, even in this country, only one state, Rhode Island, allows its judges to hold office for life.[3] As Professors Carrington and Cramton have written:

> In the last century and a half, hundreds of constitutions have been written and ratified. Many of these became the law of American states, while many others have been adopted in nations that share our commitment to individual freedom and representative democracy. None of these hundreds of constitutions has provided for a court of last resort staffed by judges who are entitled to remain in service until they die or are found guilty of very serious misfeasance. Every group of constitution makers—forced to think responsibly about the issue under modern conditions—has concluded that there must be periodic movement of persons through offices in which so much power is vested, either through . . . term limits or age limits, by requiring reelection from time to time, or by allowing for removal by legislative action.[4]

Although the Founding Fathers correctly believed that federal judges needed to be independent of the president and Congress so that they would not be beholden to other political officials when reaching judicial decisions, the Founding Fathers incorrectly thought that life tenure was the best mechanism to provide that independence. The Founding Fathers simply could not have anticipated how dramatically the Justices' life spans would increase. Supreme Court Justices are now staying on the Court well into their 80s and sometimes even into their 90s. Moreover, because the Justices are often appointed when they are in their 50s, most of them now serve for at least 20 to 25 years and many for more than 30. The most recent Justice, Elana Kagan, was 50 when appointed and could foreseeably serve for more than 40 years. Justice Thomas was only 43 when he was appointed, and, if he serves to the same age as Justice Stevens, will be on the bench for almost half a century. The most important judges in our country simply should not wield so much power for so long (the same is true for lower federal court judges but how to deal with that problem, given the large number of such judges, is beyond the scope of this discussion).

The great harms caused by life tenure are significant and include, among others, the following:

1. Justices often stay on the bench even after they are no longer fit to serve;
2. Whether a president has the opportunity to nominate a Justice often depends on luck or random events, not a well-conceived political rotation system; and
3. The president has a strong incentive to nominate young Justices who will serve for a long time. Because of that longevity, eventually Supreme Court Justices are likely to fall out of step with current American values, needs, and priorities.

These harms justify a constitutional amendment abolishing life tenure and replacing it with fixed, nonrenewable terms for Supreme Court Justices. Although such an amendment would not directly solve the problems of value-laden judicial review and the resulting overreaching by the Justices, it would lessen the antidemocratic impact of those problems because the Justices would rotate more frequently, and the Senate and the American people would have a more effective say on who gets to sit on the Court.

Incompetent Justices

Throughout American history, and in virtually every generation, Supreme Court Justices have stayed on the bench after their mental and physical capabilities had deteriorated so much that friends, family, and even the Justices on their own Court urged them (often unsuccessfully) to retire. This problem is often ignored in the media and in the law schools. In one of the few major articles on the subject,[5] noted journalist and constitutional law professor David Garrow exhaustively marshaled the evidence for the claim that Supreme Court Justices often stay on the bench too long. The examples are too numerous to catalogue in this chapter, but here are a few representative cases that illustrate the seriousness of the problem.

In 1921, Justice Joseph McKenna's mental abilities were slipping so badly that Chief Justice Taft complained to people outside the Court that the 78-year-old McKenna could no longer perform his job. Taft even suggested to McKenna (to no avail) that he consider retiring. Two years later, Taft polled his colleagues to see whether McKenna should be expressly asked to step down from the Court. Five of Taft's colleagues answered yes but Justice Oliver Wendell Holmes and Justice Louis Brandeis said no. Accordingly, Taft took no action.

The next year, several of the Justices visited Justice McKenna's doctor who agreed that McKenna should retire, but McKenna again refused. During this period, Taft only assigned McKenna the easiest opinions, but even those often had to be changed significantly or reassigned to another Justice. Finally, Taft convened a meeting in his home with all the Justices except McKenna where the Court agreed not to decide any case where McKenna's vote might be decisive. They also brought McKenna's son to the house and conveyed this message to him. A few months later, McKenna finally retired, at least four years after he was no longer fit to serve. Taft later recounted that the Court should have acted much sooner to convince the aged and infirm McKenna to give up his life tenure.[6]

On December 31, 1974, 76-year-old Justice William Douglas suffered a major stroke. He did not return to the Court until March 24, 1975. He met with reporters the next day, and his voice was "weak," and "slurred." One reporter described Justice Douglas as a "frail and fragile old man . . . most of his once remarkable vigor . . . drained away."[7]

Douglas was in and out of the hospital over the next few months and did not return to the Court to hear oral arguments. The Court decided to carry over eight cases to the next term because the Justices were divided and did not want to count Douglas's vote. On October 6, 1975, Douglas returned to the bench, but after a while it was apparent that he had been dozing during the arguments. Over the next few weeks, his colleagues observed that Douglas had "moments of lucidity and energy followed by near incoherence and sleep."[8]

On October 17, 1975, the Court again decided not to resolve any case where Douglas's vote might be crucial, and also agreed, by a vote of 7–1, not to assign him any opinions to write. Justice White so strongly disagreed with that decision that he sent a letter of protest to his colleagues saying they had no authority to take away Douglas's responsibilities and that, although it would be "better for everyone if . . . he retired," if the Court wanted Douglas to cease functioning as a Supreme Court Justice it should say so publicly and ask Congress to consider impeachment.[9]

No action was taken, but two weeks later Justice Douglas was hospitalized again and finally agreed to retire. In the words of David

Garrow, "Douglas' failure to retire eight months earlier had forced the Court into a 'crisis mentality,' for parts of two successive terms and following his official retirement the mentally incapacitated Douglas repeatedly tried to participate in the Court's consideration of pending cases even after his angry colleagues bluntly ordered him to cease and desist."[10] Life tenure did not help the legacy of Justice William O. Douglas, and it also caused great harm to our nation's highest court.

By the late 1980s, there were many reports in the press that Justice Thurgood Marshall had delegated most of his work to his law clerks and would often decide cases by asking how fellow liberal William Brennan voted, and then vote the same way.[11] On October 30, 1989, during the oral argument of an important antitrust case, Justice Marshall became openly confused and repeatedly mixed up the parties. Six weeks later, he had great difficulty reading an opinion from the bench causing enormous embarrassment in the courtroom. By this time, Marshall was 81 years old and had been losing his hearing and mental abilities for years. When Justice David Souter was nominated to replace retiring Justice Brennan in July 1990, Marshall made several strange public statements about Souter, leading numerous commentators to suggest that Marshall's physical problems were now also causing mental problems.[12] Finally, in June 1991, Marshall retired, years after he had ceased being a full, active participant in the Court's affairs.

These are just three of the many examples of Supreme Court Justices refusing to retire long after their skills had deteriorated to the point where they could not perform their job. Sometimes, a Justice's refusal to leave the Court is based on the normal human desire to retain a position of great authority and respect, sometimes it is due to misplaced ego, and sometimes it is caused by an inability because of age and sickness to honestly see how ineffectual one has become. Regardless of the reasons, the position of Supreme Court Justice is far too important to our system of government to allow people to serve on the Court when they can no longer perform the required tasks, but the guarantee of life tenure makes it virtually impossible to remove an unwilling Justice.

The Replacement Problem

The president of the United States can only nominate a Supreme Court Justice when a sitting Justice either retires or dies. Thus, the composition of the Court over time has less to do with a well-structured political process than with random events often beyond the control of the people, the president, or the Senate. Because the nomination process is the only significant check on the Supreme Court's decisions (no Justice has been successfully impeached and the constitutional amendment process is very difficult), the only way to effectuate desired change in Supreme Court decision making is to appoint Justices whose values are different from previous Justices. But, because of life tenure, changes on the Court are haphazard, inconsistent, and wholly unpredictable.

In four years in office, President William Howard Taft made five appointments to the Court, and in three years President Warren Harding made four. On the other hand, President Jimmy Carter made no appointments during his four years in office, and President Bill Clinton only made two in eight years.[13] There is no plausible justification for a political system in which the composition of the highest Court in the land is left to chance (not to mention politically motivated retirement decisions by members of the Court).

The dangers of such a random system of Supreme Court appointments can be seen by looking at how one of the most significant decisions in constitutional history came to be decided. In 1952, the Supreme Court agreed to hear five cases from the lower courts challenging the forced segregation of America's public schools, including the case of *Brown v. Board of Education.* At the time, Chief Justice Fred Vinson, along with a few of the other Justices, weren't sure that the Constitution forbid segregation, and, in any event, were concerned that the Court might not be able to enforce a decision requiring the end of this pernicious practice.[14] Justice Felix Frankfurter, a staunch opponent of segregation as a policy matter, also wasn't sure that the Court, either as a matter of history or precedent, should strike it down.[15] The case was argued in the spring of 1953, but, because the Justices were so divided over this monumental issue, they asked for reargument the following term. But, in September 1953, Chief Justice Vinson died of a heart attack and "everything changed."[16] President Dwight Eisenhower replaced Vinson with Earl Warren, the governor of California, "who had extraordinary political skills and personal warmth, along with a deep commitment to social justice. Through a combination of determination, compromise, charm, and intense work with the other justices (including visits to the hospital bed of an ailing Robert Jackson), Warren engineered something that might have seemed impossible the year before: a unanimous opinion overruling *Plessy.* Thurgood Marshall, a principal architect of the litigation strategy that led to *Brown,* recalled, 'I was so happy I was numb.'"[17] Justice Frankfurter, in a famous quote, said that the replacement of Vinson with Earl Warren, and the resulting impact on the *Brown* decision, was "the first indication that I have ever had that there is a God."[18]

Important Supreme Court decisions involving the country's most critical social problems, like school segregation, should not depend on a random event such as the heart attack of a Supreme Court Justice. A rotating system of 18-year nonrenewable terms (the most popular current proposal described in more detail below) would allow every president who made it through his first term at least two appointments, and the American people and the Senate would know that every two years a Supreme Court vacancy would need to be filled. This kind of system (which could only work by abolishing life tenure) would be more consistent, more representative, and more logical than giving some presidents three or four appointments and some presidents one or two based on factors beyond the control of the American people and our political system.

Young and Then Old Justices

Faced with the prospect of being able to influence the country through the appointment of a Supreme Court Justice, and knowing how much longer people live today than before, presidents have a strong incentive to nominate young Justices. President Reagan's nominees, for example, were 51-year-old Sandra Day O'Connor, 50-year-old Antonin Scalia, and 51-year-old Anthony Kennedy.[19] Justice O'Connor served for approximately 25 years and Justices Scalia and Kennedy are still on the bench showing no signs they are considering retirement. Recently, President Obama nominated the 54-year-old Sonia Sotomayor and the 50-year-old Elana Kagan. If they both serve until their mid-80s, which has been the norm recently, they will each serve at least 30 years on the bench. That means they will be hearing cases in 2040. Regardless of whether they are up to the task at that time physically and mentally, they will be serving a society markedly different from the one they served as lawyers and civil servants. It wasn't always this way. Between 1789 and 1970, Justices served an average of 14.9 years, whereas between 1970 and 2005 Justices served an average of 26.1 years.[20]

Numerous scholars have proposed alternatives to life tenure that would guarantee Supreme Court Justices sufficient independence to perform their responsibilities but avoid the problems with life tenure discussed in this chapter. The most popular proposal is to have the Justices serve fixed 18-year terms so that, absent extraordinary events, there would be two vacancies on the Court every four years.[21] In addition, the Justices would draw their salaries for life (so that their future economic prospects would not impact their decision making) and be able to serve on the lower courts if they wished. The advantages of this proposal are (1) every president would get the same number of appointments per term (assuming no one dies or retires in office); (2) the Justices would serve the same number of years (as opposed to some serving for short periods of time and others for long periods of time); (3) a more frequent confirmation process would give the American people and the Senate more of a say in who gets to be on the Court; and (4) fewer Justices would serve past the time that they are still qualified for the job.[22]

This proposal, of course, isn't perfect. This rotating procedure would entail many more confirmation hearings, which could be distracting for both the Senate and the president; the Court may not have its full share of members while the confirmation battles are fought; and fixed 18-year terms could still lead to Justices staying on the bench after they should retire. Although these problems aren't minor, they are not as serious as the consequences of life tenure.

The strong need for judicial independence can be served without allowing Supreme Court Justices to hold office long after they should have retired and without leaving to chance how many Justices a president has the opportunity to appoint. Fixed terms give the Justices job security, salaries for life mean they don't have to be concerned about future job prospects, and more frequent hearings involve the people and the Senate in the judicial selection process more fully (with meaningful changes, it is hoped, to the current broken confirmation process). Our democratic system of government will be considerably improved once life tenure for our highest Court is abolished.

THE COURT SHOULD DEFER TO THE DECISIONS OF OTHER POLITICAL OFFICIALS UNLESS THERE IS AN "IRRECONCILABLE VARIANCE" BETWEEN THE CONSTITUTION AND THE CHALLENGED DECISION

Humility is the most difficult virtue. . . . By and large, we are not trained economists, educators, social workers or criminologists. . . . The authority of courts to enforce the [Constitution]

can be stretched too thin. One sure way to husband that authority is to invoke it only where necessary.

—Justice Sandra Day O'Connor

Starting with the Founding Fathers, and throughout American history, there have been repeated calls by important political figures
and legal scholars urging the Supreme Court to strongly defer to the
elected branches and the states when exercising the power of judicial
review. One of the premises supporting these repeated calls is that
when the people disagree over fundamental policy questions such as
abortion, affirmative action, the separation of church and state, and
gun control, there is no persuasive justification for delegating the
final say over those questions to nine Supreme Court Justices who the
American people do not hire and cannot fire.

The first person to advocate this limited role for the Supreme
Court was the Founding Father who wrote most eloquently about judicial review and how the Justices should perform their duties under
the new Constitution. In the *Federalist Papers,* which were a series
of essays designed to persuade the people of New York to ratify the
new Constitution, Alexander Hamilton justified the power of judicial review and limited its scope. In terms of justification, he wrote
that the "interpretation of the laws is the proper and peculiar province of the courts," and therefore it made sense to give judges the
power to "ascertain" the meaning of both the Constitution, which
is the paramount supreme law, and "any particular act proceeding
from the legislative body."[23] If the Constitution was designed to limit
government, it made sense "to suppose that the courts were designed
to be an intermediate body between the people and the legislature
in order, among other things, to keep the latter within the limits assigned to their authority."[24] This rationale for judicial review, first
articulated by Alexander Hamilton, would later be explicitly adopted by Chief Justice Marshall in the landmark case of *Marbury v.
Madison.*[25]

Although Hamilton anticipated the doctrine of judicial review,
he likely had in mind a quite different form of it than the Supreme
Court has exercised throughout history. Hamilton wrote that this
great power should be used by the Court only when there was an "irreconcilable variance" between an act of the elected branches and the
clear language of the Constitution.[26] Without such an "irreconcilable
variance," there would be no justification for Supreme Court Justices

to substitute their value judgments for those of more accountable governmental officials.

As this book has demonstrated, however, the Supreme Court has repeatedly overturned the policy decisions of the elected branches and the states when constitutional text and history were vague, and no reasonable person could argue that the decision was at an "irreconcilable variance" with the Constitution. The Court has gone far beyond the limited delegation of powers that Hamilton and the other Founding Fathers believed the Court would exercise.

Almost a century after Alexander Hamilton articulated the "irreconcilable variance" standard for judicial review, a prominent legal scholar echoed and justified Hamilton's position in what has become one of the most famous law review articles ever written on that subject. In 1893, James Bradley Thayer published an essay in the *Harvard Law Review* called "The Origin and Scope of the American Doctrine of Constitutional Law."[27] In this essay, Thayer forcefully argued that a court should only strike down a piece of legislation "when those who have the right to make laws have not merely made a mistake, but have made a very clear one—so clear that it is not open to rational question."[28] Thayer urged this strong judicial deference to other political actors for numerous reasons but mostly because, when exercising judicial review, judges are reviewing the work of more accountable government officials who have a serious obligation to consider the constitutionality of the laws they are enacting. Their decisions should only be overturned when they make a clear error.[29] Thayer argued that elected officials would take their obligation to consider the constitutionality of their own actions far more seriously if judges played only a minor role in reviewing the validity of those decisions. The more seriously legislators took their obligations, the better our democracy would operate.

Although some modern scholars scoff at Thayer's possibly naïve suggestion that, without a strong Supreme Court, the Congress would take its obligation to enact constitutional laws more seriously, much in Thayer's proposal merits serious attention, as other scholars have indeed recognized. For example, Professor Jeremy Waldron has made the argument that, when the American people are divided over difficult questions involving disputed rights, the Supreme Court is a poor democratic choice for the resolution of those rights. This is so because the Court feels compelled to justify its decisions in the misleading language of text and prior cases and not by a straightforward discussion of the positives and negatives of recognizing the right at issue.[30] He gives as an example the abortion controversy and observes that the Court in *Roe* spends only a few paragraphs discussing the "importance of reproductive rights in relation to privacy," and the "other moral issues at stake."[31] The Court, concerned with its legitimacy, masks the real reasons for its decisions with the rhetoric of legal jargon, and the public is deprived of a full and serious discussion.

Professor Waldron compares how the Supreme Court has dealt with the abortion question to how England's Parliament wrestled with the issue in 1966. Debating whether or not to pass a bill liberalizing abortion, members of Parliament conducted a fierce debate. According to Waldron, they "debated the questions passionately, but also thoroughly and honorably, with attention to the rights, principles, and pragmatic issues on both sides. . . . One remarkable thing was that everyone who participated in the debate . . . paid tribute to the respectfulness with which their positions had been listened to and heard in that discussion. . . . How many times have we ever heard anybody . . . pay tribute to the attention and respectfulness with which her position was discussed . . . by the Supreme Court."[32]

When the Supreme Court debates abortion (or gun control, affirmative action, religious freedom, etc.), its deliberations are shielded from the public (except for the lucky few who get to attend the oral arguments), and its decisions are announced in the misleading language of constitutional interpretation. When legislatures debate these kinds of questions, more attention is paid to the real interests at stake and often the discussion is open for all to see and hear. There is also usually a legislative record for the public to review. This is not to suggest that the legislative process as it currently exists in this country handles these issues well, but at least the legislators can be voted out of office and public debate is supposed to influence their choices. Neither is true about the Supreme Court.

Although most Americans agree with broad ideals of personal liberty, freedom of speech, freedom of religion, and racial equality, there is substantial disagreement over concrete applications of those ideals to specific problems, as the debates over abortion, affirmative action, and prayer in school demonstrate. Why would we choose to place the ultimate resolution of those issues in the hands of unelected governmental officials who are supposed to address them, not head on, but indirectly through the lens of what a vague document written hundreds of years ago says (or doesn't say). Nowhere in the Court's abortion decisions, for example, is there a thorough examination of the issue itself—"on the ethical status of the fetus, on the predicament of pregnant women and the importance of their choices, their freedom, and their privacy, on the moral conflicts and difficulties that all this involves, and on the pragmatic issues about the role that law should play in regard to private moral questions. These are the issues that surely need to be debated when society is deciding about abortion rights, and those are the issues that are given most time in legislative debates and least time in the judicial deliberations."[33]

Waldron's modern writings support Thayer's argument that judges should only second guess the decisions of other officials (at least at the federal level) when those decisions clearly violated unambiguous constitutional text, a standard the Supreme Court has never consistently followed. Under that system, our democracy would function better and our public debates over disputed moral questions would be richer. Thayer's proposal, if implemented, would return most important constitutional questions (such as gun control, affirmative action, and abortion among others) back to the American people and their elected leaders, where those issues belong.

More than 100 years after Thayer wrote his article, two other modern nationally known constitutional law professors in addition to Waldron (and others), Mark Tushnet of Harvard Law School, and Larry Kramer, the dean of Stanford Law School, have urged that this country may be better off with either limited or possibly even no judicial review of the decisions of other governmental officials. In Professor Tushnet's book, aptly named *Taking the Constitution Away from the Courts*,[34] he argues that the American people and other political actors should play a stronger role in interpreting and understanding what the Constitution means, and that judicial supremacy negatively impacts how we think of and apply the Constitution. His call is for a more "populist" constitutional law where the "public should participate in shaping constitutional law more directly," and where the Constitution "give[s] all of us that opportunity."[35] He urges the people "to reclaim" the Constitution "from the courts."[36]

Similarly, Larry Kramer argues in his book *The People Themselves: Popular Constitutionalism and Judicial Review*[37] against the idea that the Supreme Court should have the final say on disputed questions of constitutional law. He believes that the Court's exercise of so much power is both antidemocratic and historically indefensible. For Kramer, "the very notion that the Court, composed of nine elite members of society each of whom are appointed for life and are not . . . usually subject to impeachment or other forms of accountability, should be able to have a final and unalterable say on matters of fundamental concern is not only an idea that we ought to eschew today—it is also a notion that many of our forefathers dismissed as patently inconsistent with a commitment to democratic governance."[38] Kramer agrees with Tushnet that the Supreme Court unnecessarily interferes with self-government and the ability of the people to decide for themselves how to best interpret the Constitution.

As these examples demonstrate, throughout American history numerous important legal scholars have argued that the Supreme Court's power of judicial review be severely limited. Many other voices could be added to the list, including Presidents Thomas Jefferson, Abraham Lincoln, and Franklin D. Roosevelt, all of whom made strong public statements about the dangers of allowing a strong Supreme Court to exercise too much authority over other governmental officials. Perhaps Lincoln said it best in an oft-quoted public statement concerning the infamous *Dred Scott* decision:

> I do not forget the position assumed by some, that constitutional questions are to be decided by the Supreme Court; nor do I deny that such decisions must be binding in any case, upon the parties to a suit; as to the object of that suit, while they are also entitled to very high respect and consideration in all parallel cases by all other departments of the government. . . . *At the same time, the candid citizen must confess that if the policy of the government upon vital questions, affecting the whole people, is to be irrevocably fixed by decisions of the Supreme Court, the instant they are made, in ordinary litigation between parties, in personal actions, the people will have ceased to be their own rulers, having to that extent practically resigned their government into the hands of that eminent tribunal* [emphasis added].[39]

When the Court overturns a decision of the elected branches or the states that clearly transcends an unambiguous constitutional directive, the Court is acting like a court interpreting prior law. But when the Court uses vague constitutional phrases such as *due process, equal protection,* or *establishment of religion* to set forth complex legal codes governing the decisions of elected political officials on issues like abortion, affirmative action, and the separation of church and state, it is not acting like a court of law but rather a policy-making veto council. And the decisions of this council aren't based on constitutional text and history but personal judgments, political beliefs, and subjective opinions, which is why the law on those and most other debated constitutional questions change as the values of the Justices change.

The cure for this problem of judicial overreaching is that the American people (and the Congress and the president) should insist that the Court not overturn the decisions of other governmental actors except in those rare circumstances when political officials violate clear constitutional limitations. Absent that circumstance, there is simply no democratically good reason to delegate to unelected, unaccountable judges the discretion to decide difficult policy questions not answered by the text or history of the Constitution.

It is often said in academic circles that any theory of how the Supreme Court should operate can only work if it would lead to the conclusion that *Brown v. Board of Education* was correctly decided. There is little dispute that the people who wrote and ratified the Fourteenth Amendment believed that school segregation did not violate the Fourteenth Amendment, and, thus the argument goes, a strong theory of judicial deference to elected representatives would lead to the conclusion that the Court's decision in *Brown* outlawing segregation must have been incorrect. And if that is where the theory leads, it cannot be right.

My model of deference can withstand this objection because *Brown* is one of the rare cases where the Court should have overturned the choices of other governmental officials. My theory of deference includes the fundamental notion that the Supreme Court, to act like a real court, must take the text of the Constitution as its primary guide and limitation. Although the phrase *equal protection of the laws* has many different and reasonable meanings across an infinite array of constitutional issues (where the Court should defer to other governmental officials), the deliberate segregation of the races in schools and other government facilities against the will of one of the races for the purpose of subjugating that race cannot be *equal* under the law in any meaningful sense of that term. If the drafters of the Fourteenth Amendment believed that segregation and inherently unequal schools did not violate the text of the Fourteenth Amendment, they should have used a word other than *equal*. In America in 1954, and probably even in 1896 when *Plessy* was decided, the word *equal* simply cannot mean that blacks can be treated differently under the law in a way that injures them solely because of the color of their skin. And, had the Court ruled the other way in *Plessy,* and had that been unacceptable to the people at the time, they could have amended the Constitution accordingly. But, for our purposes, it is enough to observe that the Court in *Brown* acted like a court when it gave the word *equal* its obvious meaning and ruled that officially required segregation of the races was inconsistent with our fundamental law.

What can the American people do as a practical matter to rein in the United States Supreme Court? One famous scholar has recently suggested that the president, the next time a law important to him is struck down by the Supreme Court, should "declare that there is no place in a modern democracy for unelected judges to veto twenty-first-century laws."[40] He would then "invite" those in favor of judicial supremacy to try and pass a constitutional amendment authorizing judicial review and thus "the American people would be given the choice denied them in 1803 [when Justice Marshall wrote *Marbury v. Madison*]."[41] Although this strategy, open defiance by the president, would be "risky," and "traditionalists would be outraged," it would also empower "the people to rule on judicial supremacy [and] set off a long, boisterous . . . debate on [the Court's] role in twenty-first-century American democracy."[42]

Another possibility would be a constitutional amendment requiring that two-thirds or three-fourths of the Court had to agree that a law was unconstitutional before the Court could strike it down, or an amendment specifically stating that the Court could only overturn laws upon a showing that the law is clearly inconsistent with unambiguous constitutional text. Any device that would make it more difficult for the Court to overturn the policy decisions of other governmental officials would be a move in the right direction.

One might argue that, if judicial review is so antidemocratic, why keep it at all? The answer is that we should keep it because the fundamental idea behind judicial review is a good one. We live in a country that believes in the rule of law and limited government. If a super majority of today's people wish to define themselves in an intergenerational manner by taking certain policy choices off the table for future governments, there is nothing wrong with authorizing judges to enforce those limitations. For example, if two-thirds of the American people today believe that abortion should either be (1) completely protected in the first trimester, or (2) outlawed altogether except in cases of rape or incest, or (3) in some other agreed-upon manner, and if the people feel so strongly about this question that they want it resolved definitively across the country, then saying so in a constitutional amendment and allowing judges to enforce that amendment would be consistent with how we want to govern ourselves. If, alternatively, the people do not wish to see this issue resolved on a national level, it should be decided by elected and accountable governmental officials answerable to the voters. What doesn't make sense, and what the Founding Fathers never anticipated, was that Supreme Court Justices would use vague phrases and amorphous concepts to decide fundamental policy questions never seriously considered by the people who drafted and ratified our Constitution or its 27 amendments.

CHAPTER 10

Conclusion

The words of the Constitution . . . are so unrestricted by their intrinsic meaning or by their history or by tradition or by prior decisions that they leave the individual Justice free, if indeed they do not compel him, to gather meaning not from reading the Constitution but from reading life.

—Justice Felix Frankfurter

The Supreme Court of the United States has been unduly interfering in public policy issues for far too long with serious consequences for our representative democracy. Perhaps the best and most effective way to demonstrate why dramatic reform is sorely needed is with the following hypothetical:

Imagine you are part of a special group of people charged with creating a brand-new government for a country called *New Nation*. At the first meeting, the group agrees on the following important premises:

1. New Nation will be a representative democracy with a written Constitution with both state and federal governments. At the federal level, there will be a Legislature that makes the laws, an Executive that enforces the laws, and Federal Judges who will resolve disputes when people feel they are injured by other people or the government.
2. The laws will be made and implemented by elected officials, but those officials will be limited by a set of fundamental

principles that we agree to ahead of time in our written Constitution.

3. We put into the Constitution a set of specific rules about how our Government will be structured. We do this to create intergenerational agreement over specific questions, and to relieve future generations from having to fight over these questions. For example, we decide the President has to be 35, and every State shall be represented equally in one house of the national legislature.

4. We realize we have to create a political institution, separate and independent from the elected branches, to enforce these ideals; otherwise the limitations won't work. We decide that, because the Constitution is our fundamental and paramount law, it makes sense to give judges the authority to enforce the Constitution's rules.

5. There is also a general consensus among our group that we value the broad ideals of (1) freedom of speech; (2) freedom of religion; (3) equality under the law for all people; 4) due process of law for all people; (4) voting rights for all people; and 5) a right to bear arms for the people.

Then we go home for the night and have a stiff drink.

On Day Two, we start having a debate about the specific applications of the broad principles we have been discussing. The following five questions are raised by people who have varying concerns about our new government:

1. Should the government be allowed to prohibit abortions, and, if so, under what circumstances?

2. Should the government be allowed to place religious symbols on governmental property to instill a sense of faith in our children and our people?

3. Should elected officials be allowed to use racial preferences to help historically disadvantaged minorities achieve equality under the law or would such preferences violate the rights of nonminorities to be treated equally?

4. Should the government be allowed to limit or even prohibit the private possession of firearms or would such laws violate the people's right to self-defense?

5. How far should the National Government be allowed to go in regulating local activities in light of our conflicting desires to maintain local autonomy on important policy questions but allow efficient regulation of our national economy?

Now assume that there is heated argument on each of these (and other difficult) questions with reasonable people disagreeing on how they should be resolved. After much discussion, we decide that we can't resolve these specific applications of the broad principles so we will defer their resolution to future generations. And then we authorize nine judges who work in our Capital and who almost never take part in public debate to have an ultimate veto power and regulatory authority on these and other difficult and contested questions. We give them the license to decide what *equal, due process,* and *commerce* means even though they may know little or nothing about race relations, medical ethics, or economics. These nine judges will resolve these issues for all of us unless a super majority of our elected officials at both the local and national levels are able to pass an amendment to our fundamental charter—something that will be almost impossible to do on the kinds of contested questions that divide us now and are likely to divide us in the future. These nine judges will sit on something called the Supreme Court and will announce their decisions in a specialized legal language, but in reality their subjective value preferences and personal life experiences will generate their results. They will dictate answers to questions involving individual rights, the structure of government, and educational, social, and economic policy; they will hold their offices for life; and they will all be lawyers.

This, of course, is not a hypothetical but how America's system actually operates. It is time to limit the power of the Supreme Court of the United States.

Epilogue

At the constitutional level where we work, 90 percent of any decision is emotional. The rational part of us supplies the reasons
for supporting our predilections.
—Justice William O. Douglas

As this book was being completed in the summer of 2011, the
most talked-about constitutional law issue facing the United
States was the constitutionality of President Obama's new health care
legislation. A key component of this law is the requirement that all
Americans, with narrow exceptions, either buy health insurance or
pay a penalty. The fundamental constitutional issue is whether Congress has the authority under the Commerce Clause to pass this "individual mandate" to buy health insurance.[1] Those in favor of the
constitutionality of the mandate argue that health insurance specifically, and medical care generally, are nationally important economic
issues requiring comprehensive legislation. They also argue that the
entire plan can't work unless people are required to buy health insurance before they get sick. Therefore, the argument goes, Congress's
power to regulate "commerce among the states," as well as Congress's authority to enact laws "necessary and proper" to the execution of its enumerated powers, provides Congress the authority to
pass this law.

Those who argue against the validity of the individual mandate
argue that never before in our nation's history has the federal government required private individuals to purchase a product they don't
want. Moreover, although the Commerce Clause allows Congress

to regulate *activities* that substantially affect commerce among the states, it does not give Congress the authority to regulate *inactivity* or the decision not to buy a product. If Congress can require people to buy health insurance, opponents argue, then there will be no limit on Congress's power, and we will no longer live in a country with a limited national government.

The debate over the individual mandate, like the question whether Congress has the constitutional power to issue paper money, where this book started, raises fundamental concerns about the nature and scope of the national government and its relationship to the states and the American people. And as was the case with the paper money controversy, the final say over the validity of the individual mandate will likely be determined by the Supreme Court of the United States.

On June 29, 2011, the Sixth Circuit United States Court of Appeals issued a decision in one of the cases currently pending on this issue.[2] There were three judges on the panel and each wrote a separate opinion. One judge thought that the Commerce Clause issue was relatively clear and voted to uphold the mandate, one judge thought that the Commerce Clause issue was close and also voted (reluctantly it appeared) to uphold the mandate, and one judge thought the Commerce Clause issue was relatively clear but voted to invalidate the mandate. All three judges wrote long, thoughtful opinions wrestling with the same precedents, text, and history, but all three came up with different perspectives on the constitutional validity of the individual mandate. On August 12, 2011, the Eleventh Circuit United States Court of Appeals struck down the mandate as unconstitutional by a vote of 2–1.[3] The majority and dissenting opinions totaled more than 200 pages.

If and when the Court eventually resolves this question, the decision will almost certainly reflect the three major themes of this book. First, the preexisting law of the Commerce Clause cannot definitively resolve whether the individual mandate is constitutional. All of the court of appeals opinions on the question so far have correctly summarized the prior law and set forth rational accounts of how this issue should be decided. There is simply no right or wrong legal answer.

Second, the Justices will write their opinions in the misleading language of text, history, and prior case law even though it is likely that other political, economic, and personal value judgments will play a major role in dictating the result. These nonlegal considerations will be hidden from the American people.

Third, the resolution of this issue in the Supreme Court will depend much more on who is on the Court when the issue is decided than the substance of preexisting law. If there were five members of the Court sharing Justice Thomas's strong pro–states rights views, for example, the mandate would almost certainly be invalidated, but if there were five Justices on the Court with Justice Breyer's procongressional power views, the mandate would likely be upheld. As of this writing, the conventional wisdom is that the four conservatives will overturn the mandate, the four moderates will uphold it, and the decision will come down to the Court's current swing vote, Justice Kennedy. Whether or not that wisdom is correct, the important point is that, when predicting how the Court will resolve this question, it is much more important to count heads than to review the prior law of the Commerce Clause.

President Obama's health care legislation was debated in Congress for months and discussed in town hall meetings and other political venues throughout the United States. Although our political process is far from perfect, the people felt strongly about this issue, they made their feelings known to their elected representatives, and those representatives fought and negotiated with the president of the United States. Whether or not the individual mandate is good or bad for our country is an issue well beyond my expertise. What I do know, however, is that, in the end, the decision whether or not the individual mandate is constitutional or not is much more of a public policy question than a legal question. The Justices who eventually decide this issue will resolve it, not like judges interpreting prior law, but as members of an ultimate veto council with the authority to vote thumbs up or thumbs down on this important piece of legislation. Moreover, they will not be transparent about the real reasons for their votes. And, even worse, we didn't vote for these council members, we can't fire them, and they hold their offices for life.

In 1935, the Supreme Court was striking down important New Deal legislation favored by the Congress and the president. Frustrated by the Court's interference with such important policy initiatives, a writer at the time observed:

To those interested in the future of American democracy, this suggests the question: Why should the Supreme Court have such far-reaching and often uncontrollable power over the great social and economic problems of the day? Other nations . . . have been able to progress and safeguard their liberties without entrusting a court of nine elderly men with the power to nullify the acts of a national legislature elected by, and directly responsible to, the people. . . . Some of the most profound authorities on our constitutional history have suggested that the American experiment in democracy would be more successful in the future if the control by the Supreme Court over the direction of our national development were checked. We can here merely raise this question, which is made all the more urgent by the present critical need for a more just and flexible functioning of our democratic institutions.[4]

The Supreme Court should not overturn the new health care law (or for that matter abortion laws, affirmative action laws, gun control laws, or any other law) unless the law is completely at odds with clear constitutional text. "We the People" have only authorized the Justices to enforce the legal principles contained in the Constitution, not to enforce their personal value judgments on health care or other important disputed questions. We should insist that the Justices act like judges interpreting prior law, not politicians who have the power to override the policy decisions of the elected branches, the states, and the American people.

Notes

Prologue

1. Joseph M. Cormack, *The Legal Tender Cases—A Drama of American Legal and Financial History*, 16 VA. L. REV. 132, 134 (1929).

2. Ibid., 132.

3. U.S. CONST. art. I, § 8.

4. Ibid.

5. *Hepburn v. Griswold*, 75 U.S. (8 Wall.) 603 (1870); PAUL BREST ET AL., PROCESSES OF CONSTITUTIONAL DECISION MAKING: CASES AND MATERIALS 232–33 (4th ed. 2000).

6. *Hepburn*, 75 U.S. (8 Wall.) at 603.

7. Ibid.

8. Cormack, *The Legal Tender Cases*, 141 (quoting *Hepburn*, 75 U.S. (8 Wall.) at 633).

9. BREST ET AL., PROCESSES OF CONSTITUTIONAL DECISION MAKING, 235.

10. Cormack, *The Legal Tender Cases*, 142.

11. Sidney Ratner, *Was the Supreme Court Packed by President Grant?*, 50 POL. SCI. Q. 343, 352 (1935).

12. Cormack, *The Legal Tender Cases*, 140. The author of this comment was writing in 1929.

13. 79 U.S. (12 Wall.) 457 (1871).

14. Ibid.

15. Because the decision in *Knox* was based to some degree on the necessities of war, 10 years later the Court held by a vote of 8–1 that Congress could issue legal tender paper in times of war or peace. *See* Juilliard v. Greenman (The Legal Tender Cases), 110 U.S. 421 (1884).

16. Ratner, *Was the Supreme Court Packed,* at 347–48.

17. Ibid.

18. Cormack, *The Legal Tender Cases,* 144.

19. James MacGregor Burns, Packing the Court 95–96 (2009).

Chapter 1

1. H. Jefferson Powell, Constitutional Conscience 90 (2008).

2. Richard A. Posner, *Forward: A Political Court,* 119 Harv. L. Rev. 32, 40–41 (2005).

Chapter 2

1. Joseph J. Ellis, American Sphinx: The Character of Thomas Jefferson 207–08 (1998).

2. Ibid.

3. Michael W. McConnell, *The Story of* Marbury v. Madison: *Making Defeat Look like Victory, in* Constitutional Law Stories 13, 16 (Michael C. Dorf ed., 2d ed. 2009).

4. Ibid., 17.

5. Eric J. Segall, *Why I Still Teach* Marbury *(and So Should You): A Response to Professor Levinson,* 6 U. Pa. J. Const. L. 573, 577–78 (2004).

6. McConnell, *The Story of* Marbury v. Madison, 27.

7. Ibid.

8. Ibid.

9. Ibid., 28.

10. 14 U.S. (1 Wheat.) 304 (1816).

11. U.S. Const. art. III; *Marbury,* 5 U.S. (1 Cranch), 177.

12. U.S. Const. art. III, § 2.

13. Judiciary Act of 1789, ch. 20, § 13, 1 Stat. 73, 81 (1789) (codified as amended at 28 U.S.C. § 1651 (2006)).

14. Jeffrey A. Segal & Harold J. Spaeth, The Supreme Court and the Attitudinal Model Revisited 23 (2002).

15. *Marbury,* 5 U.S. (1 Cranch), 173–76.

16. Ibid., 179 (quoting U.S. Const. art. III, § 3).

17. Ibid.

18. Ibid., 179–80.

19. *See* Citizens United v. FEC, 130 S.Ct. 876 (2010) (campaign finance); Grutter v. Bollinger, 539 U.S. 306 (2003) (affirmative action); Gratz v. Bollinger, 539 U.S. 244 (2003) (affirmative action); Planned Parenthood of Se. Pa. v. Casey, 505 U.S. 833 (1992) (abortion).

Chapter 3

1. Jed Handelsman Shugerman, Marbury *and Judicial Deference: The Shadow of* Whittington v. Polk *and the Maryland Judiciary Battle,* 5 U. PA. J. CONST. L. 58, 61 n.10 (2002).

2. Dred Scott v. Sandford, 60 U.S. (19 How.) 393 (1857), *superseded by constitutional amendment,* U.S. CONST. amend. XIV.

3. GEOFFREY R. STONE ET AL., CONSTITUTIONAL LAW 422 (4th ed. 2001).

4. Ibid.

5. 41 U.S. 539, 625–26 (1842).

6. Ibid., 625.

7. STONE ET AL., CONSTITUTIONAL LAW, 426.

8. Dred Scott v. Sandford, 60 U.S. (19 How.) 393, 431 (1857), *superseded by constitutional amendment,* U.S. CONST. amend. XIV.

9. Ibid.

10. Ibid., 427.

11. Ibid., 455.

12. Ibid., 449–55.

13. BURNS, PACKING THE COURT, 59.

14. Ibid.

15. U.S. CONST. art. IV.

16. Northwest Ordinance, ch. 8, 1 Stat. 50, 53 n.a (1789).

17. BURNS, PACKING THE COURT, 61.

18. Ibid., 60–61.

19. U.S. CONST. amend. XIII; U.S. CONST. amend. XIV; U.S. CONST. amend. XV.

20. U.S. CONST. amend XIV, § 5.

21. LAURENCE H. TRIBE, AMERICAN CONSTITUTIONAL LAW 550 (2d ed. 1998).

22. *The Slaughter-House Cases,* 83 U.S. (1 Wall.) 36 (1872).

23. Ibid., 60.

24. Ibid., 66.

25. *The Slaughter-House Cases,* 83 U.S. (16 Wall.) at 79; TRIBE, AMERICAN CONSTITUTIONAL LAW, 552.

26. *The Slaughter-House Cases,* 83 U.S. (16 Wall.) at 75.

27. Ibid., 89 (Field, J., dissenting).

28. STONE ET AL., CONSTITUTIONAL LAW, 699 (quoting ROBERT J. KACZOROWSKI, THE POLITICS OF JUDICIAL INTERPRETATION: THE FEDERAL COURTS, DEPARTMENT OF JUSTICE, AND CIVIL RIGHTS, 1866–75, 154–55, 161 (1985)).

29. TRIBE, AMERICAN CONSTITUTIONAL LAW, 1693.

30. *The Civil Rights Cases,* 109 U.S. 3 (1883).

31. TRIBE, AMERICAN CONSTITUTIONAL LAW , 1693.

32. *The Civil Rights Cases,* 109 U.S. at 17; STONE ET AL., CONSTITU-TIONAL LAW, 435.

33. *The Civil Rights Cases,* 109 U.S. at 11.

34. Ibid., 20.

35. Ibid., 24.

36. Of course, almost 100 years later, the Court did allow Congress to regulate such behavior under the Commerce Clause. *See* Katzenbach v. McClung, 379 U.S. 294 (1964).

37. *The Civil Rights Cases,* 109 U.S. at 27 (Harlan, J., dissenting).

38. Ibid., 48.

39. Ibid., 58–59.

40. BURNS, PACKING THE COURT, 89.

41. Thomas Zimmerman, "Plessy v. Ferguson," 1890s America: A Chronology, http://www.bgsu.edu/departments/acs/1890s/plessy/plessy.html (accessed November 7, 2011).

42. Ibid.

43. Plessy v. Ferguson, 163 U.S. 537 (1896), *overruled by* Brown v. Bd. of Educ., 347 U.S. 483 (1954).

44. Ibid., 540.

45. Ibid., 541, referring to *Plessy v. Ferguson* at 551, 544.

46. *Plessy,* 163 U.S. at 551.

47. *Plessy,* 163 U.S. at 552.

48. *Plessy,* 163 U.S. at 559 (Harlan, J., dissenting).

Chapter 4

1. WILLIAM B. LOCKHART ET AL., CONSTITUTIONAL LAW: CASES–COMMENTS–QUESTIONS 67–69 (8th ed. 1996).

2. ALBERT J. BEVERIDGE, THE LIFE OF JOHN MARSHALL, VOL. I (1916), *reprinted in* LOCKHART ET AL., CONSTITUTIONAL LAW, 67.

3. 22 U.S. (9 Wheat.) 1 (1824).

4. KENNETH PANZA, ODGEN VS GIBBONS (1824): BREAKING THE FULTON-LIVINGSTON MONOPOLY, STEAMBOATS OF THE HUDSON RIVER THE EARLY YEARS: 1807–1824, http://www.ulster.net/~hrmm/steamboats/monopoly.html (accessed November 7, 2011).

5. *Gibbons,* 22 U.S. (9 Wheat.) at 1, 193–94.

6. Ibid., 195.

7. LOCKHART ET AL., CONSTITUTIONAL LAW, 72.

8. Ibid.

9. Ibid.

10. U.S. CONST. amend. IX; U.S. CONST. amend. X.

11. 198 U.S. 45 (1905).

12. Ibid., 46.

13. BURNS, PACKING THE COURT, 119. For a wonderful discussion of *Lochner,* see DAVID BERNSTEIN, REHABILITATING LOCHNER (2010).

14. BERNSTEIN, REHABILITATING LOCHNER, 27.

15. *Lochner,* 198 U.S. at 53.

16. Ibid., 57.

17. Ibid., 60.

18. Ibid., 61.

19. Ibid., 70–73.

20. Ibid., 65.

21. LOUIS FISHER & NEAL DEVINS, POLITICAL DYNAMICS OF CONSTITUTIONAL LAW 78 (1st ed. 1992).

22. U.S. CONST. art. I, § 8.

23. KATHLEEN M. SULLIVAN & GERALD GUNTHER, CONSTITUTIONAL LAW 89 (16th ed. 2007).

24. Ibid.

25. 247 U.S. 251 (1918), *overruled by* United States v. Darby, 312 U.S. 100 (1941).

26. Ibid., 272.

27. Ibid., 277.

28. *See* Gibbons v. Ogden, 22 U.S. (9 Wheat.) 1 (1824).

29. *Hammer,* 247 U.S. at 276.

30. Ibid., 273.

31. Ibid., 276.

32. FISHER & DEVINS, POLITICAL DYNAMICS, 80.

33. *Hammer,* 247 U.S. at 277–80.

34. SULLIVAN & GUNTHER, CONSTITUTIONAL LAW, 373.

35. Ibid.

36. President Franklin D. Roosevelt, Fireside Chat on Reorganization of the Judiciary (Mar. 9, 1937), *in* RUSSELL D. BUHITE & DAVID W. LEVY, FDR's FIRESIDE CHATS 84 (1992).

37. The entire court-packing controversy is brilliantly recounted in JEFF SHESOL, SUPREME POWER: FRANKLIN ROOSEVELT VS. THE SUPREME COURT (2010).

38. Adkins v. Children's Hosp., 261 U.S. 525 (1923), *overruled by* W. Coast Hotel Co. v. Parrish, 300 U.S. 379 (1937).

39. *W. Coast Hotel,* 300 U.S. at 399.

40. 301 U.S. 1 (1937).

41. Ibid., 41–42.

42. *Wickard v. Filburn,* 317 U.S. 111 (1942).

43. Alphabetical List of Decisions, Common Sense Americanism, http://www.csamerican.com/sc.asp?r=317+U.S.+111 (accessed November 7, 2011).

44. Ibid.

45. Jim Chen, *The Story of* Wickard v. Filburn, *in* CONSTITUTIONAL LAW STORIES 69, 83 (Michael C. Dorf ed., 2d ed. 2009).

46. Alphabetical List of Decisions, Common Sense Americanism.

47. Ibid.

48. *Wickard v. Filburn,* 317 U.S. 111, 125 (1942).

49. Ibid., 128.

50. Ibid., 128–29.

51. 514 U.S. 549 (1995).

52. Ibid., 564.

53. Ibid., 624.

54. Ibid., 564–68.

55. Ibid., 624.

56. Ibid., 561.

57. 529 U.S. 598 (2000).

58. Ibid., 632.

59. Ibid., 630.

60. Violence Against Women Act of 1994, 42 U.S.C. § 13981 (2006), *invalidated by Morrison,* 529 U.S. 598.

61. The Court found Congress lacked power under both the Commerce Clause and the Fourteenth Amendment, but the discussion here is limited to the Commerce Clause.

62. *Morrison,* 529 U.S. at 613.

63. Ibid., 614.

64. Ibid., 653.

65. Ibid., 654.

66. Ibid.

67. Ibid., 637.

68. 545 U.S. 1 (2005).

69. Ibid., 17.

70. Ibid., 17 (quoting *Wickard v. Filburn,* 317 U.S. 111, 125 (1942)).

71. Ibid., 57–58.

72. Ibid., 49.

73. *Compare* Gonzales v. Raich, 545 U.S. 1, 23 (2005), *with* ibid., 43–45 (O'Connor, J., dissenting).

74. *United States v. Morrison,* 529 U.S. 598, 660 (2000) (Breyer, J., dissenting).

Chapter 5

1. BARRY FRIEDMAN, THE WILL OF THE PEOPLE 296 (2009); Lucinda M. Finley, *Contested Ground: The Story of Roe v. Wade and Its Impact on American Society, in* CONSTITUTIONAL LAW STORIES 233, 336 (Michael C. Dorf ed., 2d ed. 2009).

2. Finley, *Contested Ground,* 336.

3. Friedman, Will of the People, 297.

4. Finley, *Contested Ground,* 336.

5. Ibid.

6. Ibid.

7. Reva B. Seigel, *The New Politics of Abortion: An Equality Analysis of Women-Protective Abortion Restrictions,* 2007 U. Ill. L. Rev. 991, 1000–01.

8. Finley, *Contested Ground,* 337.

9. Ibid.

10. Ibid.

11. Ibid., 338.

12. Ibid., 339.

13. Ibid.

14. Ibid.

15. Friedman, Will of the People, 296.

16. Ibid.

17. Ibid., 297.

18. Ibid., 297–98.

19. Ibid., 296.

20. Finley, *Contested Ground,* 355–56.

21. Ibid., 333–82.

22. *Roe v. Wade,* 410 U.S. 113, 116 (1973).

23. Ibid., 116–17.

24. Ibid., 148–51.

25. Ibid., 152.

26. Ibid.

27. Ibid., 153.

28. *See* ibid.

29. Ibid., 159.

30. Ibid., 160–63.

31. Ibid., 162.

32. Ibid., 163–64.

33. Ibid., 173–74.

34. Ibid., 174.

35. *Doe v. Bolton,* 410 U.S. 179, 222.

36. Ibid., 222–23.

37. For a good list of critical sources, *see* http://www.endroe.org/annbio.aspx.

38. *See* John Hart Ely, *The Wages of Crying Wolf: A Comment on* Roe v. Wade, 82 Yale L.J. 920 (1973).

39. 381 U.S. 479 (1965).

40. David Kairys, With Liberty and Justice for Some: A Critique of the Conservative Supreme Court 160–61 (1993).

41. Ibid.

42. For an excellent summary of this time period, see FRIEDMAN, WILL OF THE PEOPLE, 304–07.

43. Ibid., 305–06.

44. William N. Eskridge Jr., *Pluralism and Distrust: How Courts Can Support Democracy by Lowering the Stakes of Politics,* 114 YALE L.J. 1279, 1312 (2005).

45. Cass R. Sunstein, *Three Civil Rights Fallacies,* 79 CALIF. L. REV. 751, 766 (1991).

46. Siegel, *New Politics of Abortion,* 1003–05.

47. FRIEDMAN, WILL OF THE PEOPLE, 302.

48. Ibid., 302–03.

49. Ibid., 303 (citing Thomas C. Grey, *Do We Have an Unwritten Constitution?,* 27 STAN. L. REV. 703 (1975)).

50. Ibid., 303 (citing Grey, *Unwritten Constitution,* at 711–13).

51. Ibid., 303 (citing Paul Brest, *The Misconceived Quest for the Original Understanding,* 60 B.U. L. REV. 204, 222–24 (1980)).

52. Ibid., 303.

53. Ibid.

54. Ibid. (citing Gary McDowell, *Politics of Original Intention,* in Michael J. Perry, *"Interpreting" the Constitution, in* THE CONSTITUTION, THE COURTS, AND THE QUEST FOR JUSTICE 70 (Robert A. Goldwin and William A. Schambra, eds. 1989).

55. FISHER & DEVINS, POLITICAL DYNAMICS, 212.

56. Ibid., 216.

57. Ibid., 215.

58. Ibid., 218.

59. Ibid.

60. 448 U.S. 297 (1980).

61. Ibid., 316–17.

62. Ibid., 334.

63. FRIEDMAN, WILL OF THE PEOPLE, 298.

64. FISHER & DEVINS, POLITICAL DYNAMICS, 229.

65. Ibid., 221–22; FREIDMAN, WILL OF THE PEOPLE, 313–15.

66. FRIEDMAN, WILL OF THE PEOPLE, 298.

67. 505 U.S. 833 (1992).

68. Ibid., 843–44.

69. *See* Planned Parenthood of Se. Pa. v. Casey, 947 F.2d 682 (3d Cir. 1991), *aff'd in part and rev'd in part,* 505 U.S. 833 (1992); EDWARD LAZARUS, CLOSED CHAMBERS 459–60 (1998).

70. LAZARUS, CLOSED CHAMBERS, 459–60.

71. Ibid., 465 (emphasis added).

72. *Webster v. Reprod. Health Servs.,* 492 U.S. 490, 538 (1989) (Blackmun, J., dissenting).

73. Lazarus, Closed Chambers, 482.

74. *Planned Parenthood of Se. Pa. v. Casey,* 505 U.S. 833, 887 (1992).

75. Ibid., 985–92.

76. For further discussion, see Eric J. Segall, *Justice O'Connor and the Rule of Law,* 17 U. Fla. J.L. & Pub. Pol'y 107 (2006).

77. 530 U.S. 914 (2000).

78. Julie Rovner, *"Partial-Birth Abortion": Separating Fact from Spin,* npr (Feb. 21, 2006), http://www.npr.org/templates/story/story.php?storyId=5168163 (accessed Nov. 7, 2011).

79. Ibid.

80. *See* ibid.

81. *Stenberg,* 530 U.S. at 973 (Kennedy, J., dissenting).

82. *Stenberg,* 530 U.S. 914 (2000).

83. Ibid., 920–21.

84. Ibid., 928–30.

85. Ibid.

86. Ibid., 954–55 (Scalia, J., dissenting) (emphasis added).

87. Ibid., 979 (Kennedy, J., dissenting).

88. 18 U.S.C. § 1531(b)(1)(A) (2006).

89. 550 U.S. 124 (2007).

90. Ibid.

91. *Gonzales,* 550 U.S. at 157.

92. Ibid., 159–60 (emphasis added) (citations omitted).

93. Ibid., 184–86 (Ginsburg, J., dissenting).

94. *Gonzales,* 550 U.S. at 161 (quoting *Ayotte v. Planned Parenthood of N. New England,* 546 U.S. 320 (2006)).

95. Ibid.

96. Ibid.

97. *See* Priscilla J. Smith, *Is the Glass Half-Full?:* Gonzales v. Carhart *and the Future of Abortion Jurisprudence,* Harv. L. & Pol'y Rev. (Apr. 9, 2008), http://hlpronline.com/wordpress/wp-content/uploads/2009/12/Smith_HLPR.pdf (accessed Nov. 7, 2011); Dahlia Lithwick, *Father Knows Best,* Slate (Apr. 18, 2007, 7:21 PM), http://www.slate.com/id/2164512 (accessed Nov. 7, 2011).

Chapter 6

1. 554 U.S. 570 (2008).

2. *McDonald v. City of Chi.,* 130 S. Ct. 3020 (2010).

3. *See* Jonathan Hamilton and David Burch, *Gun Ownership—It's the Law in Kennesaw,* Rense.com, (Mar. 14, 2001) http://www.rense.com/general9/gunlaw.htm (accessed Nov. 7, 2011).

4. For these and other interesting gun statistics, see James D. Agresti & Reid K. Smith, *Gun Control Facts,* JustFacts.com, http://www.justfacts.com/guncontrol.asp (accessed Nov. 7, 2011).

5. 307 U.S. 174 (1939).

6. Ibid., 175; Nelson Lund, Heller *and Second Amendment Precedent,* 13 Lewis & Clark L. Rev. 335, 337 (2009).

7. *Miller,* 307 U.S. at 178.

8. Lund, *Second Amendment Precedent,* 337.

9. Ibid., 338.

10. *Miller,* 307 U.S. at 178.

11. Ibid., 183.

12. William G. Merkel, The District of Columbia v. Heller *and Antonin Scalia's Perverse Sense of Originalism,* 13 Lewis & Clark L. Rev. 349, 350 n.3 (2009).

13. Jamal Greene, Heller *High Water? The Future of Originalism,* 3 Harv. L. & Pol'y Rev. 325, 334 (2009).

14. Ibid.

15. Ibid.

16. J. Harvie Wilkinson III, *Of Guns, Abortions, and the Unraveling Rule of Law,* 95 Va. L. Rev. 253, 304 (2009).

17. Ibid., 289–301.

18. *District of Columbia v. Heller,* 554 U.S. 570, 577 (2008).

19. Ibid.

20. Ibid., 573–636.

21. Ibid.

22. Ibid., 576–79.

23. Ibid., 651 (Stevens, J., dissenting).

24. Ibid.

25. Ibid.

26. Merkel, *Scalia's Perverse Sense of Originalism,* 352.

27. Ibid.

28. Ibid., 352–59; *see also* William G. Merkel, Heller *as Hubris, and How* McDonald v. City of Chicago *May Well Change the Constitutional World as We Know It,* 50 Santa Clara L. Rev. 1221, 1221–31 (2010).

29. *See* Robert H. Churchill, *Gun Regulation, the Police Power, and the Right to Keep Arms in Early America: The Legal Context of the Second Amendment,* 25 Law & Hist. Rev. 139 (2007).

30. *See* Eugene Volokh, *Implementing the Right to Keep and Bear Arms for Self-Defense: An Analytical Framework and a Research Agenda,* 56 UCLA L. Rev. 1443 (2009); *see also* Nelson Lund, *The Past and Future of the Individual's Right to Arms,* 31 Ga. L. Rev. 1 (1996).

31. *Heller,* 554 U.S. at 628–30.

32. Ibid., 694–95 (Breyer, J., dissenting).

33. Ibid., 696–99.

34. Ibid., 681–722.

35. Ibid., 634 (majority opinion).

36. Ibid., 721 (Breyer, J., dissenting).

37. Ibid., 681–722.

38. Ibid., 719–22.

39. Ibid., 579–83 (majority opinion).

40. *See* Merkel, Heller *as Hubris,* 1224.

41. Dawn E. Johnson, *The Creation of Fetal Rights: Conflicts with Women's Constitutional Rights to Liberty, Privacy, and Equal Protection,* 95 Yale L.J. 599 (1986).

42. Wilkinson, *Of Guns, Abortions and the Unraveling Rule of Law,* 254.

43. Ibid.

44. *Planned Parenthood of Se. Pa. v. Casey,* 505 U.S. 833, 1000–01 (1992).

Chapter 7

1. *See* Gerald Rosenberg, The Hollow Hope: Can Courts Bring About Social Change? 39–157 (2008).

2. Ibid., 47–48.

3. *See* Ronald Caldwell Jr., *The Erosion of Affirmative Action and Its Consequences for the Black-White Educational Attainment Gap,* 57 U. Kan. L. Rev. 813, 813 (2009).

4. Ibid.

5. Vernellia R. Randall, "For Whites Only—A Long History of Affirmative Action," The University of Dayton, (Dec. 10, 2010) http://academic.udayton.edu/race/04needs/affirm22.htm (accessed Nov. 7, 2011); *see also* Bridgette Baldwin, *Stratification of the Welfare Poor: Intersections of Gender, Race, & Worthiness in Poverty Discourse and Policy,* 6 Modern Am. 4, 7 (2010).

6. Randall, "For Whites Only."

7. Ibid.

8. Ibid.

9. Ibid.

10. Ibid.

11. Ibid.

12. *See* Corey A. Ciocchetti & John Holcomb, *The Frontier of Affirmative Action: Employment Preferences & Diversity in the Private Workplace,* 12 U. Pa. J. Bus. L. 283, 289–90 (2010); Michael P. Pohorylo, *The Role of Parents Involved in the College Admissions Process,* 42 Conn. L. Rev. 693, 698–99 (2009).

13. Ciocchetti & Holcomb, *The Frontier of Affirmative Action,* 289–90; Pohorylo, *The Role of Parents,* 698.

14. *See* Ciocchetti & Holcomb, *The Frontier of Affirmative Action,* 291.

15. Pohorylo, *The Role of Parents,* 699.

16. Ciocchetti & Holcomb, *The Frontier of Affirmative Action,* 293.

17. Ibid.

18. *See* Clinton White House Staff, "Affirmative Action: History and Rationale," ALMANAC OF POLICY ISSUES (Jul. 19, 1995), http://www.policyalmanac.org/culture/archive/affirmative_action_history.shtml (accessed Nov. 7, 2011).

19. Ibid.

20. *See* United States History, "Affirmative Action," www.u-s-history.compages/h1970.html (accessed Feb. 19, 2011).

21. Pohorylo, *The Role of Parents,* 700.

22. *Regents of the Univ. of Cal. v. Bakke,* 438 U.S. 265, 272 (1978).

23. *See* Ibid., 272.

24. *See* Ibid., 276.

25. *See* Ibid., 277.

26. Ibid., 269–72.

27. Ibid., 306.

28. Ibid., 387.

29. Ibid., 307.

30. Ibid., 312.

31. Ibid., 313–14.

32. Ibid., 315.

33. Ibid., 323–24.

34. Ibid., 395–96.

35. Ibid., 402.

36. Ibid., 407.

37. Ibid., 379.

38. SAMUEL LEITER & WILLIAM M. LEITER, AFFIRMATIVE ACTION IN ANTIDISCRIMINATION LAW AND POLICY 139 (2002); Stanley Kurtz, *Affirmative Signs Preferences Won't Be on Campus Forever,* OLD NATIONAL REVIEW (Nov. 17, 2003), http://old.nationalreview.com/kurtz/kurtz200311170907.asp (accessed Nov. 7, 2011).

39. *Fulliove v. Klutznick,* 448 U.S. 448, 453 (1980).

40. Ibid., 477–78.

41. *City of Richmond v. J.A. Croson Co.,* 488 U.S. 469 (1989).

42. Ibid., 490–91.

43. Ibid., 560.

44. *Metro Broad. Inc. v. FCC,* 497 U.S. 547 (1990).

45. *See* Ibid., 564.

46. *Adarand Constructors, Inc. v. Peña,* 515 U.S. 200 (1995).

47. Ibid., 204.

48. Ibid.
49. Eric J. Segall, *Reconceptualizing the Judicial Activism Debate as Judicial Responsibility: A Tale of Two Justice Kennedys*, 41 ARIZ. ST. L.J. 709, 730–32 (2009).
50. *Adarand*, 515 U.S. at 224–26.
51. *Metro Broad. Inc. v. FCC*, 497 U.S. 547 (1990).
52. Segall, *Reconceptualizing the Judicial Activism Debate*, 730–32 (citing Neil Devins, Adarand Constructors, Inc. v. Pena *and the Continuing Irrelevance of the Supreme Court's Affirmative Action Decision*, 37 WM. & MARY L. REV. 673, 706 (1996)).
53. Segall, *Reconceptualizing the Judicial Activism Debate*, 731.
54. *Grutter v. Bollinger*, 539 U.S. 306 (2003).
55. *Gratz v. Bollinger*, 539 U.S. 244 (2003).
56. *Grutter*, 539 U.S. at 316 (citing *Regents of Univ. of Cal. v. Bakke*, 438 U.S. 265 (1978)).
57. Ibid.
58. *Gratz*, 539 U.S. at 277–79.
59. Ibid., 278.
60. Ibid.
61. *Grutter*, 539 U.S. at 348.
62. *Gratz*, 539 U.S. at 294–95; *Grutter*, 539 U.S. at 334.
63. *Gratz*, 539 U.S. at 282.
64. *See* ibid.
65. Ibid., 259.
66. Ibid., 281.
67. *Grutter*, 539 U.S. at 384.
68. Ibid., 343.
69. *Parents Involved in Cmty. Sch. v. Seattle Sch. Dist. No. 1*, 551 U.S. 701 (2007).
70. Ibid., 807–12 (Breyer, J., dissenting).
71. Ibid., 808.
72. Ibid., 811.
73. *See* Washington v. Seattle School Dist. No. 1, 458 U.S. 457, 461–66 (1982).
74. *Parents Involved*, 551 U.S. at 813.
75. Ibid., 711–12.
76. Ibid., 715.
77. *Parents Involved*, 551 U.S. at 818.
78. Ibid., 716.
79. Ibid., 784–85 (Kennedy, J., concurring in part).
80. Ibid., 714 (majority opinion).
81. *See* Comfort v. Lynn Sch. Comm., 418 F.3d 1 (1st Cir. 2005), *cert. denied*, 546 U.S. 1061 (2005).
82. *Parents Involved*, 551 U.S. at 726.

83. Ibid.,747–48.

84. Ibid., 787–88 (Kennedy, J., concurring in part).

85. Ibid., 788.

86. Ibid.

87. Ibid., 797–98 (Kennedy, J., concurring).

88. Ibid., 793–99.

89. Ibid., 863–66.

90. Ibid., 867–68.

91. *See* Grutter v. Bollinger, 539 U.S. 306, 344–46 (2003) (Thomas, J., concurring in part); Adarand Constructors, Inc. v. Peña, 515 U.S. 200, 239–41 (1995) (Scalia, J., concurring).

92. *See* Parents Involved in Community Schools v. Seattle School District No. 1, 551 U.S. 701, 803–68 (2007) (Breyer, J., dissenting); Gratz v. Bollinger, 539 U.S. 244, 298–304 (2003) (Ginsburg, J., dissenting).

93. Louis H. Pollack, *Mr. Chief Justice: May It Please the Court,* in Constitutional Government in America 247, 252 (Ronald K.L. Collins ed., 1980); Jed Rubenfeld, *Affirmative Action,* 107 Yale L.J. 427, 430–31 (1997); Eric Schnapper, *Affirmative Action and the Legislative History of the Fourteenth Amendment,* 71 Va. L. Rev. 753 (1985).

94. James Boyd White, *What's Wrong with Our Talk about Race? On History, Particularity, and Affirmative Action,* 100 Mich. L. Rev. 1927 (2001–2002).

95. Ibid., 1941–42.

96. Ibid., 1942.

97. Ibid.

98. Ibid., 1949–50.

99. Cal. Const. art. I, § 31 (1996); Mich. Const. art. I, § 26 (2006); Neb. Const. art. I, § 30 (2008); Wash. Rev. Code § 49.60.400 (1998).

100. Joanne Barkan, *Alive and Not Well: Affirmative Action on Campus,* Dissent (Spring 2008), http://www.dissentmagazine.org/article/?article=1162 (accessed Nov. 8, 2011).

Chapter 8

1. U.S. Const. amend. I.

2. Thomas Jefferson, Letter to the Danbury Baptists (Jan. 1, 1802), http://www.loc.gov/loc/lcib/9806/danpre.html (accessed Nov. 8, 2011).

3. *Everson v. Bd. of Educ.,* 330 U.S. 1 (1947).

4. Ibid.

5. Ibid., 15–16.

6. Ibid., 18.

7. Ibid., 38–42.

8. Ibid., 41.

9. Ibid., 58–59.

10. Ibid., 19.

11. 392 U.S. 236 (1968).

12. *See* ibid., 243–44.

13. *See* ibid., 244.

14. Ibid., 252.

15. Ibid.

16. Ibid., 254.

17. 403 U.S. 602 (1971).

18. Ibid., 612–13.

19. Ibid., 613–14

20. Ibid., 618–20.

21. Ibid., 617.

22. Ibid., 612.

23. Ibid., 625.

24. Ibid., 662.

25. Ibid., 668.

26. 403 U.S. 672 (1971).

27. Ibid., 685–87. The Court did strike down that part of the law saying that the prohibition on using the buildings for religious purposes would lapse after 20 years. Ibid., 689.

28. Ibid., 668.

29. *Comm. for Pub. Educ. & Religious Liberty v. Nyquist,* 413 U.S. 756 (1973).

30. *Levitt v. Comm. for Pub. Educ. & Religious Liberty,* 413 U.S. 472 (1973).

31. *Nyquist,* 413 U.S. at 820 (White, J., dissenting) (emphasis added).

32. 421 U.S. 349 (1975), *overruled by* Mitchell v. Helms, 530 U.S. 793 (2000).

33. 433 U.S. 229 (1977), *overruled by* Helms, 530 U.S. 793.

34. *Wolman,* 433 U.S. at 236–38.

35. *Meek,* 421 U.S. at 365.

36. *Wolman,* 433 U.S. at 252–54.

37. Ibid., 254.

38. *See* Eric J. Segall, *Parochial School Aid Revisited: The Lemon Test, the Endorsement Test and Religious Liberty,* 28 SAN DIEGO L. REV. 263, 272–73 (1991).

39. 473 U.S. 402 (1985), *overruled by* Agostini v. Felton, 521 U.S. 203 (1997).

40. 473 U.S. 373 (1985), *overruled by* Agostini, 521 U.S. 203.

41. *Mueller v. Allen,* 463 U.S. 388 (1983).

42. *See* Segall, *Parochial School Aid,* 275 n.92.

43. *Agostini,* 521 U.S. 203.

44. Ibid., 222.
45. 530 U.S. 793 (2000).
46. Ibid., 809.
47. Ibid., 829. Justice O'Connor's concurring opinion was not quite as broad as she was slightly more concerned with ensuring that the aid not be diverted to religious use than Justice Thomas but, at the end of the day, the difference in the decisions has not made a practical difference.
48. 536 U.S. 639 (2002).
49. Ibid., 647, 653.
50. 449 U.S. 39 (1980).
51. Ibid., 40.
52. Ibid., 41–42.
53. 465 U.S. 668 (1984).
54. Ibid., 671.
55. Ibid.
56. Ibid., 672.
57. Ibid., 674.
58. Ibid., 675.
59. Ibid., 676.
60. Ibid., 676–77.
61. Ibid., 680.
62. Ibid., 683.
63. Ibid., 709.
64. Ibid., 712–13.
65. Ibid., 726–27.
66. Ibid., 690.
67. Ibid., 688.
68. Ibid., 691.
69. Ibid., 692.
70. 492 U.S. 573 (1989).
71. Ibid., 579–81.
72. Ibid., 582.
73. Ibid., 587.
74. Ibid., 601.
75. Ibid., 616.
76. Ibid., 618.
77. Ibid., 635 (O'Connor, J., concurring).
78. Ibid., 664 (Kennedy, J., dissenting).
79. Ibid., 674.
80. Ibid.
81. Ibid.
82. Ibid., 674–75.

83. Ibid., 656.

84. Ibid., 664–65 n.3.

85. Ibid., 607–08 (majority opinion).

86. Ibid., 652 (Stevens, J., dissenting).

87. Ibid., 651.

88. For a good summary of these cases, see William M. Howard, Annotation, *First Amendment Challenges to Display of Religious Symbols on Public Property,* 107 A.L.R. 5TH 1 (2003).

89. *Am. Jewish Cong. v. City of Chi.,* 827 F.2d 120, 129 (7th Cir. 1987) (Easterbrook, J., dissenting).

90. *See* McCreary Cnty. v. ACLU of Ky., 545 U.S. 844, 851 (2005); Van Orden v. Perry, 545 U.S. 677 (2005).

91. *McCreary Cnty.,* 545 U.S. at 851.

92. Ibid.

93. Ibid., 852.

94. *ACLU of Ky. v. McCreary Cnty.,* 96 F. Supp. 2d 688, 699 (E.D. Ky. 2000) (order granting preliminary injunction).

95. *McCreary Cnty.,* 545 U.S. at 856.

96. Ibid., 856–57.

97. *ACLU of Ky. v. McCreary Cnty.,* 145 F. Supp. 2d 845, 851 (E.D. Ky. 2001) (order granting extension of preliminary injunction).

98. 545 U.S. 844 (2005).

99. 545 U.S. 677 (2005).

100. Ibid., 681.

101. Ibid., 681–82.

102. Ibid., 681 n.1.

103. Ibid., 682.

104. Ibid., 688–89.

105. Ibid., 691.

106. Ibid., 691–92.

107. *McCreary Cnty.,* at 867–68.

108. Ibid., 874.

109. *Van Orden,* 545 U.S. at 738 (Souter, J., dissenting).

110. Ibid., 708 (Stevens, J., dissenting).

111. Ibid., 700 (Breyer, J., concurring).

112. Ibid., 701–05.

113. *See* Peter Irons, *Curing a Monumental Error: The Presumptive Unconstitutionality of Ten Commandments Displays,* 63 OKLA. L. REV. 1, 22–23 (2010).

114. *Van Orden,* 545 U.S. at 707 (Stevens, J., dissenting).

115. Ibid., 703 (Breyer, J., concurring).

116. Ibid.

117. Ibid., 702–04.

118. Irons, *Monumental Error,* 28.

119. Ibid., 28–36.

Chapter 9

1. Steven G. Calabresi & James Lingreen, *Term Limits for the Supreme Court: Life Tenure Reconsidered,* 29 HARV. J.L. & PUBLIC POL'Y 769, 819 (2006).

2. Ibid.

3. Ibid.

4. ROGER C. CRAMTON & PAUL D. CARRINGTON, REFORMING THE COURT: TERM LIMITS FOR SUPREME COURT JUSTICES 468 (2006).

5. David Garrow, *Mental Decrepitude on the U.S. Supreme Court: The Historical Case for a 28th Amendment,* 67 U. CHI. L. REV. 995 (2000).

6. Ibid., 9–10.

7. Ibid., 24.

8. Ibid., 25.

9. Ibid., 26.

10. Ibid.

11. Ibid., 32.

12. Ibid., 34.

13. James E. DiTullio & John B. Schochet, *Saving This Honorable Court: A Proposal to Replace Life Tenure on the Supreme Court with Staggered, Nonrenewable Eighteen-Year Terms,* 90 VA. L. REV. 1093, 1118 (2004).

14. *Separate Is not Equal, Brown v. Board of Education,* SMITHSONIAN MUSEUM OF NATURAL HISTORY, http://americanhistory.si.edu/Brown/history/5-decision/justices.html (accessed Nov. 8, 2011).

15. Cass R. Sunstein, *Did Brown Matter?,* NEWYORKER.COM (May 3, 2004), http://www.newyorker.com/archive/2004/05/03/040503crbo_books, (accessed Nov. 8, 2011).

16. Ibid.

17. Ibid.

18. Ibid.

19. DiTullio & Schochet, *Saving This Honorable Court,* 1112.

20. Calabresi & Lingreen, *Term Limits,* 775.

21. *See* ibid.

22. *See* ibid.

23. George W. Carey, *The Judicial Assault on the Constitution, in* THE MOST DANGEROUS BRANCH 5 (Edward McLean ed. 2008).

24. Ibid.

25. 5 U.S. (1 Cranch) 137 (1803).

26. THE FEDERALIST NO. 78 (Alexander Hamilton (1788)).

27. James Bradley Thayer, *The Origin and Scope of the American Doctrine of Constitutional Law,* 7 HARV. L. REV. 129 (1893).

28. Ibid., 139–40.

29. *See* Thomas Grey, *Thayer's Doctrine: Notes on Its Origin, Scope, and Present Implication,* 88 NW. U.L. REV. 28, 40 (1993).

30. *See* Jeremy Waldron, *The Core of the Case against Judicial Review,* 115 YALE L.J. 1346, 1383–84 (2006).

31. Ibid., 1383.

32. Ibid., 1384–85.

33. Ibid., 1385.

34. MARK TUSHNET, TAKING THE CONSTITUTION AWAY FROM THE COURTS (1999).

35. Ibid., 194.

36. Ibid.

37. LARRY KRAMER, THE PEOPLE THEMSELVES: POPULAR CONSTITUTIONALISM AND JUDICIAL REVIEW (2004).

38. John Michael Eden & John Paul Ryan, *The People Themselves: Popular Constitutionalism and Judicial Review,* OXFORD (2004) http://www.bsos.umd.edu/gvpt/lpbr/subpages/reviews/kramer1104.htm (accessed Nov. 8, 2011).

39. SULLIVAN & GUNTHER, CONSTITUTIONAL LAW, 23–24.

40. BURNS, PACKING THE COURT, 253.

41. Ibid.

42. Ibid.

Epilogue

1. A subsidiary issue was whether the mandate could be deemed a valid tax but, as of this writing, no court has yet upheld the mandate as a tax possibly because such a challenge, at this point, would be premature.

2. http://www.ca6.uscourts.gov/opinions.pdf/11a0168p-06.pdf, Jun. 29, 2011.

3. http://www.uscourts.gov/uscourts/courts/ca11/201111021.pdf, Aug. 12, 2011.

4. Sidney Ratner, *Was the Supreme Court Packed by President Grant?,* 50 POL. SCI. Q. 343, 358 (1935).

Index

About the Author

ERIC J. SEGALL is a Professor of Law at Georgia State University College of Law. He graduated from Emory University, Phi Beta Kappa, Summa Cum Laude, and from Vanderbilt Law School where he was the Research Editor for the *Law Review* and member of the Order of the Coif. He clerked for the Honorable Charles Moye Jr., Chief Judge for the Northern District of Georgia, and Albert J. Henderson of the Eleventh Circuit Court of Appeals. After his clerkships, he worked for Gibson, Dunn & Crutcher, and the United States Department of Justice, before joining the GSU faculty in 1991.